MTLE

Minnesota
Middle Level Science (5-8)

Teacher Certification Exam
By: Sharon Wynne, M.S.

XAMonline, INC.
Boston

Copyright © 2011 XAMonline, Inc.
All rights reserved. No part of the material protected by this copyright notice may be reproduced or utilized in any form or by any means, electronic or mechanical, including photocopying, recording or by any information storage and retrievable system, without written permission from the copyright holder.

To obtain permission(s) to use the material from this work for any purpose including workshops or seminars, please submit a written request to:

XAMonline, Inc.
25 First Street, Suite 106
Cambridge, MA 02141
Toll Free: 1-800-509-4128
Email: info@xamonline.com
Web: www.xamonline.com
Fax: 1-617-583-5552

Library of Congress Cataloging-in-Publication Data

Wynne, Sharon A.
 Minnesota Middle Level Science (5-8) Teacher Certification / Sharon A. Wynne. -1st ed.
 ISBN: 978-1-60787-081-4
  1. Minnesota Middle Level Science (5-8)   2. Study Guides   3. MTLE
  4. Teachers' Certification & Licensure   5. Careers

Disclaimer:
The opinions expressed in this publication are the sole works of XAMonline and were created independently from the National Education Association, Educational Testing Service, or any State Department of Education, National Evaluation Systems or other testing affiliates.

Between the time of publication and printing, state specific standards as well as testing formats and website information may change that is not included in part or in whole within this product. Sample test questions are developed by XAMonline and reflect similar content as on real tests; however, they are not former tests. XAMonline assembles content that aligns with state standards but makes no claims nor guarantees teacher candidates a passing score. Numerical scores are determined by testing companies such as NES or ETS and then are compared with individual state standards. A passing score varies from state to state.

Printed in the United States of America   œ-1
Minnesota Middle Level Science (5-8)
ISBN: 978-1-60787-081-4

TEACHER CERTIFICATION STUDY GUIDE

TABLE OF CONTENTS

DOMAIN I   **CONCEPTS AND APPLICATIONS IN MIDDLE LEVEL GENERAL SCIENCE**

COMPETENCY 001   **UNDERSTAND THE PRINCIPLES AND PROCESSES OF SCIENTIFIC INQUIRY AND THE NATURE AND HISTORY OF SCIENCE**

Skill 1.1   Demonstrating knowledge of the principles of scientific inquiry (e.g., asking questions, designing and conducting experiments, communicating and justifying conclusions based on logic and empirical evidence) 1

Skill 1.2   Demonstrating knowledge of appropriate methods, technology, and tools for designing and carrying out a scientific investigation

Skill 1.3   Applying methods and criteria for collecting, organizing, and communicating scientific information 3

Skill 1.4   Recognizing procedures and sources of information (e.g., state and national standards) for the safe and proper use of equipment and materials used in scientific investigations 5

Skill 1.5   Applying knowledge of ethical principles to the acquisition, care, handling, and disposal of live organisms 7

Skill 1.6   Demonstrating understanding of the history of science and the evolution of scientific knowledge, including the contributions of various cultures 9

Skill 1.7   Demonstrating knowledge of how assumptions, values, and the limitations of available data or theories can influence scientific progress 12

COMPETENCY 002   **UNDERSTAND CONNECTIONS BETWEEN SCIENCE, TECHNOLOGY, AND SOCIETY, AND CONNECTIONS BETWEEN SCIENCE AND OTHER SCHOOL SUBJECTS**

Skill 2.1   Applying the systems model (e.g., inputs, outputs, feedback) to a given technological, biological, physical, or Earth and space system 13

Skill 2.2   Demonstrating knowledge of unifying themes, principles, and relationships that connect the different branches of the sciences 13

Skill 2.3   Demonstrating knowledge of how the relationships between science and technology lead to new discoveries and advances 14

TEACHER CERTIFICATION STUDY GUIDE

Skill 2.4 Describing similarities and differences between the goals and processes of scientific inquiry and between technological and engineering design 16

Skill 2.5 Demonstrating knowledge of the use of computer models, diagrams, flowcharts, tables, graphs, and mathematical relationships to interpret, model, and solve problems 16

Skill 2.6 Analyzing social, economic, and ethical issues related to scientific and technological developments 17

Skill 2.7 Demonstrating knowledge of how the systematic approaches of science can inform courses of action for addressing problems related to personal, local, national, or global challenges 21

Skill 2.8 Demonstrating knowledge of how to assess a certain course of action in terms of alternatives, costs, risks, and benefits 22

Skill 2.9 Recognizing opportunities for further education and careers in the sciences and the role of the sciences in everyday life 22

COMPETENCY 003   UNDERSTAND THE CONTENT AND METHODS FOR DEVELOPING STUDENTS' CONTENT-AREA READING SKILLS TO SUPPORT THEIR READING AND LEARNING IN THE SCIENCES

Skill 3.1 Demonstrating knowledge of key components and processes involved in reading (e.g., vocabulary knowledge, including orthographic and morphological knowledge; background knowledge; knowledge of academic discourse, including the syntactic and organizational structures used in print and digital academic texts; print processing abilities, including decoding skills; use of cognitive and metacognitive skills and strategies) 23

Skill 3.2 Demonstrating the ability to plan instruction and select strategies that support all students' content-area reading (e.g., differentiating instruction to meet the needs of students with varying reading proficiency levels and linguistic backgrounds, identifying and addressing gaps in students' background knowledge, scaffolding reading tasks for students who experience comprehension difficulties) 24

Skill 3.3 Demonstrating knowledge of explicit strategies for facilitating students' comprehension before, during, and after reading content-area texts and for promoting their use of comprehension strategies 28

Skill 3.4	Demonstrating knowledge of explicit strategies for promoting students' academic language and vocabulary development, including their knowledge of domain-specific vocabulary words 30
Skill 3.5	Demonstrating knowledge of explicit strategies for developing students' critical literacy skills (e.g., encouraging students to question texts, developing students' ability to analyze texts from multiple viewpoints or perspectives) 31
Skill 3.6	Demonstrating the ability to plan instruction and select strategies that support students' reading and understanding of sources of information in the sciences (e.g., helping students follow laboratory instructions and interpret diagrams and graphs) 31

DOMAIN II   EARTH AND SPACE SYSTEMS

COMPETENCY 004   UNDERSTAND THE COMPONENTS AND EVOLUTION OF THE EARTH SYSTEM

Skill 4.1	Describing the formation and physical properties of Earth materials 32
Skill 4.2	Recognizing the physical, environmental, biological, structural, and tectonic processes that influence the formation of a given rock (e.g., sedimentary, igneous, metamorphic) 33
Skill 4.3	Recognizing the physical, environmental, biological, structural, and tectonic processes that influence the formation of a given rock sequence 35
Skill 4.4	Demonstrating knowledge of the formation and development of a given Earth structure (e.g., volcanic structures, rift valleys, ocean spreading center, fault-block mountains) 35
Skill 4.5	Demonstrating knowledge of how a given geologic or biologic event is recorded in a rock sequence 37
Skill 4.6	Demonstrating knowledge of how fossils and radioactive isotopes are used to determine the age of rocks and to interpret the geologic past 42

COMPETENCY 005   UNDERSTAND MATTER AND ENERGY IN EARTH SYSTEMS

Skill 5.1	Analyzing the transfer and transformation of energy as it flows between Earth systems (i.e., the lithosphere, hydrosphere, and atmosphere), including the processes of convection, conduction, and radiation 44

Skill 5.2	Analyzing processes of the lithosphere (e.g., weathering, erosion, movement of tectonic plates, volcanism, earthquakes) 44
Skill 5.3	Analyzing processes that occur in freshwater and ocean systems 48
Skill 5.4	Analyzing processes that occur in the atmosphere and sources of energy that drive those processes, including the changes that occur during the water cycle 50
Skill 5.5	Describing how global patterns of atmospheric movement influence weather 52
Skill 5.6	Demonstrating knowledge of the movement of chemical elements and compounds between different reservoirs on Earth 53
Skill 5.7	Analyzing physical models that represent the behavior of a given Earth system 53

COMPETENCY 006　　UNDERSTAND EARTH IN THE SOLAR SYSTEM AND UNIVERSE

Skill 6.1	Demonstrating knowledge of the properties and organization of different types of stars and galaxies 54
Skill 6.2	Recognizing evidence used to support the scientific understanding of the universe 57
Skill 6.3	Describing objects in the solar system (e.g., planets, comets, moons, the sun) in terms of physical, chemical, and geological processes 59
Skill 6.4	Demonstrating knowledge of the motion of objects in the solar system 61
Skill 6.5	Analyzing the orbit, rotation, and axial tilt of Earth to explain seasons, day length, and long-term changes in climate 62

COMPETENCY 007　　UNDERSTAND HUMAN INTERACTIONS WITH EARTH SYSTEMS

Skill 7.1	Analyzing the scientific evidence used to predict the occurrence of an environmental hazard on a human time frame.. 64
Skill 7.2	Describing observed changes in a given Earth system (e.g., lithosphere, hydrosphere, atmosphere) that are due to human activity 64

TEACHER CERTIFICATION STUDY GUIDE

Skill 7.3   Recognizing the causes and consequences of water pollution and the movement of water pollutants through Earth systems 64

Skill 7.4   Recognizing the causes and consequences of air pollution and the movements of air pollutants through Earth systems 65

DOMAIN III   LIFE SCIENCE

COMPETENCY 008   UNDERSTAND THE STRUCTURES AND FUNCTIONS OF LIVING ORGANISMS

Skill 8.1   Demonstrating knowledge of the macroscopic structure of a given common organism 66

Skill 8.2   Demonstrating knowledge of the structure of a plant or animal organ system and the functions of those organ systems 70

Skill 8.3   Demonstrating knowledge of processes used by common organisms (e.g., flowering and nonflowering plants, bacteria, mammals, amphibians) to sustain life 78

Skill 8.4   Recognizing how the structure and function of the components of a living system (e.g., coral reef, estuary, forest, grassland) support the overall function of that system 78

Skill 8.5   Analyzing how and why the structures (e.g., skeletal system, respiratory system) for a given function are different in different species 84

Skill 8.6   Recognizing the origins, transmission, prevention, management, or cures for human diseases (e.g., heart disease, malaria, common cold) 84

Skill 8.7   Demonstrating knowledge of how a given immunity is established and how a given active or passive immunity functions in a human 85

COMPETENCY 009   UNDERSTAND MOLECULAR AND CELLULAR LIFE PROCESSES

Skill 9.1   Demonstrating knowledge of the cellular structures and related functions of different types of plant and animal cells, including the structural and functional differences between eukaryotic and prokaryotic cells 87

Skill 9.2   Demonstrating knowledge of how plants transform energy from the sun into food through the process of photosynthesis and how energy stored in food molecules is released through cellular respiration 89

Skill 9.3   Demonstrating knowledge of the cellular processes of DNA replication and protein synthesis 93

Skill 9.4   Recognizing how the structures of different types of cells relate to their functions in tissues and organ systems 96

Skill 9.5   Recognizing the stages of mitosis and meiosis and their roles in growth and reproduction 97

Skill 9.6   Analyzing the inheritance of genetic traits and how sex is determined in plants and animals 98

Skill 9.7   Recognizing how genetic changes (i.e., mutations) are expressed as traits (i.e., phenotypes) and the role these changes play in biological evolution 101

COMPETENCY 010   UNDERSTAND THE DIVERSITY AND BIOLOGICAL EVOLUTION OF LIFE

Skill 10.1   Analyzing the physical and behavioral adaptations that can occur in a given common species in response to environmental stresses 107

Skill 10.2   Recognizing the factors (e.g., geographic location, climate, natural and human-caused disturbances, invasive species) that affect species diversity in different ecosystems 107

Skill 10.3   Demonstrating knowledge of the niches and habitats of common species in different ecosystems in the world's major biomes 108

Skill 10.4   Analyzing the process of speciation (e.g., geographic isolation, founder effect, adaptive radiation) in living populations and the fossil record 109

Skill 10.5   Identifying organisms using a classification key 109

COMPETENCY 011   UNDERSTAND THE INTERDEPENDENCE AMONG LIVING THINGS AND THE FLOW OF ENERGY AND MATTER THROUGH ECOSYSTEMS

Skill 11.1   Demonstrating knowledge of factors that influence the diversity and number of species in a given ecosystem 111

Skill 11.2   Analyzing species interactions and interdependence in ecosystems (e.g., coral reefs, grasslands, rain forests, estuaries) 111

Skill 11.3	Demonstrating knowledge of the biotic and abiotic components of a given niche, habitat, ecosystem, or biome 112
Skill 11.4	Analyzing the cycling of matter and the flow of energy in a given ecosystem, and the structure of food webs in different ecosystems, including the roles of decomposers, producers, and consumers 112
Skill 11.5	Recognizing how environmental changes in an organism's habitat can elicit a specific behavioral response in the organism 113

DOMAIN IV   PHYSICAL SCIENCE

COMPETENCY 012   UNDERSTAND LINEAR MOTION AND FORCES

Skill 12.1	Analyzing one-dimensional and two-dimensional linear motion (e.g., average speed, direction) using graphs, diagrams, vectors, and simple mathematical relationships 114
Skill 12.2	Applying Newton's laws to analyze the forces acting on an object represented in free-body vector diagrams, graphs, or descriptions of everyday phenomena 117
Skill 12.3	Analyzing changes in the kinetic and potential energy of a system (e.g., pendulum, mass on a spring) and the transfer of energy into or out of a system of interacting objects (e.g., loss of heat due to friction) 119
Skill 12.4	Analyzing the observed motion of an object in a system of interacting objects in terms of balanced and unbalanced forces and the conservation of energy 120

COMPETENCY 013   UNDERSTAND VIBRATIONS, WAVE MOTION, AND THE BEHAVIOR OF LIGHT

Skill 13.1	Analyzing the wavelength, amplitude, period, and frequency of a given oscillating object or wave, including changes in the pitch or intensity of sound waves 122
Skill 13.2	Analyzing the wave motion of a standing or traveling wave in a given medium 123
Skill 13.3	Analyzing how sound waves are affected when the source of the sound is in motion 124
Skill 13.4	Demonstrating knowledge of the chromatic composition of light and how humans perceive an object and its color 124

TEACHER CERTIFICATION STUDY GUIDE

Skill 13.5 Analyzing the reflection, refraction, transmission, and absorption of light when it encounters an object, plane or curved mirror, prism, or convex or concave lens 126

Skill 13.6 Applying the laws of reflection and refraction to explain magnification and the production of virtual and real images in a pinhole system or in a simple system of lenses and mirrors 128

COMPETENCY 014   UNDERSTAND ELECTRICITY AND MAGNETISM

Skill 14.1 Demonstrating knowledge of electrostatics and experiments, and measurements that demonstrate the charge of a given object 130

Skill 14.2 Analyzing experiments and measurements that demonstrate the movement of electrons and changes in the charge of interacting objects.... 131

Skill 14.3 Demonstrating knowledge of the properties of magnets, and experiments that demonstrate those properties 134

Skill 14.4 Analyzing the magnetic field of a straight current-carrying wire and a current-carrying solenoid 135

Skill 14.5 Recognizing a circuit consisting of batteries, bulbs, and switches that meets a given design criteria for the brightness and control of the bulbs 137

COMPETENCY 015   UNDERSTAND THE PROPERTIES AND STRUCTURE OF MATTER

Skill 15.1 Applying knowledge of the properties of matter, including mass, density, volume, concentration, melting and boiling points, and solubility limits of a given substance 138

Skill 15.2 Recognizing the differences between pure elements, compounds, solutions, suspensions, and colloids 139

Skill 15.3 Demonstrating knowledge of the processes of distillation, precipitation, extraction, and chromatography 141

Skill 15.4 Demonstrating knowledge of the basic atomic and subatomic constituents of matter.. 142

Skill 15.5 Analyzing the properties of a gas, liquid, or solid in terms of kinetic theory, intermolecular forces, and the arrangement and motion of atoms, ions, or molecules.. 143

TEACHER CERTIFICATION STUDY GUIDE

Skill 15.6 Applying knowledge of the periodic table and the principles for filling the electron orbitals of atoms in order to explain periodic trends in electrical conductivity and ionization energy and the metallic character of a given set of elements 145

Skill 15.7 Applying knowledge of the periodic table to predict the covalent, ionic, or metallic nature of a bond in a given substance 147

Skill 15.8 Analyzing the changes in matter and energy that occur in the nuclear processes of radioactive decay, fission, and fusion 148

Skill 15.9 Applying knowledge of the unique structure of carbon to explain how that structure results in the large variety of organic molecules 148

COMPETENCY 016   UNDERSTAND CHEMICAL REACTIONS, THERMODYNAMICS, AND CHEMICAL KINETICS

Skill 16.1 Demonstrating knowledge of chemical symbols, formulas, and the characteristics of different types of chemical bonds 151

Skill 16.2 Recognizing the properties of acids and bases 153

Skill 16.3 Demonstrating knowledge of balancing chemical equations, and the changes in the energy and arrangement of atoms for a given chemical reaction 156

Skill 16.4 Recognizing different types of chemical reactions (e.g., oxidation-reduction, acid-base, free radical, precipitation) 157

Skill 16.5 Demonstrating knowledge of the first and second laws of thermodynamics, and the changes in the enthalpy and entropy that occur during a given chemical reaction 157

Skill 16.6 Demonstrating knowledge of factors (e.g., effective particle collisions, temperature, concentration) that can affect the spontaneity and rate of a given chemical reaction 161

Skill 16.7 Recognizing how changes in the concentration of reactants and products, the introduction of a catalyst, or changes in temperature or pressure can be used to predict the change in the equilibrium state of a given chemical reaction 162

Middle Level Science

TEACHER CERTIFICATION STUDY GUIDE

Sample Test 164

Answer Key 183

Rigor Table 184

Rationales with Sample Questions 185

TEACHER CERTIFICATION STUDY GUIDE

Section 1 About XAMonline

XAMonline – A Specialty Teacher Certification Company
Created in 1996, XAMonline was the first company to publish study guides for state-specific teacher certification examinations. Founder Sharon Wynne found it frustrating that materials were not available for teacher certification preparation and decided to create the first single, state-specific guide. XAMonline has grown into a company of over 1800 contributors and writers and offers over 300 titles for the entire PRAXIS series and every state examination. No matter what state you plan on teaching in, XAMonline has a unique teacher certification study guide just for you.

XAMonline – Value and Innovation
We are committed to providing value and innovation. Our print-on-demand technology allows us to be the first in the market to reflect changes in test standards and user feedback as they occur. Our guides are written by experienced teachers who are experts in their fields. And, our content reflects the highest standards of quality. Comprehensive practice tests with varied levels of rigor means that your study experience will closely match the actual in-test experience.

To date, XAMonline has helped nearly 600,000 teachers pass their certification or licensing exams. Our commitment to preparation exceeds simply providing the proper material for study - it extends to helping teachers **gain mastery** of the subject matter, giving them the **tools** to become the most effective classroom leaders possible, and ushering today's students toward a **successful future**.

TEACHER CERTIFICATION STUDY GUIDE

Section 2 About this Study Guide

Purpose of this Guide
Is there a little voice inside of you saying, "Am I ready?" Our goal is to replace that little voice and remove all doubt with a new voice that says, "I AM READY. **Bring it on!**" by offering the highest quality of teacher certification study guides.

Organization of Content
You will see that while every test may start with overlapping general topics, each are very unique in the skills they wish to test. Only XAMonline presents custom content that analyzes deeper than a title, a subarea, or an objective. Only XAMonline presents content and sample test assessments along with **focus statements**, the deepest-level rationale and interpretation of the skills that are unique to the exam.

Title and field number of test
→Each exam has its own name and number. XAMonline's guides are written to give you the content you need to know for the specific exam you are taking. You can be confident when you buy our guide that it contains the information you need to study for the specific test you are taking.

Subareas
→These are the major content categories found on the exam. XAMonline's guides are written to cover all of the subareas found in the test frameworks developed for the exam.

Objectives
→These are standards that are unique to the exam and represent the main subcategories of the subareas/content categories. XAMonline's guides are written to address every specific objective required to pass the exam.

Focus statements
→These are examples and interpretations of the objectives. You find them in parenthesis directly following the objective. They provide detailed examples of the range, type, and level of content that appear on the test questions. **Only XAMonline's guides drill down to this level.**

How do We Compare with Our Competitors?
XAMonline – drills down to the focus statement level
CliffsNotes and REA – organized at the objective level
Kaplan – provides only links to content
MoMedia – content not specific to the test

Each subarea is divided into manageable sections that cover the specific skill areas. Explanations are easy-to-understand and thorough. You'll find that every test answer contains a rejoinder so if you need a refresher or further review after taking the test, you'll know exactly to which section you must return.

TEACHER CERTIFICATION STUDY GUIDE

How to Use this Book
Our informal polls show that most people begin studying up to 8 weeks prior to the test date, so start early. Then ask yourself some questions: How much do you really know? Are you coming to the test straight from your teacher-education program or are you having to review subjects you haven't considered in 10 years? Either way, take a **diagnostic or assessment test** first. Also, spend time on sample tests so that you become accustomed to the way the actual test will appear.

This guide comes with an online diagnostic test of 30 questions found online at www.XAMonline.com. It is a little boot camp to get you up for the task and reveal things about your compendium of knowledge in general. Although this guide is structured to follow the order of the test, you are not required to study in that order. By finding a time-management and study plan that fits your life you will be more effective. The results of your diagnostic or self-assessment test can be a guide for how to manage your time and point you towards an area that needs more attention.

After taking the diagnostic exam, fill out the **Personalized Study Plan** page at the beginning of each chapter. Review the competencies and skills covered in that chapter and check the boxes that apply to your study needs. If there are sections you already know you can skip, check the "skip it" box. Taking this step will give you a study plan for each chapter.

Week	Activity
8 weeks prior to test	Take a diagnostic test found at www.XAMonline.com
7 weeks prior to test	Build your Personalized Study Plan for each chapter. Check the "skip it" box for sections you feel you are already strong in.
6-3 weeks prior to test	For each of these 4 weeks, choose a content area to study. You don't have to go in the order of the book. It may be that you start with the content that needs the most review. Alternately, you may want to ease yourself into plan by starting with the most familiar material.
2 weeks prior to test	Take the sample test, score it, and create a review plan for the final week before the test.
1 week prior to test	Following your plan (which will likely be aligned with the areas that need the most review) go back and study the sections that align with the questions you may have gotten wrong. Then go back and study the sections related to the questions you answered correctly. If need be, create flashcards and drill yourself on any area that you makes you anxious.

TEACHER CERTIFICATION STUDY GUIDE

Section 3 About the Minnesota Middle Level Science (5-8) Exam

What is the Minnesota Middle Level Science (5-8) Exam?
The Minnesota Middle Level Science (5-8) exam is meant to assess mastery of the content knowledge required to teach middle level science in Minnesota public schools.

Often **your own state's requirements** determine whether or not you should take any particular test. The most reliable source of information regarding this is your state's Department of Education. This resource should have a complete list of testing centers and dates. Test dates vary by subject area and not all test dates necessarily include your particular test, so be sure to check carefully.

If you are in a teacher-education program, check with the Education Department or the Certification Officer for specific information for testing and testing timelines. The Certification Office should have most of the information you need.

If you choose an alternative route to certification you can either rely on our website at www.XAMonline.com or on the resources provided by an alternative certification program. Many states now have specific agencies devoted to alternative certification and there are some national organizations as well, for example:
National Association for Alternative Certification
http://www.alt-teachercert.org/index.asp

Interpreting Test Results
Contrary to what you may have heard, the results of the Minnesota Middle Level Science (5-8) test are not based on time. More accurately, your score will be based on the raw number of points you earn in each section, the proportion of that section to the entire subtest, and the scaling of the raw score. Raw scores are converted to a scale of 100 to 300. It is likely to your benefit to complete as many questions in the time allotted, but it will not necessarily work to your advantage if you hurry through the test.

Scores are available by email if you request this when you register. Score reports are available twenty-one days after the testing window and posted to your account for 45 days as PDFs. Scores will also be sent to your chosen institution(s).

TEACHER CERTIFICATION STUDY GUIDE

What's on the Test?
The Minnesota Middle Level Science (5-8) exam is a computer-based test and consists of two subtests, each lasting one hour. You can take one or both subtests at one testing appointment. A periodic table and a formulas/constants page are provided with your test. The breakdown of the questions is as follows:

Category	Approximate Number of Questions	Approximate Percentage of the test
SUBTEST 1	50	
I: Concepts and Applications in Middle Level General Science		43%
II: Earth and Space Systems		57%
SUBTEST 2	50	
I: Life Science		45%
II: Physical Science		55%

Question Types

You're probably thinking, enough already, I want to study! Indulge us a little longer while we explain that there is actually more than one type of multiple-choice question. You can thank us later after you realize how well prepared you are for your exam.

1. **Complete the Statement.** The name says it all. In this question type you'll be asked to choose the correct completion of a given statement. For example: The Dolch Basic Sight Words consist of a relatively short list of words that children should be able to:
    a. Sound out
    b. Know the meaning of
    c. Recognize on sight
    d. Use in a sentence

   The correct answer is C. In order to check your answer, test out the statement by adding the choices to the end of it.

2. **Which of the Following.** One way to test your answer choice for this type of question is to replace the phrase "which of the following" with your selection. Use this example: Which of the following words is one of the twelve most frequently used in children's reading texts:
    a. There
    b. This
    c. The
    d. An

   Don't look! Test your answer. ____ is one of the twelve most frequently used in children's reading texts. Did you guess C? Then you guessed correctly.

Middle Level Science

TEACHER CERTIFICATION STUDY GUIDE

3. **Roman Numeral Choices.** This question type is used when there is more than one possible correct answer. For example: Which of the following two arguments accurately supports the use of cooperative learning as an effective method of instruction?
    I. Cooperative learning groups facilitate healthy competition between individuals in the group.
    II. Cooperative learning groups allow academic achievers to carry or cover for academic underachievers.
    III. Cooperative learning groups make each student in the group accountable for the success of the group.
    IV. Cooperative learning groups make it possible for students to reward other group members for achieving.

    A. I and II
    B. II and III
    C. I and III
    D. III and IV

    Notice that the question states there are **two** possible answers. It's best to read all the possibilities first before looking at the answer choices. In this case, the correct answer is D.

4. **Negative Questions.** This type of question contains words such as "not," "least," and "except." Each correct answer will be the statement that does **not** fit the situation described in the question. Such as: Multicultural education is **not**
    a. An idea or concept
    b. A "tack-on" to the school curriculum
    c. An educational reform movement
    d. A process

    Think to yourself that the statement could be anything but the correct answer. This question form is more open to interpretation than other types, so read carefully and don't forget that you're answering a negative statement.

5. **Questions That Include Graphs, Tables, or Reading Passages.** As ever, read the question carefully. It likely asks for a very specific answer and not broad interpretation of the visual. Here is a simple (though not statistically accurate) example of a graph question: In the following graph in how many years did more men take the NYSTCE exam than women?

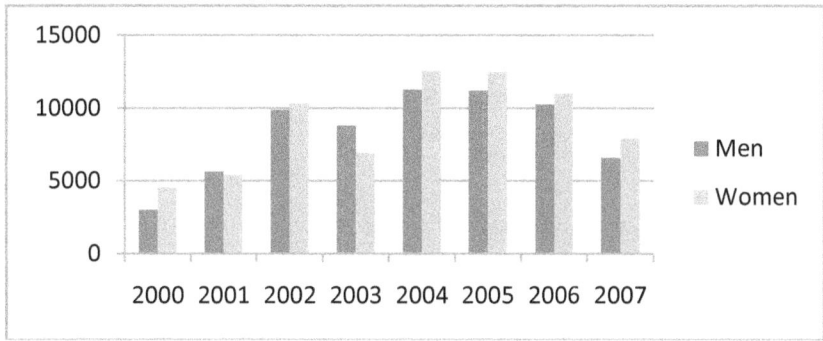

    a. None
    b. One
    c. Two
    d. Three

It may help you to simply circle the two years that answer the question. Make sure you've read the question thoroughly and once you've made your determination, double check your work. The correct answer is C.

TEACHER CERTIFICATION STUDY GUIDE

Section 4 Helpful Hints

Study Tips
1. **You are what you eat.** Certain foods aid the learning process by releasing natural memory enhancers called CCKs (cholecystokinin) composed of tryptophan, choline, and phenylalanine. All of these chemicals enhance the neurotransmitters associated with memory and certain foods release memory enhancing chemicals. A light meal or snacks from the following foods fall into this category:
   - Milk
   - Nuts and seeds
   - Rice
   - Oats
   - Eggs
   - Turkey
   - Fish

   The better the connections, the more you comprehend!

2. **See the forest for the trees.** In other words, get the concept before you look at the details. One way to do this is to take notes as you read, paraphrasing or summarizing in your own words. Putting the concept in terms that are comfortable and familiar may increase retention.

3. **Question authority.** Ask why, why, why. Pull apart written material paragraph by paragraph and don't forget the captions under the illustrations. For example, if a heading reads *Stream Erosion* put it in the form of a question (why do streams erode? Or what is stream erosion?) then find the answer within the material. If you train your mind to think in this manner you will learn more and prepare yourself for answering test questions.

4. **Play mind games**. Using your brain for reading or puzzles keeps it flexible. Even with a limited amount of time your brain can take in data (much like a computer) and store it for later use. In ten minutes you can: read two paragraphs (at least), quiz yourself with flash cards, or review notes. Even if you don't fully understand something on the first pass, your mind stores it for recall, which is why frequent reading or review increases chances of retention and comprehension.

5. **The pen is mightier than the sword.** Learn to take great notes. A by-product of our modern culture is that we have grown accustomed to getting our information in short doses. We've subconsciously trained ourselves to assimilate information into neat little packages. Messy notes fragment the flow of information. Your notes can be much clearer with proper formatting. ***The Cornell Method*** is one such format. This method was popularized in *How to Study in College,* Ninth Edition, by Walter Pauk. You can benefit from the method without purchasing an additional book by simply looking the method up online. Below is a sample of how *The Cornell Method* can be adapted for use with this guide.

TEACHER CERTIFICATION STUDY GUIDE

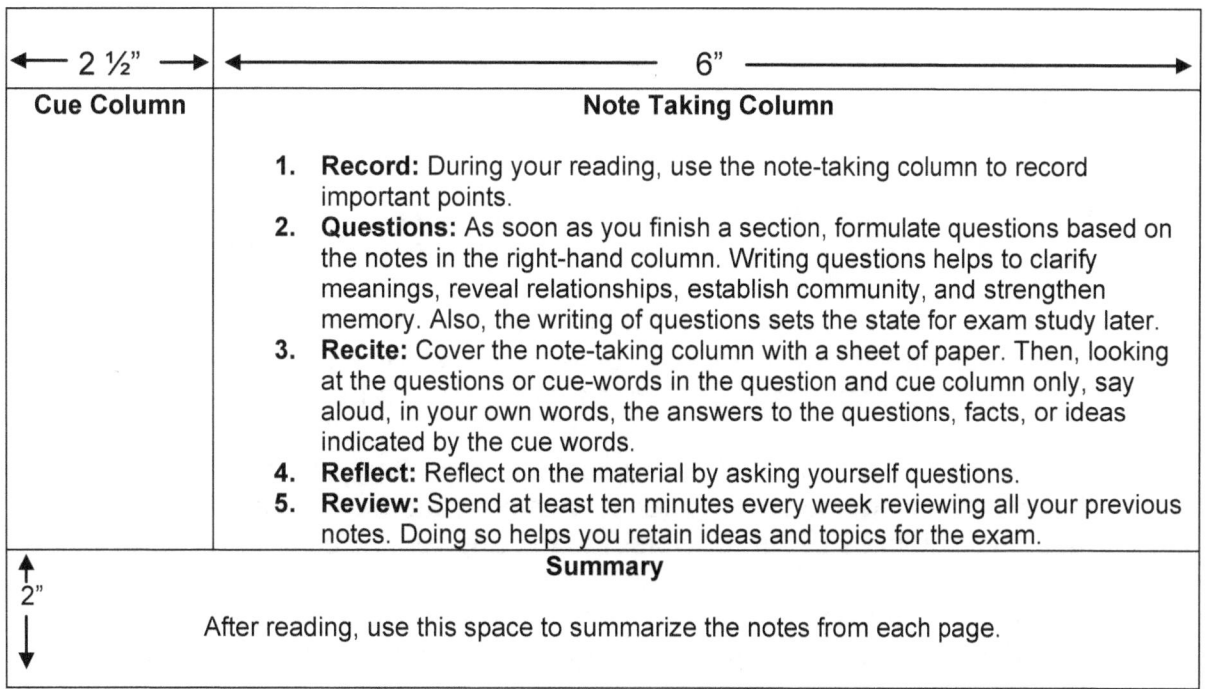

*Adapted from *How to Study in College,* Ninth Edition, by Walter Pauk, ©2008 Wadsworth

6. **Place yourself in exile and set the mood.** Set aside a particular place and time to study that best suits your personal needs and biorhythms. If you're a night person, burn the midnight oil. If you're a morning person set yourself up with some coffee and get to it. Make your study time and place as free from distraction as possible and surround yourself with what you need, be it silence or music. Studies have shown that music can aid in concentration, absorption, and retrieval of information. Not all music, though. Classical music is said to work best.

7. **Get pointed in the right direction.** Use arrows to point to important passages or pieces of information. It's easier to read than a page full of yellow highlights. Highlighting can be used sparingly, but add an arrow to the margin to call attention to it.

8. **Check your budget.** You should at least review all the content material before your test, but allocate the most amount of time to the areas that need the most refreshing. It sounds obvious, but it's easy to forget. You can use the study rubric above to balance your study budget.

> The proctor will write the start time where it can be seen and then, later, provide the time remaining, typically 15 minutes before the end of the test.

TEACHER CERTIFICATION STUDY GUIDE

Testing Tips

1. **Get smart, play dumb.** Sometimes a question is just a question. No one is out to trick you, so don't assume that the test writer is looking for something other than what was asked. Stick to the question as written and don't overanalyze.

2. **Do a double take.** Read test questions and answer choices at least twice because it's easy to miss something, to transpose a word or some letters. If you have no idea what the correct answer is, skip it and come back later if there's time. If you're still clueless, it's okay to guess. Remember, you're scored on the number of questions you answer correctly and you're not penalized for wrong answers. The worst case scenario is that you miss a point from a good guess.

3. **Turn it on its ear.** The syntax of a question can often provide a clue, so make things interesting and turn the question into a statement to see if it changes the meaning or relates better (or worse) to the answer choices.

4. **Get out your magnifying glass.** Look for hidden clues in the questions because it's difficult to write a multiple-choice question without giving away part of the answer in the options presented. In most questions you can readily eliminate one or two potential answers, increasing your chances of answering correctly to 50/50, which will help out if you've skipped a question and gone back to it (see tip #2).

5. **Call it intuition.** Often your first instinct is correct. If you've been studying the content you've likely absorbed something and have subconsciously retained the knowledge. On questions you're not sure about trust your instincts because a first impression is usually correct.

6. **Graffiti.** Sometimes it's a good idea to mark your answers directly on the test booklet and go back to fill in the optical scan sheet later. You don't get extra points for perfectly blackened ovals. If you choose to manage your test this way, be sure not to mismark your answers when you transcribe to the scan sheet.

7. **Become a clock-watcher.** You have a set amount of time to answer the questions. Don't get bogged down laboring over a question you're not sure about when there are ten others you could answer more readily. If you choose to follow the advice of tip #6, be sure you leave time near the end to go back and fill in the scan sheet.

TEACHER CERTIFICATION STUDY GUIDE

Do the Drill

No matter how prepared you feel it's sometimes a good idea to apply Murphy's Law. So the following tips might seem silly, mundane, or obvious, but we're including them anyway.

1. **Remember, you are what you eat, so bring a snack.** Choose from the list of energizing foods that appear earlier in the introduction.

2. **You're not too sexy for your test.** Wear comfortable clothes. You'll be distracted if your belt is too tight, or if you're too cold or too hot.

3. **Lie to yourself.** Even if you think you're a prompt person, pretend you're not and leave plenty of time to get to the testing center. Map it out ahead of time and do a dry run if you have to. There's no need to add road rage to your list of anxieties.

4. **Bring sharp, number 2 pencils.** It may seem impossible to forget this need from your school days, but you might. And make sure the erasers are intact, too.

5. **No ticket, no test.** Bring your admission ticket as well as **two** forms of identification, including one with a picture and signature. You will not be admitted to the test without these things.

6. **You can't take it with you.** Leave any study aids, dictionaries, notebooks, computers and the like at home. Certain tests **do** allow a scientific or four-function calculator, so check ahead of time if your test does.

7. **Prepare for the desert.** Any time spent on a bathroom break **cannot** be made up later, so use your judgment on the amount you eat or drink.

8. **Quiet, Please!** Keeping your own time is a good idea, but not with a timepiece that has a loud ticker. If you use a watch, take it off and place it nearby but not so that it distracts you. And **silence your cell phone.**

To the best of our ability, we have compiled the content you need to know in this book and in the accompanying online resources. The rest is up to you. You can use the study and testing tips or you can follow your own methods. Either way, you can be confident that there aren't any missing pieces of information and there shouldn't be any surprises in the content on the test.

If you have questions about test fees, registration, electronic testing, or other content verification issues please visit www.mtle.nesinc.com.

Good luck!
Sharon Wynne
Founder, XAMonline

Middle Level Science

TEACHER CERTIFICATION STUDY GUIDE

DOMAIN I: CONCEPTS AND APPLICATIONS IN MIDDLE LEVEL GENERAL SCIENCE

COMPETENCY 001 UNDERSTAND THE PRINCIPLES AND PROCESSES OF SCIENTIFIC INQUIRY AND THE NATURE AND HISTORY OF SCIENCE

Skill 1.1 Demonstrating knowledge of the principles of scientific inquiry (e.g., asking questions, designing and conducting experiments, communicating and justifying conclusions based on logic and empirical evidence)

THE SCIENTIFIC METHOD

The scientific method is the basic process behind scientific experimentation. It involves several steps, beginning with formulating a hypothesis and working through the discovery process to make a conclusion based on observation and testing.

Posing a Question
Although many discoveries happen by chance, a scientist's standard thought process begins with forming a question to test by conducting research. The more limited the question, the more readily an experiment can be designed to answer that question.

Forming a Hypothesis
Once the question is formulated, a scientist makes an educated guess about the answer to the problem or question. This "best guess" is called the **hypothesis**.

Doing the Test
Next, a series of steps known as an experiment are outlined to test this hypothesis. To make a test fair, data from an experiment must have a **variable** or any condition that can be changed, for example temperature or mass. A good test will try to manipulate as few variables as possible. This allows the researcher to more readily identify the variable or condition that produces a particular result. Experiments also require a second factor known as a control. A **control** is a factor that remains unchanged throughout the experiment, which allows the researcher to verify that the experiment worked correctly. When using a control, all the conditions are the same except for the variable being tested.

Observing and Recording the Data
Once the experiment is conducted, data must be gathered based on the results obtained. Data reporting should state specifics of how the measurements were made during the experiment. For example, a graduated cylinder needs to be read with proper procedures. For beginning students, technique must be part of the instructional process to give validity to the data.

Drawing a Conclusion
Careful analysis of the recorded data allows the experimenter to draw a conclusion based on the evidence. After recording data, the experimenter compares data with that of other researchers that conducted similar experiments. A conclusion is the judgment derived from the data results.

Communicating Results
Scientific findings are usually documented in the form of a lab report. All lab reports should include a specific title and tell exactly what is being studied. The abstract is a summary of the report that is placed at the beginning of the paper. The purpose should always be defined, clearly stating the question the experiment was designed to answer. The purpose should include the hypothesis (educated guess) of the expected outcome of the experiment. The entire experiment should relate to this problem. It is important to accurately describe what was done to prove or disprove a hypothesis. Observations and results of an experiment should be recorded, including all results from data. Drawings, graphs, and illustrations should be included to support information. Observations are objective, whereas analysis and interpretation are subjective. A conclusion should explain why the results of the experiment either proved or disproved the hypothesis.

Scientific theory and experimentation must be repeatable. It is also possible that previously established theories can be disproved and may be changed on the basis of new scientific proof. Science depends on communication, agreement, and disagreement among scientists. It is built on theories, laws, and hypotheses.

MODELS

A model is a basic element of the scientific method. Many topics in science are studied with models. A model is a simplification or representation of a problem that is being studied or predicted. A model is a substitute, but it is similar to what it represents. We encounter models at every step of our daily living. The periodic table of the elements is a model that chemists use for predicting the properties of the elements. Physicists use Newton's laws to predict how objects, such as planets and spaceships, will interact. In geology, the continental drift model estimates the past positions of continents. Samples, ideas, and methods are all examples of models. At every step of scientific study, models are extensively used. The primary activity of hundreds of thousands of U.S. scientists is to produce new models; these models are presented to the scientific community and the general public in tens of thousands of scientific papers published every year.

TEACHER CERTIFICATION STUDY GUIDE

Skill 1.2 Demonstrating knowledge of appropriate methods, technology, and tools for designing and carrying out a scientific investigation

LABORATORY EQUIPMENT

Bunsen Burners

Hot plates should be used whenever possible to avoid the risk of burns or fire. If Bunsen burners are used, the following precautions should be followed:

- Know the location of fire extinguishers and safety blankets, and train students in their use. Long hair and long sleeves should be secured and out of the way.
- Turn on the gas slowly to about a quarter of maximum and make a spark with the striker. The preferred method to light burners is to use strikers, rather than matches.
- Adjust the air valve at the bottom of the Bunsen burner until the flame shows an inner cone.
- Adjust the flow of gas to the desired flame height by using the adjustment valve.
- Do not touch the barrel of the burner (it is hot).

Graduated Cylinders

Graduated cylinders are used for precise measurements. They should always be placed on a flat surface. The surface of the liquid will form a **meniscus** (lens-shaped curve). The measurement is read at eye level, reading the bottom of this curve.

Balances

Electronic balances are easy to use but are expensive. An electronic balance should always be used on a flat surface and **tared** (returned to zero) before measuring. Substances should always be placed on a piece of weighing paper to avoid spills and/or damage to the instrument.

Triple beam balances must be used on a level surface and can be adjusted using the screws located at the bottom of the balance. Start with the largest counterweight first and proceed toward the last notch that does not tip the balance. Do the same with the next largest, and so on, until the pointer remains at zero. The total mass is the total of all the readings on the beams. Again, use weighing paper under the substance to protect the equipment.

Buret

A buret is used to dispense precisely measured volumes of liquid. A stopcock is used to control the volume of liquid being dispensed at a time.

Light Microscopes

Light microscopes commonly are used in laboratory experiments. Several procedures should be followed to properly care for this equipment:

- Clean all lenses with lens paper only.

- Carry microscopes with two hands; one on the arm and one on the base.
- Always begin focusing on low power; then switch to high power.
- Store microscopes with the low power objective down.
- Always use a cover slip when viewing wet mount slides.
- To avoid breaking the slide or scratching the lens, bring the objective down to its lowest position then adjust the fine focus.
- Wet mount slides should be made by placing a drop of water on the specimen and then putting a glass cover slip on top of the drop of water. Placing the cover slip on the slide at a 45-degree angle will help avoid air bubbles. The total magnification is determined by multiplying the ocular (usually 10X) and the objective (usually 10X on low, 40X on high).

LABORATORY PROCEDURES

Chromatography
Chromatography uses the principles of capillary action to separate substances such as plant pigments. Molecules of a larger size will migrate up the paper more slowly, whereas smaller molecules will move more quickly and produce lines of pigments.

Spectrophotometry
Spectrophotometry uses percent light absorbance to measure a color change, thus giving qualitative data a quantitative value.

Centrifugation
Centrifugation is used to separate substances of varying densities, which is achieved by spinning substances at a high speed. The denser part of a solution will settle out at the bottom of the test tube, while the lighter material will stay on top. For example, centrifugation is used to separate blood into blood cells and plasma, with the heavier blood cells settling on the bottom.

Electrophoresis
Electrophoresis uses electrical charges of molecules to separate them according to their size. The molecules, such as DNA or proteins, are pulled through a gel toward either the positive end of the gel box (if the material has a negative charge) or the negative end of the gel box (if the material has a positive charge).

TECHNOLOGY

Computer technology has greatly improved the collection and interpretation of scientific data. Molecular findings have been enhanced through the use of computer images. Technology has revolutionized access to data via the Internet and shared databases. The manipulation of data is enhanced by sophisticated software capabilities. Computer engineering advances have produced such products as MRIs and CT scans in medicine. Laser technology has numerous applications with refining precision.

Satellites have improved our ability to communicate and transmit radio and television signals. Navigational abilities have been greatly improved through the use of satellite signals.

Sonar technology uses sound waves to locate objects and is especially useful underwater. The sound waves bounce off the object and are used to assist in location. Seismographs record vibrations in the earth and allow us to measure earthquake activity.

USING LABORATORY CHEMICALS AND SOLUTIONS

All laboratory solutions should be prepared as directed in the lab manual. Care should be taken to avoid contamination of solutions and samples. All glassware should be rinsed thoroughly with distilled water before use and cleaned well after use. Safety goggles should be worn while working with glassware, to protect the eyes. All solutions should be made with distilled water, since tap water contains dissolved particles that may affect the results of an experiment. Chemicals should be stored in a secured, dry area and in accordance with the material safety data sheet (MSDS). Acids are to be locked in a separate area. Used solutions should be disposed of according to local disposal procedures. Any questions regarding safe disposal or chemical safety may be directed to the local fire department.

Skill 1.3 Applying methods and criteria for collecting, organizing, and communicating scientific information

THE INTERNATIONAL SYSTEM OF UNITS (SI)

In science, the International System of Units is the global standard of measurement; this allows for easier comparison among experiments done by scientists around the world. The seven base units are presumed to be mutually independent. A kilogram, for example, is the mass of a platinum-iridium cylinder maintained in a laboratory near Paris, France. It used to be the mass of a liter of water.

Seven base units

Base quantity	Unit	Symbol
length	meter	m
mass	kilogram	kg
time	second	s
electric current	Ampere	A
temperature	Kelvin	K
amount of substance	mole	mol
luminous intensity	candela	cd

Prefixes

- **Deca-** = 10X the base unit.
- **Hecto-** = 100X the base unit
- **Kilo-** = 1000X the base unit
- **Deci-** = 1/10 the base unit
- **Centi-** = 1/100 the base unit
- **Milli-** = 1/1000 the base unit

GRAPHING

Graphing is an important way to visually display data for analysis. The two types of graphs most commonly used are the line graph and the bar graph (histogram).

Line Graphs
A line graph shows change over time. They are set up to show two variables. The x-axis is the horizontal axis; this is where the **independent variable** of the experiment is plotted. The y-axis is the vertical axis; the **dependent variable** is plotted here. Dependent variables are manipulated by the experimenter. The axes of a graph should be labeled at equal intervals. If one interval represents one day, the next interval should not represent ten days. A "best fit" line is a smooth curve or straight line drawn through the points of the graph to show the relationship between the variables. Both axes should always be labeled for a graph to be accurately interpreted. Graphs must always include a descriptive title; a good title will describe both the dependent and the independent variables.

Bar Graphs
Bar graphs are set up with category labels along the horizontal axis. An appropriate scale is chosen for the vertical axis that will show the responding variable. A bar is drawn for each category with a height equal to the data along the vertical axis. Each bar represents a separate piece of data and is not joined by a continuous line. Bar graphs should also be given a descriptive title.

Uses for Graphs
The type of graph used to represent one's data depends on the type of data collected. Line graphs are used to compare different sets of related data or to predict data that has not yet be measured. For example, a line graph would be used to compare the rate of activity of different enzymes at varying temperatures. A bar graph or histogram is used to compare different items and make comparisons based on this data. A bar graph would be used to compare the range of ages of children in a classroom. A pie chart is useful when organizing data as part of a whole. A pie chart would be used to display the percent of time students spend on various after-school activities.

TEACHER CERTIFICATION STUDY GUIDE

EXPERIMENTAL ERROR

All experimental uncertainty is due to either random errors or systematic errors.

Random Errors
Random errors are statistical fluctuations in the measured data due to the precision limitations of the measurement device. Random errors usually result from the experimenter's inability to take the same measurement in exactly the same way to get exactly the same number.

Systematic Errors
Systematic errors, by contrast, are reproducible inaccuracies that are consistently made during an experiment at the same point. Systematic errors are often due to a problem that persists throughout the entire experiment.

Systematic and random errors refer to problems associated with making measurements. Mistakes made in the calculations or in reading the instrument are not considered in error analysis.

Appropriate measuring devices
There is an appropriate measuring device for each aspect of science and an appropriate way to measure each variable. A microscope is used to view microscopic objects. A centrifuge is used to separate two or more parts in a liquid sample. The Internet and teaching guides offer resources for laboratory ideas.

The common instrument used for measuring volume is the graduated cylinder. The unit of measurement is usually in milliliters (mL), read for accuracy at the bottom of the meniscus, the curved surface of the liquid.

The common instrument for measuring mass, the triple beam balance measures in tenths of a gram and can estimate mass to hundredths of a gram.
The ruler or meter sticks are the most commonly used instruments for measuring length.

Skill 1.4   Recognizing procedures and sources of information (e.g., state and national standards) for the safe and proper use of equipment and materials used in scientific investigations

All laboratory solutions should be prepared as directed in the lab manual. Care should be taken to avoid contamination. All glassware should be rinsed thoroughly with distilled water before using and cleaned well after use. All solutions should be made with distilled water since tap water contains dissolved particles that may affect the results of an experiment. Unused solutions should be disposed of according to local disposal procedures.

The "Right to Know Law" covers science teachers who work with potentially hazardous chemicals. Briefly, the law states that employees must be informed of potentially toxic chemicals. If requested, an inventory must be made available of the kind, hazards, and properties of the chemicals and checked against the "Substance List." Training must be provided on the safe handling and interpretation of the Material Safety Data Sheet.

The following chemicals are potential carcinogens and are not allowed in school facilities:

- Acrylonitrile
- Arsenic compounds
- Asbestos
- Benzidine
- Benzene
- Cadmium compounds
- Chloroform
- Chromium compounds
- Ethylene oxide
- Ortho-toluidine
- Nickel powder
- Mercury

Chemicals should not be stored on bench tops or heat sources. They should be stored in groups based on their reactivity with one another and in protective storage cabinets in a secured, dry area. All containers within the lab must be labeled. Acids are to be locked in a separate area. Suspect and known carcinogens must be labeled as such and segregated within trays to contain leaks and spills.

Waste should be separated based on its reactivity with other chemicals. Chemical waste should be disposed of in properly labeled containers according to local disposal procedures. Any questions regarding safe disposal or chemical safety may be directed to the local fire department.

Biological material should never be stored near food or water used for human consumption. All biological material should be appropriately labeled. All blood and body fluids should be put in a secure container with a lid to prevent leaking. All biological waste should be disposed of in biological hazardous waste bags.

Material safety data sheets are available— either directly from the company of acquisition or the Internet— for every chemical and biological substance. The manuals for equipment used in the lab should be read and understood before using them. Safety goggles should be worn while working with glassware in case of an accident.

Lab materials are readily available from the many school suppliers that routinely send their catalogues to schools. Many times, common materials are available at the local grocery store. The use of locally available flora and fauna both reduces cost and familiarizes students with local organisms.

Skill 1.5 Applying knowledge of ethical principles to the acquisition, care, handling, and disposal of live organisms

DISSECTIONS

Animals that are not obtained from recognized sources should not be used for laboratory experiments. Decaying animals or those of unknown origin may harbor pathogens and/or parasites that could be harmful to an experimenter's health. Specimens should be rinsed before handling. Non-latex gloves are desirable because some people have latex allergies. If gloves are not available, students with sores or scratches should be excused from the activity. Formaldehyde is a carcinogen and should be avoided or disposed of according to district regulations. Students objecting to dissections for moral reasons should be given alternative assignments.

LIVE SPECIMENS

Biological experiments may be done with all animals except mammalian vertebrates and birds. Lower-order life forms and invertebrates may be used for experimentation. No physiological harm should be inflicted upon the animal. All animals housed and cared for in the school must be handled in a safe and humane manner. Animals are not to remain on school premises during extended vacations unless adequate care is provided. Many state laws stipulate that any instructor who intentionally refuses to comply with the laws may be suspended or dismissed.

MICROBIOLOGY

Pathogenic organisms must never be used for experimentation. Students should adhere to the following rules at all times when working with microorganisms to avoid accidental contamination:

- Treat all microorganisms as if they were pathogenic.
- Maintain sterile conditions at all times.

Check with the Minnesota Department of Education to determine what the state expects of you—not only for the teacher certification test but also for performance in the classroom and for the welfare of your students.

Skill 1.6   Demonstrating understanding of the history of science and the evolution of scientific knowledge, including the contributions of various cultures

The following are some of the major events in the history of science.

CONDEMNATION OF 1277

In 1277, the Bishop of Paris, acting upon the advice of scholars from the University of Paris and in response to a letter from Pope John XXI, condemned certain propositions from Aristotle. An example is the Aristotelian idea that a perfect vacuum is impossible. The Roman Catholic Church maintained such an idea was heretical because it implied that God did not have the power to create a vacuum.

COPERNICAN REVOLUTION

In the third century B.C., Aristarchus suggested that Earth rotated around the sun. Nicolaus Copernicus (1473–1543) expanded this theory to the planets. The heliocentric view is that the sun and the stars are fixed in space and Earth and the other planets revolve around the sun. Planets were called "wandering stars" because of their irregular motion as seen from Earth. According to heliocentrism, the apparent motion of the sun and stars during the day is caused by the 24-hour rotation of Earth around an axis through the North and South Poles.

Using the precise knowledge of the motion of planets observed by Tycho Brahe (1546–1601), Johannes Kepler (1571–1630) discovered three laws of planetary motion:

- The orbit of every planet is an ellipse with the sun at one of the two foci.
- A line joining a planet and the sun sweeps out equal areas during equal intervals of time.
- The square of the time for one rotation around the sun is directly proportional to the cube of the distance from the sun.

In 1616, the Roman Catholic Church condemned heliocentrism because it conflicted with the Bible. In fairness to the church, it should be pointed out that telescopes at the time were not good enough to observe the small yearly motion of the stars caused by Earth's rotation around the sun.

SCIENTIFIC REVOLUTION

The scientific revolution refers to the great advances in scientific knowledge in all fields that occurred from the 17th century to the end of the 19th century. In physics, the universal law of gravity, Newton's laws of motion, statistical mechanics, and electricity and magnetism became fully developed. In chemistry, the atomic theory of matter and the periodic table were understood. There were comparable advances in biology and earth science. An important development in biology was the discovery of evolution by

Charles Darwin.

MODERN PHYSICS

In the early part of the 20th century, there were a number of phenomena that could not be explained by the existing theories of what was called classical physics. For example, it was correctly known that light was a wave. But it was incorrectly thought that a "luminiferous aether" permeated all of space and was the medium light travelled through. The Michaelson-Morley experiment performed in 1897 showed that light traveled in a vacuum at a speed independent of the speed of the observer. This is one of the grounds for Albert Einstein's theory of relativity.

Another example of inexplicable phenomena was that radioactive atoms decayed into other atoms for no apparent reason at all. Furthermore, it could not be predicted when a particular atom would decay. Also, there was no explanation for the wavelengths of the light emitted by gases when stimulated with an electron beam. The development of quantum mechanics and the theory of relativity brought new depth in understanding physics.

BEGINNINGS OF MICROBIOLOGY

Anton van Leeuwenhoek is known as the father of microscopy. In the 1650s, Leeuwenhoek made tiny lenses that produced magnifications up to 300×. He was the first scientist to see and describe bacteria, yeast, plants, and microscopic organisms found in water. Over the years, light microscopes have been refined to produce greater clarity and magnification. The scanning electron microscope (SEM) was developed in the 1950s. Instead of light, a beam of electrons is passed through the specimen. Scanning electron microscopes have a resolution about 1,000 times greater than that of light microscopes. The disadvantage of the SEM is that the chemical and physical methods used to prepare the samples result in the death of the specimen.

In the late 1800s, Louis Pasteur discovered that microorganisms play a causal role in the onset of disease. He also pioneered the pasteurization process and the development of the rabies vaccine. Robert Koch took Pasteur's observation that microorganisms cause disease one step further by postulating that specific diseases were caused by specific pathogens. Koch's postulates, as his discoveries are called, are still used as guidelines in the field of microbiology.

The postulates state that:

- The same pathogen must be found in every person with the same disease.
- The pathogen must be isolated and grown in culture.
- When the organism is re-introduced into an experimental animal, that animal should develop the same disease originally seen.
- The same pathogen must be isolated from the re-infected, experimental animal.

DISCOVERY OF DNA

DNA structure was another key discovery in biological study. In the 1950s, James Watson and Francis Crick discovered that the DNA molecule was organized into a double helix. The discovery of this structure made it possible to explain DNA's ability to replicate and to control protein synthesis.

EXPERIMENTAL MODELS

The use of animals in biological research has expedited many scientific discoveries, including the workings of the circulatory and reproductive systems. One significant use of animals is for the testing of drugs, vaccines, and other products (such as perfumes and shampoos) before use or consumption by humans. Along with the pros of animal research, the cons are also significant. The debate about the ethical treatment of animals has been ongoing since the introduction of animals in research. Many people believe the use of animals in research is cruel and unnecessary. Animal use is federally and locally regulated. The purpose of the Institutional Animal Care and Use Committee (IACUC) is to oversee and evaluate all aspects of an institution's animal care and use program.

Skill 1.7   Demonstrating knowledge of how assumptions, values, and the limitations of available data or theories can influence scientific progress

Scientific hypotheses lead to tests that produce data. Data analysis through statistical methodologies allows conclusions to be drawn, theories to be advanced, and science to progress. Assumptions about hypotheses, tests, data, and conclusions generally should be excluded from science because assumptions typically are partially or wholly incorrect. For example, deep-seated and commonly held assumptions may cause an investigator erroneously to reject some test results not because they do not conform to reality, but because they do not conform to the investigator's assumptions. Likewise, values—religious, social, personal, moral, etc.—should be excluded from the scientific process because they do not add to scientific advancement. This is not to say applied science should not conform with societal values, but rather that scientific investigation should not be hampered by extraneous or external value systems.

Investigators should always remember that no scientific system can be completely understood—a complete set of data is not available for any system. Science progresses as new data are discovered and validated. Because of this, no scientific theory should be considered perfect, complete, or rigidly inflexible. To do so makes the erroneous assumption that the result of some scientific investigation is completely correct and perfect. Investigators therefore must realize that all scientific theory, no matter how well established, is subject to revision based on additional data.

COMPETENCY 002 UNDERSTAND CONNECTIONS BETWEEN SCIENCE, TECHNOLOGY, AND SOCIETY, AND CONNECTIONS BETWEEN SCIENCE AND OTHER SCHOOL SUBJECTS

Skill 2.1 Applying the systems model (e.g., inputs, outputs, feedback) to a given technological, biological, physical, or Earth and space system

The systems model is a graphical representation of any scientific system—from a flashlight to a door latch to brakes on a car to photosynthesis. The systems model helps simplify complex processes. It breaks a system down into four steps:

1. **Input**, such as energy, matter, or food
2. **Process**, such as energy conversion or applied mechanical force
3. **Output**, such as electricity generation, sound, or light
4. **Feedback** uses information from the output to regulate the input and process, and the process repeats.

See Skill 1.1 for more information about models.

Skill 2.2 Demonstrating knowledge of unifying themes, principles, and relationships that connect the different branches of the sciences

Science typically is taught as a variety of discreet disciplines such as physics, chemistry, biology, and so forth. Mathematical studies usually are taught independently of science. Both of these statements are especially true for low- and mid-level curricula. These divisions, while somewhat arbitrary, are enormously useful in limiting curriculum development and in aligning scientific topics with educational schedules. All science disciplines demonstrate numerous unifying themes, principles, and relationships. Some of these major unifying principles are enumerated below:

- The nature of science itself is the process of accumulating scientific knowledge by aggregate investigation into scientific themes through time—and the fact that science is flexible to accommodate newly-discovered data.
- The scientific process seeks to position statistically relevant data as theories that lead to further scientific inquiry.
- All science deals with systems and transformations involving energy transfer.
- Science is measured and modeled on different scales that are related through measurement standards.
- Science seeks to understand and illuminate the processes and patterns of change in existing systems.
- Science establishes the interrelatedness of form and function in the natural world.

Skill 2.3 **Demonstrating knowledge of how the relationships between science and technology lead to new discoveries and advances**

Most modern scientific investigation requires large amounts of capital outlay to proceed. Some of this capital comes from public sources such as government grants; much of this capital comes from private sources such as for-profit entities seeking return on investment. This funding situation tends to direct scientific investigation into areas of technology that are believed to have commercially viable outcomes. As technology increases, additional areas of scientific investigation become possible because additional methods of observation and measurement are available. Thus, advances in science tend to drive advances in technology and, likewise, advances in technology tend to drive advances in science. These mutually supporting processes explain at least in part the phenomenal rate of both scientific and technological advances in modern times.

SCIENCE AND CONSUMER PRODUCTS

An important application of science and technology is the production, storage, use, management, and disposal of consumer products and energy. Scientists from many disciplines work to produce a vast array of consumer products. Energy production and management is another area in which science plays a key role.

Production and Use
The production of a large number of popular consumer products requires scientific knowledge and technology. A few examples of science-based consumer goods are

- Genetically modified foods
- Pharmaceuticals
- Plastics
- Nylon
- Cosmetics
- Household cleaning products
- Color additives

In addition to consumer product production, science helps determine the proper use and storage of consumer goods. Safe use and storage is a key component of successful production. For example, perishable products like food must be stored and used in a safe and sanitary way. Science helps establish limits and guidelines for the storage and use of perishable food products.

Disposal
The management and disposal of consumer products is also an important concern. Scientists help establish limits for the safe use of potentially hazardous consumer products. For example, household cleaning products are potentially hazardous if used improperly. Scientific testing determines the proper uses and potential hazards of such products.

Disposal of waste from consumer product production and use is of great concern. Proper disposal of hazardous waste and recycling of durable materials is important for the health and safety of human populations, as well as for the long-term sustainability of Earth's resources and environment.

USES OF GENETIC ENGINEERING

Many microorganisms are used to detoxify toxic chemicals and to recycle waste. Sewage treatment plants use microbes to degrade organic compounds. Some compounds, like chlorinated hydrocarbons, cannot be easily degraded. Scientists are working on genetically modifying microbes so they can degrade the harmful compounds that the current microbes cannot.

Genetic engineering has also benefited agriculture. For example, many dairy cows are given bovine growth hormone to increase milk production. Commercially grown plants often are genetically modified for optimal growth.

Strains of wheat, cotton, and soybeans have been developed to resist herbicides used to control weeds. This allows for the successful growth of the plants while destroying the weeds. Crop plants are also being engineered to resist infections and pests. Scientists can genetically modify crops to contain a viral gene that does not affect the plant but will "vaccinate" the plant from a virus attack. Crop plants are now being modified to resist insect attacks. This allows farmers to reduce the amount of pesticide used on plants.

ENERGY

Energy production and management is an increasingly important topic in scientific research because of the increasing scarcity of energy-yielding resources, such as petroleum. With traditional sources of energy becoming more scarce and costly, a major goal of scientific energy research is the creation of alternative, efficient means of energy production. Examples of potential sources of alternative energy include:

- Wind
- Water
- Solar
- Nuclear
- Geothermal
- Biomass

An important concern in the production and use of energy, both from traditional and alternative sources, is the affect on the environment and the safe disposal of waste products. Scientific research and study helps determine the best method for energy production, use, and waste product disposal, balancing the need for energy with the associated environmental and health concerns.

Skill 2.4 **Describing similarities and differences between the goals and processes of scientific inquiry and between technological and engineering design**

Scientific inquiry in its purest sense encapsulates the idea that knowledge about the physical world is intrinsically valuable. Thus, the pursuit of knowledge via scientific investigation is its own reward, and any knowledge obtained is worthwhile. Many researchers closely align with this viewpoint and thus pursue investigations into the natural world, which (to the lay person) perhaps have no discernable purpose beyond the accumulation of data. In tandem with this ideology is the purely abstracted scientific process that tolerates no external morality or influence and indeed seeks to eliminate all subjectivity of interpretation. This stance can be summarized by the phrase "science for the sake of science."

On the other hand, technological design and engineering design have vastly different goals that generally are driven by economic pressures. For example, technological design usually seeks a solution to an existing problem in a commercial commodity; engineering design usually seeks a solution to an existing problem or an enhancement to a given process in some commercial commodity. As these processes are therefore driven primarily by economic concerns, they rarely are performed simply for the sake of experimentation and information gathering.

Nevertheless, similarities between the processes exist. They are all rigorous disciplines that require good education and training. These processes often result in failure. They often require extensive testing and result in large amounts of data. They often use mathematics and statistical analysis to demonstrate cause-and-effect. And often, so-called pure-science investigations open the doorway for subsequent technological and engineering exploitation.

Skill 2.5 **Demonstrating knowledge of the use of computer models, diagrams, flowcharts, tables, graphs, and mathematical relationships to interpret, model, and solve problems**

Most complex processes or paradigms can be described with words to some degree of clarity, but sometimes "a picture is worth one thousand words." Diagrams attempt to illustrate a process using graphical elements. Diagrams can use photographic, realistic, or schematic portrayals of objects and often use some type of arrow or directional indicator to indicate relatedness or direction of process flow through time. Flowcharts usually are schematically presented and tightly couple the flow of time to the presentation of information—they are especially useful to illustrate events happening through time.

Graphs are used to present large amounts of aggregated numerical data in easily interpreted formats; numerous types of graphs exist, all more or less suited to specific types of data presentation. In modern times computer models have become quite complex and accurate in predicting the behavior of complex systems.

Computer models usually also have the added benefit of rapid execution. These types of tools can and should be used in the pursuit of scientific knowledge because they accurately and rapidly present large amounts of data in formats that would otherwise be fairly inaccessible to a typical reader. Most of them can be color-coordinated or use other visual artifacts to accent salient details. However, thought must be given to readers with potential visual impairments, however. In other words, alternative textual descriptions should also be provided.

These methods are suitable for use at any point during a process—they can be used before an investigation commences to predict results; they can be used during an investigation to demonstrate progress; and they can be used so summarize final results. In this way, these tools can help interpret, model, and solve problems. They should not, of course, replace rigorous design. Care must also be taken to ensure that computer models do not mischaracterize the system under study.

Skill 2.6 Analyzing social, economic, and ethical issues related to scientific and technological developments

ETHICS AND SCIENCE

Genetic engineering has drastically advanced biotechnology, but, along with these advancements, has raised safety and ethical questions. Many safety concerns have been answered by government regulations. The FDA, USDA, EPA, and National Institutes of Health are a few of the government agencies that regulate pharmaceutical, food, and environmental technology advancements.

Several ethical questions arise when discussing biotechnology. Should embryonic stem cell research be allowed? Is animal testing humane? These are just a couple of ethical questions that arise when discussing biotechnology. There are strong arguments for both sides of the issues, as well as some government regulations in place to monitor the application of biotechnology.

Politics

Concepts that reflect on a person's ethics may be used for political purposes, either to further one's agenda or to hurt an opponent. Recent political issues with ethical and scientific ties include abortion, stem-cell research, and cloning. There are at least two sides to each issue, and as such, they can easily become a partisan topic that can affect the outcome of elections.

Increasingly, local, state, national, and global governments and organizations must consider policy issues related to science and technology. For example, local and state governments must analyze the impact of proposed development and growth on the environment. Governments and communities must balance the demands of an expanding human population with the local ecology to ensure sustainable growth.

ECONOMY AND SCIENCE

Another segment of society affected by science is the economy. Scientific and technological breakthroughs greatly influence other fields of study and the job market. All academic disciplines use computer and information technology to simplify research and information sharing. In addition, advances in science and technology influence the types of available jobs and the desired work skills. For example, machines and computers continue to rapidly replace unskilled laborers. In addition, computer and technological literacy is now a requirement for many jobs and careers. Finally, science and technology continue to change the very nature of careers. Because of science and technology's great influence on all areas of the economy, careers are far less stable than in past eras. Workers can thus expect to change jobs and companies much more often than in the past.

SCIENTIFIC PROGRESS

Society faces many issues associated with medical advances. Many medical advances require us to examine our beliefs, and these ethical issues were addressed earlier. Another aspect is the length of human life. As we develop cures for illnesses and learn how to better care for ourselves and the environment, we are pushing back nature's hold. In previous centuries, the average person would live to be sixty, and, in a family of thirteen children, only two might live to adulthood. Many died from polio, measles, and mumps. Children today are routinely vaccinated for all three of these diseases. People were also susceptible to death by infection, sometimes from a cut or abscessed tooth. We have created antibiotics to prevent prolonged biotic growth and subsequent illness.

These are common examples, but we have also found ways to cure less common, lethal diseases, and to provide amazing surgical aid, such as organ transplants. While many used to die from cancer, our cure rates are improving. Screening is essential and expensive, but not nearly as expensive as the chemotherapy and radiation drugs available for these diseases. While it is wonderful to live a longer, healthier life, it has created challenges. The procedures that enable us to live longer are not free.

MANAGEMENT OF NATURAL RESOURCES

How long our natural resources will last depends on future demand and willingness on the part of governments to efficiently manage their energy needs and resources. Likewise, industry can help by getting more deeply involved by modifying existing, or developing new techniques and procedures to effectively use our natural materials. Unfortunately, natural resources are not evenly distributed throughout the earth, and political considerations, to date, have hampered cooperation in conservation efforts and development of alternative energy sources on a global scale.

As grim as the projected shortfalls may seem, there is some hope. There is a growing awareness of the problems we face, and, although not usually coordinated on a global scale, some countries are taking steps to address the issues.

Better agricultural techniques to prevent soil depletion, reclamation of waterways, banning use of chemicals damaging to the atmosphere, recycling plastics and metals, and seeking alternative energy sources are all examples of ongoing initiatives to ensure resources for future generations.

Water conservation
We live on a watery planet. Unfortunately, a large percentage (97 percent) of the water is not fit for human consumption or agricultural use because of its high salinity.

Plants and animals (including humans) require water for survival. In fact, statistics show that every person in the United States uses 300 liters of water per day, and when industrial uses are included, that number soars to roughly 5,000 liters per day, per person. Groundwater provides drinking water for 53 percent of the population in the United States. Much groundwater is clean enough to drink without any type of treatment. Impurities in the water are filtered out by the rocks and soil through which it flows.

Nonrenewable resource concerns
The focus in nonrenewable resources is the ever-increasing demand for energy. The key concern about nonrenewable resources is that once they are depleted, they are permanently gone.

Despite a finite supply of fossil fuels and radioactive fuels such as uranium, at our present rate of consumption, there are only an estimated 28 years of petroleum reserves and 40 years of uranium reserves left. To alleviate this predictable energy gap, scientists are exploring new methods of recovering additional fuels from once economically unfeasible sites and researching alternative energy sources.

ALTERNATIVE ENERGY RESOURCES

The research efforts into alternative energy sources are directed at producing viable renewable energy sources.

Hydroelectric power: Producing power from falling water is not a new idea since waterwheels have been in use for centuries. The drawback to this energy source lies in the availability of suitable locations for dams and the expense of construction.

Wind power: Windmills are another ancient technology being revisited by engineers, but wind generators produce very little electricity for the expense involved, and suitable locations (with steady, high winds) for wind fields are limited.

Tidal power: Another concept in use in some areas of the world is generating electricity by deflecting and diverting strong tidal currents through offshore turbines that drive electric generators. Again, the presence of proper conditions (strong tidal power) is necessary, and suitable locations are limited.

Geothermal energy: In some areas of the world, such as New Zealand, Iceland, and Italy, energy is produced from hot, igneous rocks within the earth. Rainwater percolates through porous strata near an **active magma chamber** and flashes to steam. Some of the steam returns to the surface through natural fissures or is extracted through drilled vents. The steam is captured and routed to turbine-powered electrical generators to produce geothermal power or may be used to directly heat buildings. For example, Reykjavik, Iceland, uses the captured steam to directly heat buildings. The limitations of this alternative energy source are obvious: the majority of metropolitan locations are not situated near an active magma chamber, but New Zealand does manage to gather enough geothermal power to meet approximately 5% of its electrical needs.

Solar energy: Solar power can be used directly as a source of heat or indirectly to produce electricity. The most common use is to heat water. An array of dark colored piping is placed on the roof of a structure and, as water circulates through the piping, it heats.

Solar cells: Solar cells produce electricity from solar radiation. **Photons** striking the junction between two semiconductors (usually selenium) induce an electrical current that is stored in batteries. Although this source of power is pollution free, there are two main limitations.

First, the production of power is limited by the distribution and periods of **insolation**, and atmospheric conditions can easily interfere with collection efforts (i.e., winter months, cloud cover, pollution, and storms).

Second, the solar cells individually produce small amounts of electricity (trickle changes) and must be arrayed in large banks. For example, a solar power plant with a capacity of 100 MW would cover a surface area of approximately 4 km2.

Solar cells have been used successfully in outer space where atmospheric conditions and cell-size restraints are of less concern. Spacecraft and satellites use solar cells to charge batteries that provide electrical power for communications equipment and operating power.

Biomass: Plant and animal wastes (decaying or decayed) can be burned to produce heat for steam turbine electrical generators. In most highly developed countries, the biomass is first converted to either methane gas (given off by decaying biomass) or alcohol, but in some underdeveloped countries, the biomass is still burned directly as a fuel source. For example, for centuries, peat bogs have been exploited as a traditional source of home heating and cooking fuel.

Fusion power: Although the technology does not currently exist, researchers are actively pursuing the means to make nuclear **fusion** power a reality. Unlike **fission**, the other form of nuclear energy currently in use, fusion does not rely on splitting atoms of uranium or other potentially deadly radioactive elements. Instead, fusion energy mimics the same process that produces the energy of the sun.

Energy is produced when small atomic nuclei fuse together to form new atoms. In a fusion reaction, two isotopes of hydrogen, deuterium, and tritium combine to make helium. The most significant advantage offered by fusion power as compared to fission power is that no dangerous radioactive isotopes are produced. The reaction produces only harmless helium that easily diffuses into the atmosphere and escapes into outer space. Additionally, the elements required for a fusion reaction are abundant on Earth (i.e., deuterium and tritium are extracted from seawater), and readily renew themselves through natural processes.

GLOBAL WARMING

Global warming is an increase in the earth's average temperature, resulting, at least in part, from the burning of fuels by humans. Global warming is hazardous because it disrupts the earth's environmental balance and can negatively affect weather patterns. Ecological and weather pattern changes can promote the natural disasters listed above.

Skill 2.7   **Demonstrating knowledge of how the systematic approaches of science can inform courses of action for addressing problems related to personal, local, national, or global challenges**

Scientific research and results should not rigidly dictate a course of action according to any given paradigm. Instead, systematic approaches to science should be used to inform decisions made to select a course of action for addressing problems related to personal, local, national, and global challenges. For example, if scientific studies indicate two available medications provide substantively different outcomes in the treatment of a given disease, policy makers should take note of this fact and presumably select the medication that provides the best outcome. This fact must be weighed against other factors however. Perhaps the cost of the better medication is prohibitive.

Thus, while the raw scientific data might suggest one course of action, the entire situation may suggest another course of action. Science should not be relied upon as infallible, nor should it be viewed as the ultimate source of authority. Instead, science and scientific data should be fed into the decision-making process. Often, science is viewed as the ultimate source of authority because policymakers are intimidated by data they do not understand. This attitude should be avoided and, if necessary, experts should be consulted to explain the scientific data in layman's terms.

Skill 2.8 Demonstrating knowledge of how to assess a certain course of action in terms of alternatives, costs, risks, and benefits

Political and policy decisions should be informed by available substantive scientific data. These data, however, should not be viewed as infallible nor should they be taken as the ultimate authority. Instead, these data should supplement the decision-making process and form a framework of understanding to approach the situation with a logical methodology. Decisions should take into consideration all available alternatives, weighing the costs, risks, benefits, and potential outcomes of each alternative. Scientific data should be used to answer questions about risks, benefits, and potential outcomes. Ultimately, the policy-making individuals should consider all information prior to making an informed and rational decision. In politics, these decisions may further be complicated by compromise.

Skill 2.9 Recognizing opportunities for further education and careers in the sciences and the role of the sciences in everyday life

Scientific education is commonly available through established and accredited institutions of higher learning. A variety of programs are available, from the standard course of study leading to degrees through certification in specific areas. Interested persons should consult with local and regional educational organizations. Careers in science are quite varied and include educators, technicians, investigators, researchers, and sales representatives. The medical field offers excellent opportunities in combining scientific research with medical practice and pharmaceuticals.

The sciences have impacted our everyday life in manifold ways. Research into information systems and mass communication methodologies have revolutionized the developed world, while research into agriculture, public health, and pharmaceuticals impinge on every corner of the globe. Indeed, the modern way of life is based on a combination of technological and medical advances made possible through prolonged and constant scientific research.

COMPETENCY 003	UNDERSTAND THE CONTENT AND METHODS FOR DEVELOPING STUDENTS' CONTENT-AREA READING SKILLS TO SUPPORT THEIR READING AND LEARNING IN THE SCIENCES

Skill 3.1 Demonstrating knowledge of key components and processes involved in reading (e.g., vocabulary knowledge, including orthographic and morphological knowledge; background knowledge; knowledge of academic discourse, including the syntactic and organizational structures used in print and digital academic texts; print processing abilities, including decoding skills; use of cognitive and metacognitive skills and strategies)

In 2000, the National Reading Panel released its now well-known report on teaching children to read. This report partially put to rest the debate between phonics and whole language. It essentially argued that word–letter recognition is as important as understanding what the text means. The report's "Big 5" critical areas of reading instruction are explained in the following sections.

PHONEMIC AWARENESS

Phonemic awareness is the acknowledgement of sounds and words; for example, a child's realization that some words rhyme is one of the skills that fall under this category. **Onset** and **rhyme** are skills that might help students learn that the sound of the first letter "b" in the word "bad" can be changed with the sound "d" to make it "dad." The key in phonemic awareness is that it can be taught with the students' eyes closed; in other words, it's all about understanding sounds, not ascribing written letters to sounds.

PHONICS

As opposed to phonemic awareness, the study of phonics must be done with the eyes open. **Phonics** is the connection between sounds and the letters on a page. In other words, students learning phonics might see the word "bad" and sound each letter out slowly until they recognize that they just said the word.

FLUENCY

When students practice **fluency**, they practice reading connected pieces of text. In other words, instead of looking at a word as just a word, they might read a sentence straight through. The point of fluency is for the student to comprehend what he or she is reading by putting words in a sentence together quickly. If a student is NOT fluent in reading, he or she would sound each letter or word out slowly and pay more attention to the phonics of each word. A fluent reader, on the other hand, might read a sentence out loud using appropriate intonations.

The best way to test for fluency is to have a student read something out loud, preferably a few sentences in a row. Most students just learning to read will not be very fluent right away, but with practice, they will increase their fluency. Even though fluency is not the same as comprehension, fluency is a good predictor of comprehension; when the student is freed from focusing on sounding out each word, he or she can shift attention to the meaning of the words.

COMPREHENSION

Comprehension simply means that the reader can ascribe meaning to text. Even though students may be good with phonics and may know what many words on a page mean, some of them are not able to demonstrate comprehension because they do not have the tools to help them comprehend. For example, students should know that stories often have structures (beginning, middle, and end). They should also know that when they are reading something and it does not make sense, they will need to employ "fix-up" strategies where they go back into the text they just read and look for clues. Teachers can use many strategies to teach comprehension, including questioning, asking students to paraphrase or summarize, utilizing graphic organizers, and focusing on mental images.

VOCABULARY

Students will be better at comprehension if they have a stronger working vocabulary. Research has shown that students learn more vocabulary when it is presented in context, rather than in vocabulary lists, for example. Furthermore, the more students get to use particular words in context, the more they will remember each word and utilize the words in the comprehension of sentences that contain the words.

Also see Skill 3.4.

Skill 3.2   **Demonstrating the ability to plan instruction and select strategies that support all students' content-area reading (e.g., differentiating instruction to meet the needs of students with varying reading proficiency levels and linguistic backgrounds, identifying and addressing gaps in students' background knowledge, scaffolding reading tasks for students who experience comprehension difficulties)**

READING ASSESSMENT

Assessment is the practice of collecting information about children's progress, and **evaluation** is the process of judging the children's responses to determine how well they are achieving particular goals or demonstrating reading skills. Assessment and evaluation are intricately connected in the literacy classroom. Assessment is necessary because teachers need ways to determine what students are learning and how they are progressing. In addition, assessment is a tool that can also help students take ownership of their own learning and become partners in their ongoing development as readers and writers. In this day of public accountability, clear, definite, and reliable assessment creates confidence in public education. There are two broad categories of assessment.

Formal assessment is composed of standardized tests and procedures carried out under prescribed conditions. Formal assessments include state tests, standardized achievement tests, NAEP tests, and the like.

Informal assessment is the use of observation and other non-standardized procedures to compile anecdotal and observational data/evidence of children's progress. Informal assessment includes but is not limited to checklists, observations, and performance tasks.

Skills to be evaluated

- The ability to use syntactic cues when encountering an unknown word. Good readers will expect the word to fit the syntax they are familiar with. Poor readers may substitute a word that does not fit the syntax and will not correct themselves.
- The ability to use semantic cues to determine the meaning of an unknown word. Good readers will consider the meanings of all the known words in the sentence. Poor readers may read one word at a time with no regard for the other words.
- The ability to use schematic cues to connect words with prior knowledge. Good readers will incorporate what they know with what the text says or implies. Poor readers may think only of the word they are reading without associating it with prior knowledge.
- The ability to use phonics cues to improve ease and efficiency in reading. Good readers will apply letter and sound associations almost subconsciously. Poor readers may have one of two kinds of problems: They may have underdeveloped phonics skills, and use only an initial clue without analyzing vowel patterns before quickly guessing the word. Or, they may use phonics skills in isolation, becoming so absorbed in the word "noises" that they ignore or forget the message of the text.
- The ability to process information from the text. Good readers should be able to get information from the text as well as store, retrieve, and integrate it for later use.
- The ability to use interpretive thinking to make logical predictions and inferences.
- The ability to use critical thinking to make decisions and insights about the text.
- The ability to use appreciative thinking to respond to the text, whether emotionally, mentally, or ideologically.

Methods of evaluation

- Assess students at the beginning of each year to determine grouping for instruction.
- Judge whether a student recognizes that a word does not make sense.
- Monitor whether the student knows when to ignore a reading mistake and read on or when to reread a sentence.
- Look for skills such as recognizing cause and effect, finding main ideas, and using comparison and contrast techniques.
- Keep dated records to follow individual progress. Focus on a few students each day. Grade them on a scale of one to five according to how well they perform certain reading abilities (such as making logical predictions). Include informal observations such as, "Ed was able to determine the meaning of the word 'immigrant' by examining the other words in the sentence."
- Remember that evaluation is important but fostering an enjoyment of reading is the ultimate goal. Keep reading pressure-free and fun so that students do not become intimidated by reading. Even if the students are not meeting standards, if they continue to want to read each day, that is a success!

DIFFERENTIATION OF INSTRUCTION

Teachers can differentiate instruction in order to address the needs of students with varying levels of reading proficiency.

Differentiation of instruction occurs when the teacher will vary the content, process, or product used in instruction (Tomlinson, 1995).

There are three primary ways to differentiate:

- **Content**: The specifics of what is learned. This does not mean that whole units or concepts should be modified. However, within certain topics, specifics can be modified.
- **Process**: The route to learning the content. All students do not have to learn the content using exactly the same method.
- **Product**: The result of the learning. Usually, a product is the result or assessment of learning. For example, not all students are going to demonstrate complete learning on a quiz; likewise, not all students will demonstrate complete learning on a written paper.

There are two keys to successful differentiation:

- **Knowing what is essential in the curriculum**: Although certain things can be modified, other things must remain intact and in a specific order. Disrupting central components of a curriculum can actually damage a student's ability to learn something successfully.

- **Knowing the needs of the students**: While this can take quite some time to figure out, it is very important that teachers pay attention to the interests, tendencies, and abilities of their students so that they understand how each of their students will best learn.

Many students will need certain concepts explained in greater depth; others may pick up on concepts rather quickly. For this reason, teachers will want to adapt the curriculum in a way that gives students the opportunity to learn at their own pace while also keeping the class together as a community. Although this can be difficult, the more creative a teacher is with the ways in which students can demonstrate mastery, the more fun the experience will be for students and teachers. Furthermore, teachers will reach students more successfully if they tailor lesson plans, activities, groupings, and other elements of curriculum to each student's need. The reasons for differentiating instruction are based on two important differences in children: interest and ability.

Differentiating Reading Instruction
Differentiating reading instruction is a bit complex. When a teacher wants to ensure that each student in his class is getting the most out of the reading instruction, the teacher will need to consider the level at which the student is proficient in reading—as well as the specific areas in which each student struggles. It is first important to use a variety of sources of data to make decisions on differentiation, rather than rely on just one test, for example.

When teachers have proficient readers in their classrooms, they usually feel that these students need less attention and less work. This is a mistake. If these students are not provided appropriate instruction and challenging activities to increase their reading abilities further, they may become disengaged with school. These students benefit greatly from integrating classroom reading with other types of reading, perhaps complementing the whole-class novel with some additional short stories or nonfiction pieces.

They also benefit from sustained silent reading, in which they can choose their own books and read independently. Discussion groups and teacher-led discussion activities are also very useful for these students. It is important, however, to ensure that these students do not feel that they have to do more work than everyone else. Remember, differentiation does not distinguish differences in quantity; it distinguishes differences in types of work.

Average readers may benefit from many of the things that highly proficient readers do; however, they may need more skill instruction. Most likely, they will not need as much skill instruction as weak readers, but they will benefit highly from having a teacher who knows which skills they are lacking and teaches them to use those skills in their own reading.

Weak readers need to focus highly on skills. Teachers will want to encourage them to make predictions, connect ideas, outline concepts, evaluate, and summarize. The

TEACHER CERTIFICATION STUDY GUIDE

activities that these students engage in should be developed to instill reading strategies that they can use in their independent reading and to propel them toward higher levels of reading.

Alternatives to Textbooks

There is a wide variety of materials available to today's teachers. Personal computers with Internet connections are becoming more common in classrooms, and teachers can bring the content of a reference book alive in text, motion, and sound. Textbook publishers often provide video, recordings, and software to accompany the text, as well as overhead transparencies and colorful posters to help students visualize what is being taught. To stay current in the field, teachers can scan the educational publishers' brochures that arrive at their principal's or department head's office or attend workshops, conferences, and presentations by educational publishers.

Skill 3.3 **Demonstrating knowledge of explicit strategies for facilitating students' comprehension before, during, and after reading content-area texts and for promoting their use of comprehension strategies**

Content-area texts are usually nonfiction. Therefore, students can use specific strategies to better comprehend the text. Content area subjects often have texts with a great deal of information. More information is included than is necessary for students to know at one time. Therefore, it is necessary for students to develop specific skills to help them take in the important information while weeding out the less important.

- **Highlighting**: this is a difficult strategy for students to master. Even at the college level, it seems that students have a hard time determining what is most important. Students have a tendency to highlight too much information. Encourage students to highlight less: Key ideas and vocabulary are a good place to start.
- **Outlining**: this is a skill that many teachers use to help students understand the most important facts. Creating outlines can be difficult for some students, so teachers may want to provide the outline to the students to use as a guide when taking their own notes. In this way, the students know what to focus on when reading.
- **Summarizing**: this strategy helps students identify key information. To create a summary, a student should identify the main idea of a passage, and then find the details that support the main idea. Using this information, the student can then write a short summary.
- **Question answering**: While this tends to be overused in many classrooms, it is still a valid method of teaching students to comprehend. Students answer questions regarding a text, either out loud, in small groups, or individually on paper. The best questions are those that cause students to think about the text (rather than just find an answer within the text).
- **Question generating**: This is the opposite of question answering, although students can then be asked to answer their own questions or the questions of

peers. In general, we want students to constantly question texts as they read. This is important because it causes students to become more critical readers. To teach students to generate questions helps them to learn the types of questions they can ask and it gets them thinking about how best to be critical of texts.

- **Monitoring comprehension**: Students need to be aware of their comprehension, or lack of it, in particular texts. So, it is important to teach students what to do when suddenly text stops making sense. For example, students can go back and reread the description of a character. Or, they can go back to the table of contents or the first paragraph of a chapter to see where they are headed.
- **Discussion**: Small group or whole-class discussion stimulates thoughts about texts and gives students a larger picture of the impact of those texts. For example, teachers can strategically encourage students to discuss related concepts to the text. This helps students learn to consider texts within larger societal and social concepts. Or teachers can encourage students to provide personal opinions in discussion. By listening to various students' opinions, this will help all students in a class to see the wide range of possible interpretations and thoughts regarding one text.
- **Textual features**: these facilitate the location of pertinent information. Headings, bold text, text in boxes, diagrams, photos, and captions bring attention to important information and clarify key concepts and ideas. The table of contents and index allow students to search for information, and the glossary lists key terms and their definitions.
- **Graphic organizers**: This is the opposite of question answering, although students can then be asked to answer their own questions or the questions of peers. In general, we want students to constantly question texts as they read. This is important because it causes students to become more critical readers. To teach students to generate questions helps them to learn the types of questions they can ask and it gets them thinking about how best to be critical of texts.
- **Textual marking**: This is where students interact with the text as they read. For example, armed with sticky notes, students can insert questions or comments regarding specific sentences or paragraphs within the text. This helps students focus on the importance of the small things, particularly when they are reading larger works (such as novels in high school). It also gives students a reference point on which to go back into the text when they need to review something.

The point of comprehension instruction is not necessarily to focus just on the text(s) students are using at the very moment of instruction, but rather to help them learn the strategies that they can use independently with any other text.

Skill 3.4 Demonstrating knowledge of explicit strategies for promoting students' academic language and vocabulary development, including their knowledge of domain-specific vocabulary words

Here are some strategies that teachers can use to increase the development of vocabulary skills in students:

Context clues help readers determine the meanings of words they are not familiar with. The **context** of a word is the text that surrounds the word. Context clues can appear within the sentence itself, within the preceding and/or following sentences, or within the passage as a whole. Read the following sentences and attempt to determine the meaning of the word in bold print:

> The **luminosity** of the room was so incredible that there was no need for lights.

If there was no need for lights, then one must assume that the word luminosity has something to do with giving off light. The definition of luminosity, therefore, is "the emission of light."

Word classification helps students draw comparisons between different types of words. Young children might begin by looking at parts of speech. Older students might begin by classifying the words in more specific categories based on the content area or other classification system.

Etymology is the study of the history of words. Understanding the language basis of words can help in determining the meaning and in building comprehension. It is particularly useful to know the definitions of prefixes, suffixes, and root words; these can help determine the meaning of several other words. For example, the Latin root "bene" means "good" or "well." English words from this root include "benefit," "beneficial," and "beneficiary." In math, knowing Greek and Latin roots can help students learn the names of geometrical shapes and other mathematical terms.

Application of Vocabulary Words in New Situations: Understanding what a word means in one context helps the student for that one reading passage. Learning to transfer that understanding to new and varied situations helps the student become a life-long learner and reader. This transfer of knowledge can be done by asking students to think of other situations where the word can be used, or by providing examples from other content areas.

Content area vocabulary is the specific vocabulary related to particular concepts of various academic disciplines (social science, science, math, art, etc). While teachers tend to think of content area vocabulary as something that should be focused on just at the secondary level (middle and high school), even elementary school students studying various subjects will understand concepts better when the vocabulary used to describe them is explicitly explained. But it is true that in the secondary level, where students go to different teachers for each subject, content area vocabulary becomes more emphasized.

Often, educators believe that vocabulary should just be taught in a language arts class, not realizing that there is not enough time for students to learn the enormous vocabulary in only one class in order to be successful with a standards-based education and that the teaching of vocabulary related to a particular subject is a very good way to help students understand the subject better.

First and foremost, teachers should teach strategies to determine the meanings for difficult vocabulary when students encounter it on their own. Teachers can do this by teaching students how to identify the meanings of words in context (usually through activities where the word is taken out, and the students have to figure out a way to make sense of the sentence). In addition, dictionary skills must be taught in all subject areas. Teachers should also consider that teaching vocabulary is not just the teaching of words; rather, it is the teaching of complex concepts, each with histories and connotations.

When teachers explicitly teach vocabulary, it is best if they can connect new words to ideas, words, and experiences with which students are already familiar. This will help to reduce the strangeness of the new words. Furthermore, the more concrete the examples, the more likely students will be able to use the word in context.
Finally, students need plenty of exposure to the new words. They need to be able to hear and use the new words in many naturally produced sentences. The more one hears and uses a sentence in context, the more the word is solidified in the person's long-term vocabulary.

Also see Skill 3.1.

Skill 3.5 **Demonstrating knowledge of explicit strategies for developing students' critical literacy skills (e.g., encouraging students to question texts, developing students' ability to analyze texts from multiple viewpoints or perspectives)**

See Skill 3.3.

Skill 3.6 **Demonstrating the ability to plan instruction and select strategies that support students' reading and understanding of sources of information in the sciences (e.g., helping students follow laboratory instructions and interpret diagrams and graphs)**

See Skills 1.2, 1.3, and 3.2.

TEACHER CERTIFICATION STUDY GUIDE

DOMAIN II: EARTH AND SPACE SYSTEMS

COMPETENCY 004   UNDERSTAND THE COMPONENTS AND EVOLUTION OF THE EARTH SYSTEM

Skill 4.1   Describing the formation and physical properties of Earth materials

STRUCTURE OF THE EARTH

The interior of the earth is divided into three chemically distinct layers. Starting from the middle and moving toward the surface are the **core**, the **mantle**, and the **crust**. Much of what we know about the inner structure of the earth has been inferred from various data. Subsequently, there is still some uncertainty about the composition and conditions in the earth's interior.

Core
The outer core of the earth begins about 3,000 km beneath the surface and is a liquid, though far more viscous than that of the mantle. Even deeper, approximately 5,000 km beneath the surface, is the solid inner core. The inner core has a radius of about 1,200 km. Temperatures in the core exceed 4,000°C. Scientists agree that this inner core is extremely dense. This conclusion is based on the fact that the earth is known to have an average density of 5,515 kg/m3, even though the material close to the surface has an average density of only 3,000 kg/m3. Therefore, a denser core must exist. Additionally, it is hypothesized that when the earth was forming, the densest material sank to the middle of the planet. Thus, it is not surprising that the core is about 80% iron. In fact, there is some speculation that the entire inner core is a single iron crystal, while the outer core is a mix of liquid iron and nickel.

Mantle
The earth's mantle begins about 35 km beneath the surface and stretches all the way to 3,000 km beneath the surface, where the outer core begins. Since the mantle stretches so far into the earth's center, its temperature varies widely; near the boundary with the crust, it is approximately 1,000°C, while near the outer core it may reach nearly 4,000° C. Within the mantle, there are silicate rocks that are rich in iron and magnesium. The silicate rocks exist as solids, but the high heat means they are ductile enough to "flow" over a long time period. In general, the mantle is a semi-solid/plastic, and the viscosity varies as pressures and temperatures change at varying depths.

Crust
It is not clear how long the earth actually has had a solid crust; most of the rocks are less than 100 million years old, though some are 4.4 billion years old. The crust of the earth is the outermost layer and is between 5 and 70 km thick. Thin areas generally exist under ocean basins (oceanic crust), and thicker crust underlies the continents (continental crust). Oceanic crust is composed largely of iron magnesium silicate rocks, while continental crust is less dense and consists mainly of sodium potassium aluminum silicate rocks. The crust is the least dense layer of the earth, and so it is rich in those

materials that floated, theoretically, during Earth's formation. Additionally, some heavier elements that bound to lighter materials are present in the crust.

INTERACTIONS BETWEEN THE LAYERS

These layers do not exist as separate entities, with little interaction between them. For instance, it is generally believed that swirling of the iron-rich liquid in the outer core results in the earth's **magnetic field**, which is readily apparent on the surface. Heat also moves out from the core to the mantle and crust. The core still retains heat from the formation of the earth, and additional heat is generated by the decay of radioactive isotopes. While most of the heat in our atmosphere comes from the sun, radiant heat from the core does warm oceans and other large bodies of water.

There is also a great deal of interaction between the mantle and the crust. The slow convection of rocks in the mantle is responsible for the shifting of tectonic plates on the crust. Matter can also move between the layers, as during the rock cycle. During the rock cycle, igneous rocks are formed when **magma**, or lava, escapes from the mantle during volcanic eruption. Rocks may also be forced back into the mantle, where the high heat and pressure recreate them as metamorphic rocks.

Skill 4.2 Recognizing the physical, environmental, biological, structural, and tectonic processes that influence the formation of a given rock (e.g., sedimentary, igneous, metamorphic)

MINERALS

Minerals must adhere to five criteria. A mineral must be

- Inorganic
- Formed in nature
- Solid in form
- Its atoms must form a crystalline pattern
- Its chemical composition must be fixed within narrow limits

There are over 3,000 different types of minerals in Earth's crust, which are classified by composition. The major groups of minerals are silicates, carbonates, oxides, sulfides, sulfates, and halides. The largest group of minerals is the silicates. Silicates are made of silicon, oxygen, and one or more other elements.

ROCKS

Rocks are made of minerals. There are three different types of rocks:

- Sedimentary
- Igneous

- Metamorphic

Rocks are classified according to where they form, how they form, and what their composition is.

Sedimentary Rocks
Lithification is the process by which sedimentary rocks are formed from sediment. Compaction and cementation of sediment is one of the main ways that sedimentary rocks are formed. Compaction occurs when the weight of overlying materials compresses and compacts the deeper sediments. Often there is some sort of substance that acts as a glue to hold sediment together. This is the process of **cementation**. Minerals such as quartz or calcite may take on the role of this glue.

Sedimentary rocks are typically formed in layers. Rocks such as shale and limestone are sedimentary rocks. In such sedimentary rocks as sandstone, conglomerate, and breccia, one can often see how sediment has been glued together to form the rock. Sedimentary rocks usually form in the presence of water. Whether it is in the deep ocean, along a riverbed, or at a beach, these are the areas where sediment is often glued and compacted together.

Igneous Rocks
Igneous rocks can be classified according to their texture, their composition, and their formation process. Igneous rocks form from melted rock. This melted rock is called **magma** when it is under Earth's surface. The same melted rock is called **lava** when it is on the surface of Earth.

As magma cools, the elements and compounds begin to form crystals. The slower the magma cools, the larger the crystals grow. Rocks with large crystals are said to have a coarse-grained texture. Granite is an example of a coarse-grained rock.

When lava is exposed at Earth's surface, it will cool very rapidly. The rocks formed from cooling lava will have a very fine-grained texture. The igneous rock basalt is an example of such a fine-grained rock. Sometimes the lava will cook so quickly that no crystals have time to form. This produces a rock with a glassy texture, such as obsidian.

Metamorphic Rocks
Metamorphic rocks are formed by high temperatures and great pressures. The process by which the rocks undergo these changes is called metamorphism. The outcome of metamorphic changes includes:

- Deformation by extreme heat and pressure
- Compaction
- Destruction of the original characteristics of the parent rock
- Bending and folding while in a plastic stage
- The emergence of completely new and different minerals due to chemical reactions with heated water and dissolved minerals

Metamorphic rocks are classified into two groups, foliated rocks and unfoliated rocks. Foliated rocks consist of compressed, parallel bands of minerals, which give the rocks a striped appearance. Examples of such rocks include slate, schist, and gneiss. Unfoliated rocks are not banded, and examples of such rocks include quartzite, marble, and anthracite rocks.

Skill 4.3 **Recognizing the physical, environmental, biological, structural, and tectonic processes that influence the formation of a given rock sequence**

See Skills 4.2 and 4.5.

Skill 4.4 **Demonstrating knowledge of the formation and development of a given Earth structure (e.g., volcanic structures, rift valleys, ocean spreading center, fault-block mountains)**

MOUNTAINS

Orogeny is the process of natural mountain building.

A **mountain** is terrain that has been raised high above the surrounding landscape by volcanic action or some form of tectonic plate collisions. The plate collisions could be either intercontinental or ocean floor collisions with a continental crust (subduction). The physical composition of mountains would include igneous, metamorphic, or sedimentary rocks; some may have rock layers that are tilted or distorted by plate collision forces.

There are many different types of mountains. The physical attributes of a mountain range depends upon the angle at which plate movement thrusted layers of rock to the surface. Many mountains (Adirondacks, Southern Rockies) were formed along high-angle faults.

Some types of mountains include:

- **Folded mountains** (Alps, Himalayas) are produced by the folding of rock layers during their formation. The Himalayas are the highest mountains in the world and contain Mount Everest, which rises almost 9 km above sea level. The Himalayas were formed when India collided with Asia. The movement that created this collision is still in process at the rate of a few centimeters per year.
- **Fault-block mountains** (Utah, Arizona, and New Mexico) are created when plate movement produces tension forces instead of compression forces. The area under tension produces normal faults, and rock along these faults is displaced upward.

- **Dome mountains** are formed as magma tries to push up through the crust but fails to break the surface. Dome Mountains resemble a huge blister on the earth's surface.
- **Upwarped mountains** (Black Hills of South Dakota) are created in association with a broad arching of the earth's crust. They can also be formed by rock thrust upward along high angle faults.

For more on mountain building, see Skill 5.2

VOLCANIC ACTIVITY

When lava cools, igneous rock is formed. This formation can occur either above ground or below ground. **Intrusive rock** includes any igneous rock that was formed below the earth's surface. Batholiths are the largest structures of intrusive rock, and they are composed of near-granite materials. They are the core of the Sierra Nevada Mountains. **Extrusive rock** includes any igneous rock that was formed at the earth's surface.

Dikes are old lava tubes formed when magma entered a vertical fracture and hardened. Sometimes, magma squeezes between two rock layers and hardens into a thin horizontal sheet called a **sill**. A **laccolith** is formed in much the same way as a sill, but the magma that creates a laccolith is very thick and does not flow easily. It pools and forces the overlying strata, creating an obvious surface dome.

A **caldera** is normally formed by the collapse of the top of a volcano. This collapse can be caused by a massive explosion that destroys the cone and empties most, if not all, of the magma in the chamber below the volcano. The cone collapses into the empty magma chamber forming a caldera.

An inactive volcano may have magma solidified in its pipe. This structure, called a **volcanic neck**, is resistant to erosion, and today, may be the only visible evidence of the past presence of an active volcano.

There are three types of volcanic mountains:

- Shield volcanoes
- Cinder cones
- Composite volcanoes

Shield volcanoes are associated with quiet eruptions. Lava emerges from the vent or opening in the crater and flows freely out over the earth's surface until it cools and hardens into a layer of igneous rock. A repeated lava flow builds this type of volcano into the largest type of volcanic mountain. Mauna Loa, found in Hawaii, is the largest volcano on Earth.

Cinder cone volcanoes are associated with explosive eruptions as lava is hurled high into the air in a spray of droplets of various sizes. These droplets cool and harden into cinders and particles of ash before falling to the ground. The ash and cinder pile up around the vent to form a steep, cone-shaped hill called the cinder cone. Cinder cone volcanoes are relatively small but may form quite rapidly.

Composite volcanoes are described as being built by both lava flows and layers of ash and cinders. Mount Fuji in Japan, Mount St. Helens in Washington State in the United States, and Mount Vesuvius in Italy are all famous composite volcanoes.

Skill 4.5 Demonstrating knowledge of how a given geologic or biologic event is recorded in a rock sequence

THE ARCHEAN EON

Life began in the oceans of the **Archean eon** (3.8 to 2.5 billion years ago). The oldest fossil found is approximately 3.4 – 3.5 billion years old.

By our present day standards, the early earth was very hot with a warm, toxic ocean. Totally devoid of oxygen, Earth was composed of hydrogen sulfide, methane, ammonia, and carbon dioxide. Life began in the ocean. Simple logic proves this contention: There wasn't an **ozone** (O_3) layer because there wasn't any **oxygen** (O_2) to be altered into ozone. Without ozone, **ultra-violet (UV) radiation** from the sun scrambles the DNA in a cell. Therefore, no life could have existed because the earliest single-celled organism couldn't handle the UV rays.

This logic caused research scientists Stanley Miller and Harold Urey to investigate the development of life in a primordial oceanic environment. They simulated the primordial ocean atmosphere in laboratory tests, and although they didn't create life, they did create **amino acids**, which are the building blocks of life. Proteins form amino acids that are able to form complex organic molecules.

Between 4.6 and 3.6 billion years ago, something occurred that still isn't scientifically clear. We transition from an earth that was uninhabited to the appearance of simple, **single-celled bacteria**. Around 2.5 billion years ago, the bacteria developed the ability to **photosynthesize** (convert carbon dioxide into sugars) which released oxygen as a by-product. As the bacteria multiplied, they released a massive amount of oxygen called the **Oxygen Revolution**. Concurrently, it marks the beginning of the Proterozoic eon.

TEACHER CERTIFICATION STUDY GUIDE

LIFE IN THE EARLY, MIDDLE, AND LATE PROTEROZOIC

The Proterozoic eon: 2.5 billion years ago (bya) to 570 million years ago (mya), is divided into 3 periods:

- Early: 2.5 to 1.6 bya.
- Middle: 1.6 to 1.0 bya.
- Late: 1.0 bya to 570 mya

Early Proterozoic
Formation of Red Beds: These Red Beds (formed 3.8 to 2.5 billion years ago) are important because they herald the appearance of significant amounts of oxygen on Earth. Their red color is produced by rust and indicates the presence of oxygen acting upon ferrous material present in the ocean, and eventually, on land. The presence of significant amounts of oxygen allowed ozone to form, which in turn, screened out the harmful ultra-violet (UV) rays and made life possible outside of the protective confines of the ocean.

Stromatolites are blue-green algae or **cyanobacteria**. Cyanobacteria produced oxygen by **photosynthesis**. Through the discovery of the **Gunflint Chert,** an assemblage of many different types of bacterial fossils, we know that around 1.9 billion years ago there was an abundance of primitive bacteria, which began to diversify.

Middle Proterozoic
The Middle Proterozoic saw the rise and development of **eukaryotic cells** (cells other than bacteria), some of whose fossils have been preserved.

Late Proterozoic
The first evidence of multi-cellular organisms, called Edicaran fauna, occurred in the Late Proterozoic: At 1.0 billion years ago, cells were starting to be organized into tissues, and tissues were being organized into organs. The early Edicaran fauna, however, didn't grow exterior cells.

THE PHANEROZOIC EON

The Phanerozoic eon (570 mya to present time), is divided into 3 eras: the Paleozoic, the Mesozoic, and the Cenozoic. Because of the extent of life form diversity that occurred during this time frame, each era is addressed separately in regard to its respective evolutionary patterns.

Paleozoic Era (570 to 245 million years ago)
Paleozoic periods:

- Cambrian: 570 to 505 mya
- Ordovician: 505 to 438 mya
- Silurian: 438 to 408 mya

- Devonian: 408 to 360 mya
- Mississippian: 360 to 320 mya
- Pennsylvanian: 320 to 286 mya
- Permian: 286 to 245 mya

The Paleozoic era was a time of great evolutionary change and begins with the development of organisms' ability to secrete hard parts. Calcium phosphate shells appeared 570 mya; calcium carbonate shells appeared 540 mya.

The Mesozoic Era: The Age of Reptiles (245 to 66 million years ago)
Mesozoic periods:

- Triassic: 245 to 208 mya
- Jurassic: 208 to 144 mya
- Cretaceous: 144 to 66 mya

Significant Mesozoic geological events
As the supercontinent of Pangea broke up, massive orogenies occurred in North America, salt domes and petrified forests formed, and the Atlantic Ocean opened up. Europe and North America underwent transgression and regression events as Africa, India, and North America moved northward. Additionally, Australia and Antarctica were connected, and South America split off from Africa and North America.

Mesozoic-era life
The mass extinction in the late Permian period of the Paleozoic left only ten percent of all life forms extant. New life forms and species evolved rapidly to fill the void left behind by the extinctions.

At the beginning of the Mesozoic, conifers (**Gymnosperms**) dominated. Conifers are nonflowering, seed-bearing plants. In the middle Cretaceous, **Angiosperms**—flowering plants with enclosed seeds—evolved.

Flowering plants had several advantages over the nonflowering species. Where non-flowering plants were solely dependent on the wind for pollination, the flowering species with their enclosed seeds had a greater potential to reproduce far away from the parent plant. The flowering plants were attractive to insects and other animals; animals ate their seeds and deposited them in their waste distances away.

The flourishing of the angiosperms encouraged insect pollination and forced insect evolution. The increased competition among insects caused a spurt in evolution to take better advantage of the new food source. The insects became more efficient plant eaters.

Likewise, as the angiosperms evolved and nut- and fruit-bearing species appeared, the plant itself became a food source and caused it to develop defenses to ward off predators. Thorns, acidic sap, spines, etc., were mechanisms to ensure the continuation of the plant species.

The pterosaurs first appeared in the Triassic period. Most had teeth, and all were predators with hair and skin stretched between the body and the limbs. Some had tails while others were tailless. Some of the Pterosaurs became very big and grew claws on their limbs. The Pterandon had a 23' wingspan; Ouetzalcoatlus had a 50' wingspan.

Marine dinosaurs evolved from land-based dinosaurs, not from marine-based organisms. They had streamlined bodies, modified reproductive organs to allow for birth at sea, and paddle-shaped limbs. Significantly, the marine dinosaurs did not have gills but were air-breathers with more efficient lungs.

Mesozoic mammals
The first true mammal dates from the Triassic period. It was a small, rodent-like creature. During the Mesozoic, the mammals went through major evolutionary change, experimentation, and development and ended up with improved nervous, circulatory, and reproductive systems, including the capacity for warm-bloodedness (the ability to regulate body temperature). Mammals are differentiated in the fossil record by having

- One bone in the lower jaw in contrast to the reptiles' many smaller bones in the jaw
- Several ear bones
- A larger skull cavity in relation to size, than reptiles

The Cenozoic era: The Age of Mammals (66 million years ago to present)
Cenozoic periods:

- Tertiary: 65 to 1.8 mya
    - Paleocene: 65 to 54.8 mya
    - Eocene: 54.8 to 33.7 mya
    - Oligocene: 33.7 to 23.8 mya
    - Miocene: 23.8 to 5.3 mya
    - Pliocene: 5.3 to 1.8 mya

- Quaternary: 1.8 mya to today
    - Pleistocene: 1.8 mya to 10,000 years ago
    - Holocene: 10,000 years ago to today

The mass extinction of almost all reptiles at the end of the Mesozoic era left a void in the biosphere that precipitated an explosion in the diversity and number of mammals. From this point on to the present day, mammals became the dominant species.

Cenozoic-era plant life

Angiosperms evolved and spread significantly during the Cenozoic era. Grasses appeared in the Miocene Epoch of the tertiary period. Adapted and suited to the dry climate of the interior, they spread over the continents, becoming dominant on the steppes of Russia, the pampas of South America, the African veldt, and the great plains of the United States. The grasslands put enormous environmental pressure on the animals, because there are problems associated with living in the grasslands.

Cenozoic-era animal life

Marine invertebrates: The massive numbers of marine phytoplankton species that went extinct during the K/T boundary period were replaced by new species such as coccolithores and diatoms.

Fish: Fish, especially sharks, continue to diversify, evolve, and become abundant. Sharks went through a giant phase but eventually returned to their modern size.

Amphibians: The few remaining amphibians remained virtually unchanged.

Reptiles: Poisonous snakes appeared during the Miocene epoch of the Tertiary period in direct response to the corresponding evolution in mammal species. The poisons are either neurotoxins or hemotoxins. A **neurotoxin**, such as that from an African puff adder, affects the nervous system and kills the victim within minutes. A **hemotoxin**, such as that from a diamondback rattlesnake, affects the blood and is slower acting.

Birds: Birds had just started to appear in the late Mesozoic era. During the Cenozoic era, the birds underwent an explosion of evolution as they diversified and multiplied. In the Eocene Epoch, large flightless birds were abundant. Some, similar to a giant parrot at nine feet tall, used their powerful beaks to crush their victims. Some flightless species, like the now-extinct dodo, survived until the 16th and 17th centuries of modern times.

Cenozoic-era mammals

Monotremes: A monotreme lays eggs but still suckles the young with mammary glands. Only two species are still alive: the platypus and the spiny anteater.

Marsupials: Pouched animals give birth to inviable young, which then develop in the mother's pouch. Marsupials like the kangaroo, koala, and wombat were highly successful in the isolated landmass of Australia. Placental animals dominated in North and South America. The marsupials went totally extinct in South America and are virtually extinct in North America except for the opossum.

Placentals: Placental mammals are the most common type of mammal, whose young are gestated longer, but are also born viable. Placental mammals first appeared in the Cretaceous period.

Primate evolution

Primates first appeared in the fossil record around 48 million years ago. Around 10 million years ago, orangutans appeared in the fossil record. Approximately 8 to 6 million years ago, **hominids** (humans), split from the **hominoids** (apes). Paleontologists still have not discovered the so-called "missing link"—the fossil that embodies both hominid and hominoid features and, presumably, gave rise to both branches of primates—in part because very few rock units have been found that date from 4 to 8 million years ago. Scientists have used DNA protein structural studies to project a biological clock of change. They counted the differences in DNA structures between chimpanzees and humans to postulate a common ancestry.

Skill 4.6   **Demonstrating knowledge of how fossils and radioactive isotopes are used to determine the age of rocks and to interpret the geologic past**

HISTORICAL GEOLOGY

Earth's history extends over more than four billion years and is reckoned in terms of a scale. Paleontologists who study the history of the earth have divided this huge period of time into four large time units called **eons** (the Hadean, the Archean, the Proterozoic, and the Phanerozoic). The oldest (Hadean), from 4.6 to 3.9 bya, predated life. Subsequent eons, which encompass the biological history of the earth, are divided into four smaller units of time called **eras**, which are further divided into major **periods**. Periods are refined into groupings called **epochs**.

An era refers to a time interval in which particular plants and animals were dominant or present in great abundance. The end of an era is most often characterized by:

- A general uplifting of the crust
- The extinction of the dominant plants or animals
- The appearance of new life forms

Methods of Geologic Dating

Estimates of the earth's age have been made possible with the discovery of radioactivity and the invention of instruments that can measure the amount of radioactivity in rocks. The use of radioactivity to make accurate determinations of Earth's age is called **absolute dating**. This process depends upon comparing the amount of radioactive material in a rock with the amount that has decayed into another element. Studying the radiation given off by atoms of radioactive elements is the most accurate method of measuring the earth's age. These atoms are unstable and are continuously breaking down or undergoing decay. The radioactive element that decays is called the **parent element**. The new element that results from the radioactive decay of the parent element is called the **daughter element.** The time required for one half of a given amount of a radioactive element to decay is called the **half-life** of that element or compound. Geologists commonly use **carbon dating** to calculate the age of a fossil substance.

Inferring the History of an Area Using Geologic Evidence

The determination of the age of rocks by cataloging their composition has been outmoded since the middle 1800s. Today, a sequential history can be determined by the fossil content (using the principle of **fossil succession**) of a rock system, as well as its superposition within a range of systems. This classification process was termed **stratigraphy** and permitted the construction of a **geologic column,** in which rock systems are arranged in their correct chronological order.

Principles of Catastrophism and Uniformitarianism

Uniformitarianism is a fundamental concept in modern geology. It simply states that the physical, chemical, and biological laws that operated in the geologic past operate in the same way today. The forces and processes that we observe presently shaping our planet have been at work for a very long time. This idea is commonly stated as "the present is the key to the past." **Catastrophism** is the concept that the earth was shaped by catastrophic events of a short-term nature.

Fossils

A fossil is the remains or trace of an ancient organism that has been preserved naturally in the earth's crust. Sedimentary rocks usually are rich sources of fossil remains. Those fossils, found in layers of sediment, were embedded in the slowly forming sedimentary rock strata. The oldest fossils known are the traces of 3.5-billion-year-old bacteria found in sedimentary rocks. Few fossils are found in metamorphic rock, and virtually none are found in igneous rocks. The magma is so hot that any organism trapped in the magma would have been destroyed.

Fossil Examples

The fossil remains of a woolly mammoth embedded in ice were found by a group of Russian explorers. The best-preserved animal remains, however, have been discovered in natural tar pits. When an animal accidentally fell into the tar, it became trapped, sinking to the bottom. Preserved bones of the saber-toothed cat have been found in tar pits. Prehistoric insects have been found trapped in ancient amber or fossil resin that was excreted by some extinct species of pine trees.

Molds, Casts, and Tracks

Fossil molds are the hollow spaces in a rock previously occupied by bones or shells. A fossil cast is a fossil mold that fills with sediments or minerals that later hardens forming a cast. Fossil tracks are the imprints in hardened mud left behind by birds or other animals.

COMPETENCY 005   **UNDERSTAND MATTER AND ENERGY IN EARTH SYSTEMS**

Skill 5.1   Analyzing the transfer and transformation of energy as it flows between Earth systems (i.e., the lithosphere, hydrosphere, and atmosphere), including the processes of convection, conduction, and radiation

While the **hydrosphere** (water layer), **lithosphere** (solid outer layer), and **atmosphere** (gasses surrounding Earth) can be described and considered separately, they are actually constantly interacting with one another. Energy flows freely between these different spheres by means of convection, conduction, and radiation.

Significant events in one sphere almost always have effects in the other spheres. The recent increase in greenhouse gases provides an example of this ripple effect. Additional greenhouse gases produced by human activities were released into the atmosphere where they built up and caused global warming and widening holes in certain areas of the atmosphere. These increasing temperatures have had many effects on the hydrosphere: rising sea levels, increasing water temperature, and climate changes. These have led to even more changes in the lithosphere, such as glacier retreat and alterations in the patterns of water-rock interaction (run-off, erosion, etc).

See Skill 16.5 for more details about convection, conduction, and radiation.

Skill 5.2   Analyzing processes of the lithosphere (e.g., weathering, erosion, movement of tectonic plates, volcanism, earthquakes)

PLATE TECTONICS

Data obtained from many sources led scientists to develop the **theory of plate tectonics**. This theory is the most current model that explains not only the movement of the continents, but also the changes in the earth's crust caused by internal forces.

The Earth's Layers
Although no one has ever drilled through the earth's crust, geologists know the composition of the earth through the study of seismic shock waves.

The composition and density of the materials in the earth cause sound waves to either slow down or speed up. By measuring the speed of the seismic wave, scientists are able to determine the approximate location and composition of the material. The latest research indicates that the earth's solid iron and nickel inner core actually is spinning around. The Earth has three layers surrounding its core.

Lithosphere: The term lithosphere is Greek for "rock layer." Comprised of the crust and uppermost part of the mantle, the lithosphere consists of cool, rigid, and brittle materials. Most earthquakes originate in the lithosphere. Because the lithosphere is close to the surface, both temperatures and pressures are relatively low in comparison to the other layers.

The lithosphere is divided into two different crusts:

- **Continental plates** are very thick and composed of light (in density and color) materials.
- **Oceanic plates** are very thin and composed of heavy (in density and color) materials.

Since the lithosphere has a lower density than the layer below it, it "floats" on the asthenosphere similar to the way an iceberg or a block of wood floats on water.

Asthenosphere: The asthenosphere is the semi-plastic molten rock material located directly below the lithosphere. At the base of the asthenosphere, the mantle again becomes more rigid and less plastic, and it remains in that rigid state all the way to the core.

Mesosphere: The lower mantle is rigid, hard, and brittle and makes up 80% of the earth's material.

The Earth's Moving Plates

The earth's lithosphere is broken into nine, large moving slabs and several smaller ones, all called **plates**. The major plates are named after the continents they are "transporting." The plates float on and move with a layer of hot, plastic-like rock in the upper mantle. Geologists believe that the heat currents circulating within the mantle cause this plastic zone of rock to slowly flow, carrying along the overlying crustal plates.

Movement of these crustal plates creates areas where the plates **diverge** as well as areas where the plates **converge**. The Mid-Atlantic is a major area of divergence. Currents of hot mantle rock rise and separate at this point of **divergence**, creating new oceanic crust at the rate of 2 to 10 centimeters per year. **Convergence** occurs when two plates collide. When an oceanic crust collides with either another oceanic plate or a continental plate, the oceanic crust sinks, forming an enormous trench and generating volcanic activity. Convergence also includes continent-to-continent plate collisions. When two plates slide past one another, a transform fault is created.

Where the Action Is: Plate Boundaries

These movements produce many major features of the earth's surface, such as mountain ranges, volcanoes, and earthquake zones. Most of these features are located at **plate boundaries**, where the plates interact by spreading apart, pressing together, or sliding past each other. These movements are very slow, averaging only a few centimeters a year.

Boundaries form between spreading plates where the crust is forced apart in a process called **rifting**. Rifting generally occurs at mid-ocean ridges. Rifting can also take place within a continent, splitting the continent into smaller landmasses that drift away from each other, thereby forming an ocean basin (for instance, the Red Sea) between them. As the seafloor spreading takes place, new material is added to the inner edges of the separating plates. In this way, the plates grow larger, and the ocean basin widens. This is the process that broke up the super continent Pangaea and created the Atlantic Ocean.

Boundaries between plates that are colliding are zones of intense crustal activity. When a plate of ocean crust collides with a plate of continental crust, the denser oceanic plate slides under the lighter continental plate and plunges into the mantle. This process is called **subduction**, and the site where it takes place is called a subduction zone. A subduction zone is usually seen on the seafloor as a deep depression called a **trench**.

The crustal movement characterized by plates sliding sideways past each other produces a plate boundary characterized by major faults that are capable of unleashing powerful earthquakes. The San Andreas Fault forms such a boundary between the Pacific plate and the North American plate.

MOUNTAIN-BUILDING PROCESSES

Most major mountain ranges are formed by the processes of **folding** and **faulting**. Folded mountains are produced by folding of rock layers. Crustal movements may press horizontal layers of sedimentary rock together from the sides, squeezing them into wavelike folds. Up-folded sections of rock are called **anticlines**; down-folded sections of rock are called **synclines**. The Appalachian Mountains are an example of folded mountains with long ridges and valleys in a series of anticlines and synclines formed by folded rock layers.

Faults are fractures in the earth's crust that have been created by either tension or compression forces transmitted through the crust. These forces are produced by the movement of separate blocks of crust.

Faulting is categorized on the basis of the relative movement between the blocks on both sides of the fault plane. The movement can be horizontal, vertical, or oblique.

For more on mountain-building (orogeny), see Skill 4.4.

Volcanism
Volcanic mountains are built up by successive deposits of volcanic materials. **Volcanism** is the term given to the movement of magma through the crust and its emergence as lava onto the earth's surface. An active volcano is one that is presently erupting or building to an eruption. A dormant volcano is one that is between eruptions but still shows signs of internal activity that might lead to an eruption in the future. An extinct volcano is said to be no longer capable of erupting. When lava cools, igneous

rock is formed. This formation can occur either above ground or below ground.

For more about igneous rocks, see Skill 4.4

EROSION

Erosion is the inclusion and transportation of surface materials by another moveable material, usually water, wind, or ice. The most important cause of erosion is running water. Streams, rivers, and tides are constantly at work removing weathered fragments of bedrock and carrying them away from their original location.

A stream erodes bedrock by the grinding action of sand, pebbles, and other rock fragments. This grinding against each other is called **abrasion**. Streams also erode rocks by **dissolving** or **absorbing** their minerals. Limestone and marble are readily dissolved by streams.

Types of Erosion
The breaking down of rocks at or near the earth's surface is known as weathering. Weathering breaks down these rocks into smaller and smaller pieces. There are two types of weathering: physical weathering and chemical weathering.

Physical weathering is the process by which rocks are broken down into smaller fragments without undergoing any change in chemical composition. Physical weathering is mainly caused by the freezing of water, the expansion of rock, and the activities of plants and animals.

Frost wedging is the cycle of daytime thawing and refreezing at night. This cycle causes large rock masses, especially the rocks exposed on mountaintops, to be broken into smaller pieces.

The peeling away of the outer layers from a rock is called **exfoliation**. Rounded mountain tops are called **exfoliation domes** and have been formed in this way.

Chemical weathering is the breaking down of rocks through changes in their chemical composition. An example would be the change of feldspar in granite to clay. Water, oxygen, and carbon dioxide are the main agents of chemical weathering. When water and carbon dioxide combine chemically, they produce a weak acid that breaks down rocks.

Skill 5.3   Analyzing processes that occur in freshwater and ocean systems

OCEANOGRAPHY

Approximately 70 percent of the earth's surface is covered by oceans (large bodies of saline water). They are divided into five principal oceans and thirteen smaller seas.

- **Arctic Ocean:** Smallest ocean, located in the Arctic, the polar region of the northern hemisphere.
- **Atlantic Ocean:** Second largest ocean, located between the Americas on the west and Eurasia and Africa to the east. Connected in the north to the Arctic Ocean, in the southwest to the Pacific Ocean, in the southeast to the Indian Ocean, and in the south to the Southern Ocean.
- **Indian Ocean:** Third largest ocean, located between Asia to the north, Africa to the west, the Malay Peninsula, Sunda Islands, and Australia to the east, and the Southern Ocean to the south.
- **Pacific Ocean:** Largest ocean, extending from the Arctic Ocean in the north to the Southern Ocean in the south. Bounded by Asia and Australia to the west and the Americas to the east.
- **Southern Ocean:** Fourth largest ocean consisting of the southernmost portions of the Pacific, Atlantic, and Indian Oceans.

OCEAN CURRENTS AND WAVES

World weather patterns are greatly influenced by **ocean surface currents** in the upper layer of the ocean. These currents continuously move along the ocean surface in specific directions. Ocean currents that flow deep below the surface are called **sub-surface currents**. These currents are influenced by such factors as the location of landmasses in the current's path and the earth's rotation.

Current Types
Surface currents are caused by winds and are classified by temperature. **Cold currents** originate in the polar regions and flow through surrounding water, which is measurably warmer. The currents with a higher temperature than the surrounding water are called **warm currents** and can be found near the equator. These currents follow swirling routes around the ocean basins and the equator. The Gulf Stream and the California Current are the two main surface currents that flow along the coastlines of the United States. The Gulf Stream is a warm current in the Atlantic Ocean that carries warm water from the equator to the northern parts of the Atlantic Ocean. Benjamin Franklin studied and named the Gulf Stream. The California Current is a cold current that originates in the Arctic regions and flows southward along the west coast of the United States.

Water Density and Currents
Differences in water density also create ocean currents. Water found near the bottom of the ocean is the coldest and the densest. It tends to flow from a denser area to a less dense area. Currents that flow because of a difference in the density of the ocean's water are called **density currents**. Water with a higher salinity is denser than water with a lower salinity. Water that has a salinity that is different from the surrounding water may form a density current.

Causes and Effects of Waves
The movement of ocean water is caused by the wind, the sun's energy, the earth's rotation, the moon's gravitational pull on Earth, and by underwater earthquakes. Most ocean waves are caused by the impact of winds. When wind blows over the surface of the ocean, it transfers energy (friction) to the water and causes waves to form. Waves are also formed by seismic activity on the ocean floor. A wave formed by an earthquake is called a **seismic sea wave**. These powerful waves can be very destructive, with wave heights increasing to 30m or more near the shore.

Ocean Water and Salinity
Pure water is a combination of hydrogen and oxygen. These two elements make up about 96.5 percent of ocean water. The remaining portion is made up of dissolved solids. The concentration of these dissolved solids determines the water's **salinity**.

Salinity is the number of grams of these dissolved salts in 1,000 grams of seawater. The average salinity of ocean water is about 3.5 percent. In other words, one kilogram of seawater contains about 35 grams of salt. Sodium chloride, or salt (NaCl), is the most abundant of the dissolved salts. The dissolved salts also include smaller quantities of magnesium chloride, magnesium and calcium sulfates, and traces of several other salt elements. Salinity varies throughout the world's oceans; the total salinity of the oceans varies from place to place and also varies with depth. Salinity is low near river mouths where the ocean mixes with fresh water, and salinity is high in areas of high evaporation rates.

Ocean Temperatures
The temperature of the ocean water varies with different latitudes and with ocean depths. Ocean water temperature is about constant to depths of 90 meters (m). The temperature of surface water will drop rapidly from 28 degrees C at the equator to -2 degrees C at the Poles. The freezing point of seawater is lower than the freezing point of pure water. Pure water freezes at 0 degrees C, but the dissolved salts in the seawater keep it at a freezing point of –2 degrees C. The freezing point of seawater may vary depending on its salinity in a particular location.

The ocean can be divided into three temperature zones. The **surface layer** consists of relatively warm water and exhibits most of the wave action present. The area where the wind and waves churn and mix the water is called the **mixed layer**. It is in this layer where most living creatures are found, due to an abundance of sunlight and warmth. The second layer is called the **thermocline**, where it becomes increasingly cold as its depth increases. This change is due to the lack of energy from sunlight. The layer below the thermocline continues to the deep, dark, very cold, and semi-barren **ocean floor**.

Skill 5.4 **Analyzing processes that occur in the atmosphere and sources of energy that drive those processes, including the changes that occur during the water cycle**

STRUCTURE AND PROPERTIES OF THE ATMOSPHERE

Dry air is composed of three basic components; dry gas, water vapor, and solid particles (dust from soil, etc.)

The most abundant dry gases in the atmosphere are

- (N_2) Nitrogen, 78.09 percent
- (O_2) Oxygen, 20.95 percent
- (AR) Argon, 0.93 percent
- (CO_2) Carbon Dioxide, 0.03 percent

Atmospheric Layers
The atmosphere is divided into four main layers based on temperature: troposphere, stratosphere, mesosphere, and thermosphere. Below is a brief description of each:

- **Troposphere:** This layer is the closest to the earth's surface with an average thickness of 7 miles (11 km). All weather phenomena occur here, since it is the layer with the most water vapor and dust. Air temperature decreases with increasing altitude.
- **Stratosphere:** This layer contains very little water; clouds within this layer are extremely rare. The ozone layer is located in the upper portions of the stratosphere. Air temperature is fairly constant but does increase somewhat with height due to the absorption of solar energy and ultra violet rays from the ozone layer.
- **Mesosphere:** Air temperature again decreases with height in this layer. It is the coldest layer with temperatures in the range of -100 degrees C at the top.
- **Thermosphere:** This layer extends upward into space. Oxygen molecules in this layer absorb energy from the sun, causing temperatures to increase with height. The lower part of the thermosphere is called the **ionosphere**. Here, charged particles, or ions and free electrons, can be found. When gases in the Ionosphere are excited by solar radiation, the gases give off light and glow in the sky. These glowing lights are called the **Aurora Borealis** in the Northern Hemisphere and **Aurora Australis** in the Southern Hemisphere. The upper portion of the thermosphere is called the **exosphere**. Gas molecules are very far apart in this layer. Layers of exosphere are also known as the **Van Allen Belts** and are held together by Earth's magnetic field.

AIR MASSES

Air masses moving toward or away from the earth's surface are called **air currents**. Air moving parallel to Earth's surface is called **wind**. Weather conditions are generated by winds and air currents carrying large amounts of heat and moisture from one part of the atmosphere to another. Wind speeds are measured by instruments called **anemometers**.

Wind Belts

The **wind belts** in each hemisphere consist of convection cells that encircle the earth like belts. There are three major wind belts on Earth:

- Trade winds
- Prevailing westerlies
- Polar easterlies

Wind belt formation depends on the differences in air pressures that develop in the **doldrums, the horse latitudes,** and the **polar regions**. The doldrums surround the equator; within this belt, heated air usually rises straight up into Earth's atmosphere. The horse latitudes are regions of high barometric pressure with calm and light winds. Finally, the polar regions contain cold, dense air that sinks to the earth's surface.

Breezes and Monsoons

Winds caused by local temperature changes include sea breezes and land breezes.

Sea breezes are caused by the unequal heating of the land and an adjacent, large body of water. Since land heats up faster than water, it creates the movement of cool, ocean air toward the land, which is called a sea breeze. Sea breezes usually begin blowing about mid-morning and end about sunset.

A breeze that blows from the land to the ocean or a large lake is called a **land breeze.**

Monsoons are huge wind systems that cover large geographic areas and that reverse direction seasonally. The monsoons of India and Asia are examples of these seasonal winds, where they alternate wet and dry seasons. As denser, cooler air over the ocean moves inland, a steady, seasonal wind called a **summer**, or **wet, monsoon** is produced.

CLOUDS

The following are the major types of clouds and two variations of the major types:

- **Cirrus clouds:** white and feathery, high in the sky
- **Cumulus:** thick, white, fluffy
- **Stratus:** layers of clouds covering most of the sky
- **Nimbus:** heavy, dark thunderstorm cloud

- **Cumulo-nimbus:** formed from Cumulus clouds; tall, dense clouds involved in extreme weather
- **Strato-nimbus:** dark flat, low clouds, mostly containing liquid droplets

The air temperature at which water vapor begins to condense is called the **dew point.**

Relative humidity is the actual amount of water vapor in a certain volume of air compared to the maximum amount of water vapor this air could hold at a given temperature.

Skill 5.5   Describing how global patterns of atmospheric movement influence weather

The Earth's atmosphere is very similar to a fluid. Like the fluids of the ocean, our atmosphere is driven by heat, primarily solar radiation.

Warmer air masses are formed near the tropics, both over the ocean and over the continents. Cold air masses are formed in polar regions. Dryer air masses are formed over continents, while moisture-laden air masses are formed over the ocean. As an air mass moves, it may gain moisture if it moves over the water, or lose moisture as it moves over land.

As with ocean currents, warm air masses tend to move toward the poles, losing heat as they go. Cold, polar air masses will move down toward the equator. Because of coriolis forces, air masses move in a circular manner, and also circulate upward from the Earth and back down again.

Areas where hot air masses are rising away from the Earth create low-pressure zones, and areas where cold air masses are sinking down create high-pressure zones. Surface air masses generally move toward latitudes of low pressure and away from latitudes of high pressure. These latitudes of high and low pressure are known as **pressure belts**. Locally, the movement of air masses may also be affected by continental landforms, such as mountains.

FRONTS

A **front** is a narrow zone of transition between air masses of different densities that is usually due to temperature differences. Because they are associated with temperature, fronts are usually referred to as either warm or cold.

Warm front: a front whose movement causes the lighter warm air to advance, while the denser cold air retreats. A warm front usually triggers a cloud development sequence of cirrus, cirrostratus, altostratus, nimbostratus, and stratus. It may result in an onset of light rain or snowfall immediately ahead of the front, which gives way, as the cloud sequence forms, to steady precipitation (light to moderate), until the front passes, a time frame that may exceed 24 hours.

The gentle rains associated with a warm front are normally welcomed by farmers. However, if it is cold enough for snow to fall, the snow may significantly accumulate. If the air is unstable, cumulonimbus clouds may develop, and brief, intense thunderstorms may punctuate the otherwise gentler rain or snowfall.

Cold front: a front whose movement causes the denser cold air to displace the lighter warm air. The results of cold front situations depend on the stability of the air. If the air is stable, nimbostratus and altostratus clouds may form, and brief showers may immediately precede the front.

If the air is unstable, there is greater uplift. Cumulonimbus clouds may tower over nimbostratus, and cirrus clouds may be blown downstream from the cumulonimbus by high-altitude winds. Thunderstorms may occur, accompanied by gusty surface winds and hail, as well as other, more violent weather. If the cold front moves quickly (roughly 28 mph or greater), a squall line of thunderstorms may form either right ahead of the front or up to 180 miles ahead of it.

Occluded front: a front formed when a cold front has caught up to a warm front and has intermingled, usually by sliding under the warmer air. Cold fronts generally move faster than warm fronts and occasionally overrun slower-moving warm fronts. The weather ahead of an occluded front is similar to that of a warm front during its advance but switches to that of a cold front as the cold front passes through.

Stationary front: a front that shows no overall movement. The weather produced by this front can vary widely and depends on the amount of moisture present and the relative motions of the air pockets along the front. Most of the precipitation falls on the cold side of the front.

Skill 5.6 Demonstrating knowledge of the movement of chemical elements and compounds between different reservoirs on Earth

See Skill 5.1.

Skill 5.7 Analyzing physical models that represent the behavior of a given Earth system

Physical models that represent the behavior of Earth systems range from a terrarium or a simple model of a volcano to complex computerized models that predict weather patterns. Many middle school lab experiments are models for Earth systems. An experiment using a light bulb can represent solar radiation. An experiment using ice cubes can represent rising sea levels.

COMPETENCY 006   **UNDERSTAND EARTH IN THE SOLAR SYSTEM AND UNIVERSE**

Skill 6.1   **Demonstrating knowledge of the properties and organization of different types of stars and galaxies**

CONSTELLATIONS AND GALAXIES

Astronomers use groups or patterns of stars, called **constellations**, as reference points to locate other stars in the sky. Familiar constellations include Ursa Major (meaning big bear) and Ursa Minor (meaning little bear). Within the Ursa Major, the smaller constellation, the Big Dipper is found. Within the Ursa Minor, the smaller constellation, the Little Dipper is found. Different constellations appear as the earth continues its revolution around the sun with the seasonal changes.

Magnitude stars are 21 of the brightest stars that can be seen from Earth. These are the first stars noticed at night. In the Northern Hemisphere, there are 15 commonly observed first magnitude stars.

Vast collections of stars are defined as **galaxies**. Galaxies are classified as irregular, elliptical, and spiral. They are described here:

An **irregular galaxy** has no real structured appearance; most are in their early stages of life.

An **elliptical galaxy** consists of smooth ellipses, containing a little dust and gas, but composed of millions or trillions of stars.

Spiral galaxies are disk-shaped and have extending arms that rotate around its dense center. Earth's galaxy is found in the Milky Way, and it is a spiral galaxy.

DEEP SPACE

Here are some important terms related to deep space:

A **pulsar** is defined as a variable radio source that emits signals in very short, regular bursts. A pulsar is believed to be a rotating neutron star.

A **quasar** is defined as an object that photographs like a star but has an extremely large red shift and a variable energy output. A quasar is believed to be the active core of a very distant galaxy.

A **black hole** is defined as an object that has collapsed to such a degree that light cannot escape from its surface; that light is trapped by the intense gravitational field.

THE SUN

The sun is the nearest star to Earth, and it produces solar energy. By the process of **nuclear fusion**, hydrogen gas is converted to helium gas. Energy flows out of the core to the surface, allowing radiation to escape into space.

Parts of the sun include:

- **Core:** the inner portion of the sun where fusion takes place.
- **Photosphere:** the surface of the sun that produces sunspots, which are cool, dark areas that can be seen on its surface.
- **Chromosphere:** the portion of the sun turned red by hydrogen gas. Also found here are **solar flares** (sudden brightness of the chromosphere) and **solar prominences** (gases that shoot outward from the chromosphere).
- **Corona:** the transparent area of sun visible only during a total eclipse.

ORIGIN AND LIFE CYCLE OF STARS

Stars form in **planetary nebulae**, cold clouds of dust and gas within a galaxy, and go through different stages of development in a specific sequence. This theory of star development is called the **condensation theory**.

Stellar sequence of development

In the initial stage, the diffuse, cloudlike spheres of the nebula begin to shrink under the influence of its own weak gravity into a knot of gasses called a **Protostar**. The original diameter of the protostar is many times greater than the diameter of our solar system, but gravitational forces cause it to continue to contract. This compression raises the internal temperature of the protostar.

When the protostar reaches a temperature of around 10 million degrees C (18 million degrees F), nuclear fusion starts, which stops the contraction of the protostar and changes its status to a star. Nuclear fusion is the process in which hydrogen atoms fuse together to form helium atoms, releasing massive amounts of energy. It's the fusion of atoms, not combustion, which causes stars to shine.

A star's life cycle depends on its initial mass. **Red stars** have a small mass. **Yellow stars** have a medium mass. **Blue stars** have a large mass. Large-mass stars consume their hydrogen at a faster rate and have a shorter life cycle in comparison to small-mass stars that consume their hydrogen at a much slower rate. All stars eventually convert a large percentage of their hydrogen to heavier atoms and begin to die. Just as a star's mass determines its length of life, however, it also determines the pattern it follows in the last stages of its existence.

Lower main sequence stars

When small and medium mass stars (such as the sun) consume all of their hydrogen, their inner cores begin to cool. The stars begin to consume the heavier elements

Middle Level Science

produced by fusion (carbon and oxygen) and the star's shell expands tremendously outward, causing the star to become a **giant star.** A giant star is a large, cool, extremely luminous body, 10 to 100 times the diameter of the sun. In roughly 4.6 billion years from now our sun will become a giant star. As it expands, its outer layers will reach halfway to Venus.

The dying giant gives off thermal pulses approximately every 200,000 years, throwing off concentric shells of light gasses enriched with heavy elements. As it enters its last phases of the life cycle, its depleted inner core begins to contract, and the giant becomes a **white dwarf star**, a small, slowly cooling, extremely dense star, no larger than 10,000 km in diameter.

The final phase of a lower main sequence star life cycle can take two paths: After a few billion years, most main sequence white dwarfs completely burn out to become **black dwarfs:** cold, dead stars.

The path is different, however, if a white dwarf is part of a binary star, one of two suns in the same solar system. Instead of slowly cooling to become a black dwarf, it may capture hydrogen from its companion star. If this happens, the temperature of the white dwarf soars, and when it reaches approximately 10 million degrees C, a nuclear explosion occurs, creating a **nova**. A nova is the sudden brightening of a lower main sequence star to approximately 10,000 times its normal luminosity caused by the explosion of the star. A nova reaches its maximum brightness in a short time (one or two days) and then gradually dims as the gasses and cosmic dust cool.

Upper Main Sequence Stars
The initial sequence of the high-mass, upper main sequence stars is identical to the lower-mass stars: planetary nebula to protostar. If the protostar accretes enough material, however, it forms as a blue star. When a blue star has consumed all of its hydrogen it, too, expands outward, but on a much larger scale than a lower-mass star. It becomes a **supergiant star,** an exceptionally bright star, 10 to 1,000 times the diameter of the sun.

The supergiant's now-depleted core cannot support such a vast weight and collapses inward, causing its temperature to soar. When it reaches roughly 599 million degrees C, it implodes and then explodes, creating a **supernova**, the massive explosion of an upper main sequence Supergiant star caused by the detonation of carbon within the star.

A supernova releases more energy than Earth's sun will produce in its entire life cycle. The luminosity of a supernova is as bright as 500 million suns. Chinese astronomers in 1054 recorded the sudden appearance of a new star in what is now known as the Taurus Constellation. Bright enough to be seen during daytime for over a month, it remained visible for over two years.

The explosive release of energy in a supernova is so great (1,028 megatons of TNT) as to literally blow the atomic nuclei of the carbon to bits. The shattered mass is accelerated outward at nearly the speed of light (300,000 km/sec. or 186,000 mph).

Ninety percent of the shattered mass scatters into space, becoming planetary nebulae from which the life cycle may begin anew. The other ten percent, the core of the star, is blown inward, becoming a **neutron star,** the very small—10 km diameter—imploded core of a collapsed supergiant star that rotates at a high speed (60,000 rpm) and has a strong magnetic field (1012 gauss).

A neutron star may capture gas from space, a companion star, or a nearby star and become a **pulsar**, a neutron star that emits a sweeping beam of ionized-gas radiation. As the pulsar rotates, the beams of light sweep into space similar to a beacon from a lighthouse. Since first discovered in 1967, over 350 pulsars have been catalogued.

The alternate product of a supernova is a **black hole,** a volume of space from which no form of radiation can escape. Black holes are created when a supergiant star with a mass roughly three times that of the sun implodes. The inner core of the star is compacted by the supernova into a **singularity**, an object of zero radius and infinite density.

A singularity is difficult to picture. Zero radiuses imply objects with size less than an electron, but also possessing a density that precludes the escape of all radiation including light. Although a singularity has yet to be detected, theoretically, they exist in and cause the effects exhibited by black holes.

Skill 6.2 Recognizing evidence used to support the scientific understanding of the universe

ASTRONOMICAL THEORIES AND HYPOTHESES

Two main theories that explain the origins of the universe are: The Steady State theory and the Big Bang theory.

Steady State Theory
This theory held that the universe was static and that it did not evolve, having always maintained a balance of the same general properties through replacement of dying stars and galaxies by new stars and galaxies. This theory was simultaneously both a popular and controversial explanation of the universe during its heyday in the 1950s and 1960s, but astronomers have not found any evidence to prove it.

All astronomers, however, did not accept the concept of a static universe, and they proposed an alternate theory centered on a nonstatic, expanding universe. Steady-state supporter, American astronomer Fred Hoyle sarcastically dubbed this theory the "Big Bang."

The controversy between supporters and opponents of the steady state theory continued until the late 1960s when detection of primordial background radiation dealt a decisive blow to the steady state theory. In a static state the background radiation should be uniform. Since it clearly was not, however, this indicated that something had occurred to cause it to "clump" together. The logical explanation was a massive explosion that disordered the radiation.

Big Bang Theory
This theory proposes that all the mass and energy of the universe originally was concentrated at a single geometric point, which, for unknown reasons, experienced a massive explosion that scattered mass, matter, and energy throughout the universe that then formed galaxies as matter cooled during the next half-billion years.

The concept of a massive explosion is supported by the distribution of background radiation and the measurable fact that the galaxies are moving away from each other at great speed.

The universe originated around 15 billion years ago with the "Big Bang" and continued to expand for the first 10 billion years. The universe originally was unimaginably hot, but around 1 million years after the Big Bang, it cooled enough to allow for the formation of atoms from the energy and particles.

Most of these atoms were hydrogen, and they comprise the most abundant form of matter in the universe. Around a billion years after the Big Bang, the matter had cooled enough to begin congealing into the first stars and galaxies.

The Big Bang theory has been widely accepted by many astronomers.

ORIGINS OF THE SOLAR SYSTEM

Two main hypotheses of the origin of the solar system are

- The tidal hypothesis
- The condensation hypothesis

The **tidal hypothesis** proposes that the solar system began with a near collision of the sun and a large star. Some astronomers believe that as these two stars passed each other, the great gravitational pull of the large star extracted hot gases out of the sun. The mass from the hot gases started to orbit the sun, which began to cool and then condensed into the nine planets. Few astronomers support this example, however.

The **condensation hypothesis** proposes that the solar system began with rotating clouds of dust and gas. Condensation occurred in the center forming the sun and the smaller parts of the cloud formed the nine planets. This example is widely accepted by many astronomers.

TEACHER CERTIFICATION STUDY GUIDE

Skill 6.3 Describing objects in the solar system (e.g., planets, comets, moons, the sun) in terms of physical, chemical, and geological processes

There are nine planets in our solar system: Mercury, Venus, Earth, Mars, Jupiter, Saturn, Uranus, Neptune, and Pluto. These nine planets are divided into two groups based on distance from the sun. The inner planets include: Mercury, Venus, Earth, and Mars. The outer planets include Jupiter, Saturn, Uranus, Neptune, and Pluto. Recent proposals for altering the definition of a planet, if accepted, would reduce Pluto to a celestial body, not a planet.

THE PLANETS

Mercury is the closest planet to the sun, named after the Roman messenger god. Mercury's surface has craters and rocks, and its atmosphere is composed of hydrogen, helium, and sodium.

Venus has a slow rotation when compared to Earth's. Venus and Uranus rotate in opposite directions from the other planets, called retrograde rotation. The surface of Venus is not visible due to extensive cloud cover whose sulfuric acid droplets give Venus a yellow appearance. The atmosphere is composed mostly of carbon dioxide, which, combined with the dense cloud cover, traps heat. Thus Venus has a greater greenhouse effect than observed on Earth. Venus was named after the Roman goddess of love.

Earth is considered a water planet, with seventy percent of its surface covered with water. Gravity holds the masses of water in place. The different temperatures observed on Earth allow for the different states of water to exist: solid, liquid, or gas. The atmosphere is composed mainly of oxygen and nitrogen. Earth is the only planet that is known to support life.

Mars has a surface that contains numerous craters, active and extinct volcanoes, and ridges and valleys with extremely deep fractures. Iron oxide found in the dusty soil makes the surface seem rust colored and the skies seem pink. The atmosphere is composed of carbon dioxide, nitrogen, argon, oxygen, and water vapor. Mars has polar regions with ice caps composed of water. Mars has two satellites. Mars was named after the Roman war god.

Jupiter is largest planet in the solar system. Jupiter has 16 moons. The atmosphere is composed of hydrogen, helium, methane, and ammonia. White-colored bands of clouds indicate rising gases, and dark-colored bands of clouds indicate descending gases, caused by heat Jupiter's core. Jupiter's Great Red Spot is thought to be a hurricane-type cloud. Jupiter has a strong magnetic field. Jupiter was named after the Roman king of the gods.

Saturn is the second largest planet in the solar system. Saturn has beautiful rings of ice, rock, and dust particles circling it. Saturn's atmosphere is composed of hydrogen, helium, methane, and ammonia. Saturn has 20-plus satellites. Saturn was named after the Roman god of agriculture.

Uranus is a gaseous planet with 10 dark rings, 15 satellites, and retrograde revolution. Its atmosphere is composed of hydrogen, helium, and methane. Uranus was named after the Greek god of the heavens.

Neptune is another gaseous planet with an atmosphere consisting of hydrogen, helium, and methane. Neptune has 3 rings and 2 satellites. Neptune was named after the Roman sea god because its atmosphere is the color of the seas.

Pluto is the smallest planet in the solar system, with one satellite. Pluto's atmosphere probably contains methane, ammonia, and frozen water. Pluto revolves around the sun every 250 years. Pluto was named after the Roman god of the underworld.

All the planets revolve around the sun, and all the planets except Venus and Uranus, rotate on their axis in the same direction. Except for Pluto, all the planets follow roughly the same elliptical orbital planes around the sun. Neptune and Pluto occasionally change places in the order. Pluto's orbit is so erratic compared to the other planets that sometimes it carries Pluto inside of Neptune's orbit.

The **asteroid belt** is located between Mars and Jupiter and may be the remnants of a planet crushed by the massive gravitational force of Jupiter. Some astronomers believe that asteroids are rocky fragments that may have been the remains of the birth of the solar system and that never formed into a planet.

Comets are masses of frozen gases, cosmic dust, and small rocky particles. Astronomers think that most comets originate in a dense comet cloud beyond Pluto. A comet consists of a nucleus, a coma, and a tail that always points away from the sun. The most famous comet, Halley's Comet, is named after the person who first discovered it in 240 B.C. It returns to the skies near Earth every 75 to 76 years.

Meteoroids are composed of particles of rock and metal of various sizes floating in space. When a meteoroid travels through the earth's atmosphere, friction causes its surface to heat up and it begins to burn. The burning meteoroid falling through the earth's atmosphere then is called a meteor or a "shooting star."

Meteorites are meteors that strike the earth's surface. A physical example of the impact of a meteorite—the Barringer Crater—can be seen in Arizona.

TEACHER CERTIFICATION STUDY GUIDE

Skill 6.4 Demonstrating knowledge of the motion of objects in the solar system

According to the **nebular theory,** the solar system was formed by a gravitational collapse of a giant molecular cloud approximately 4.6 billion years ago. From the time of its formation, the solar system has undergone constant change, often as a result of planetary impacts and collisions.

ECLIPSES

An eclipse is a phenomenon that occurs when a stellar body is shadowed by another and as a result, is rendered invisible.

The earth, moon, and sun must be in perfect alignment with each other to produce an eclipse. The sun never moves in between the earth and the moon. The orbits of the earth and moon cause them to move in and out of the shadow areas. The **umbra** is the central region of the shadow caused by an eclipse that receives no light from the sun. The **penumbra** is the lighter outer edges of the shadow created during a partial eclipse where some light hits.

There are two types of eclipses:

- **Lunar eclipse:** The earth is between the sun and the moon. The moon is in the earth's shadow, making the moon invisible.
- **Solar eclipse:** The moon is between the sun and the earth. The earth is in the moon's shadow, making the sun invisible.

Both types of eclipses have two forms: partial and full.

A **total (full) eclipse** can only be seen in the equatorial regions. Most total eclipses are spaced six months apart and normally last only two to ten minutes. During a total solar eclipse, the moon covers most of the sun, usually only showing a flaming **corona** around the sun's edges.

A **partial lunar eclipse** occurs when the moon does not completely enter the earth's shadow, so part of the moon is visible.

A **partial solar eclipse** (or **annular eclipse**) occurs when the moon appears as a small, dark spot in the center of the sun.

Just as the earth follows an orbit around the sun, the moon follows an eastward-moving orbit around the earth.

Middle Level Science

Because the moon's rotational period matches the earth's, and its period of revolution is 27.3 days (called the **sidereal period**), this keeps one side of the moon always facing Earth. The side always facing us is called the near side, and the darkened side we never see is called the far side.

The **phases of the moon** are the apparent change in the shape of the moon caused by the absence or presence of reflected sunlight as the moon orbits around the earth. The orbital pattern of the moon in relation to the sun and earth determines the extent of lunar illumination, and consequently, what illuminated shape is presented to the earth.

When the moon is between the sun and the earth, the side facing us is darkened, and we refer to this as a **new moon**. The opposite pattern occurs in the second half of the complete lunar cycle, when the moon is fully illuminated and bright in the night sky. This is called a **full moon**. The other phases between these extremes reflect the orbital point of the moon as it completes its journey around the earth.

A day is a unit of time equivalent to 24 hours on Earth. This is because it takes earth one **sidereal day**, or 23.934 solar hours, to complete a single rotation on its axis. The day is then further divided into equal periods of hours and seconds.

Skill 6.5   **Analyzing the orbit, rotation, and axial tilt of Earth to explain seasons, day length, and long-term changes in climate**

The distribution of solar energy is called **insolation**. Solar radiation isn't distributed evenly across the earth because of the earth's curvature, axial tilt, and orbit. This results in uneven heating of the atmosphere and is why the temperature is warmer at the equator and colder at the poles.

Because of the curvature and tilt, the energy striking the polar areas is spread over a larger area, which dilutes the energy received by a particular area. At the equator the energy is more concentrated.

The effect of insolation is important to life on Earth. The absence of solar radiation would cause the creation of very cold air masses and the thermal blanket of the atmosphere would not have heat to hold and reradiate. In short order, the world would become an icy rock.

Externalists put forth the concept that the axial tilt of the earth is responsible for the ice ages. This tilt does vary over time relative to the earth's orbital plane. Although these changes do not change the total amount of sunlight striking the planet, they do affect the distribution of the solar radiation.

Milankovitch Cycles: Based on the earth's relationship to the sun, this theory proposes that the axial tilt and wobble of the earth's orbit is responsible for warming or cooling.

Technically, the theory deals with these terms:

- **Precession:** the wobble of the earth on its axis.
- **Obliquity:** the tilt of the earth's axis. This ranges between 22.5 to 25.5 degrees. Today the tilt is 23.5 degrees.
- **Eccentricity:** the shape of an orbit. The earth's orbital shape changes periodically from elliptical to circular.

If there is a change in the tilt and orbit, then the amount of incoming solar radiation will change over time. The tilt of the axis is key in determining where most of the solar radiation strikes. It causes either longer or shorter summers and winters. A shorter summer increases the snow pack in the mountains. As this builds over time, it causes a glacial period.

The cycle is between 18,000 to 100,000 years. With the exception of one period, ice core O-18 ratio data correlates with this cycle and also shows a possible correlation between the Milankovitch Cycles and the oceans as a CO_2 sink.

SEASONS

The result of the tilt of the earth's axis allows for the seasonable changes called summer, spring, autumn, and winter. As the earth continues to revolve around the sun, it is the angle of the earth's axis that contributes to the amount of sunlight that is received on Earth, resulting in the changing seasons.

- **Summer solstice** occurs when the North Pole is tilted toward the sun on June 21st or 22nd, providing increased daylight hours for the Northern Hemisphere and shorter daylight hours for the Southern Hemisphere.
- **Winter solstice** occurs when the South Pole is tilted toward the sun on December 21st or 22nd, providing shorter daylight hours in the Northern Hemisphere and longer daylight hours in the Southern Hemisphere.
- The **spring or vernal equinox** occurs on March 20th or 21st, when the direct energy from the sun falls on the equator providing equal lengths of day and night hours in both hemispheres.
- The **autumnal equinox** occurs on September 22nd or 23rd providing equal amounts of day and night hours in both hemispheres.

TEACHER CERTIFICATION STUDY GUIDE

COMPETENCY 007   UNDERSTAND HUMAN INTERACTIONS WITH EARTH SYSTEMS

Skill 7.1   Analyzing the scientific evidence used to predict the occurrence of an environmental hazard on a human time frame

Modern technology is a tremendous tool for predicting environmental hazards. There are sensors that detect harmful contaminants in the air, water, and soil. There is technology that accurately predicts when a volcano will erupt and when a hurricane will reach land. There are complex computer-based systems that collect massive amounts of data and predict the likelihood tsunamis and earthquakes.
Also see Skills 7.2, 7.3, and 7.4.

Skill 7.2   Describing observed changes in a given Earth system (e.g., lithosphere, hydrosphere, atmosphere) that are due to human activity

As our population grows, the demand for lumber and wood products has grown exponentially. The increased urbanization has claimed once-vast tracts of forests, replacing them with concrete paving and closely packed structures.

This same drive to urbanization also affects our soil. Arable farmland is shrinking as the press to develop home and commercial sites increases. Of the approximately 15 billion hectares of dry land on the earth, only 2 billion are suitable for agriculture. If the same land is used year after year, there is a definite danger of soil exhaustion as vital nutrients are depleted.

Farmland is not the only victim of urbanization. Grazing lands for our cattle and other domesticated animals are also shrinking, and, as a consequence, many of the remaining areas are being overgrazed. Overgrazing leads to the loss of the grassland's topsoil cover, leaving it vulnerable to erosion.

Also see Skills 7.3 and 7.4.

Skill 7.3   Recognizing the causes and consequences of water pollution and the movement of water pollutants through Earth systems

Groundwater sources are contaminated by a wide range of pollutants. Septic tanks, broken pipes, agriculture fertilizers, garbage dumps, rainwater runoff, leaking underground tanks all pollute groundwater. Toxic chemicals from farmland mix with groundwater. Removal of large volumes of groundwater can cause collapse of soil and rock underground, causing the ground to sink. Along shorelines, excessive depletion of underground water supplies allows the intrusion of salt water into the freshwater field, making the groundwater supply undrinkable.

Organic wastes—sewage—are produced by both humans and animals. Left untreated, these wastes, and the wastes from food treatment plants can enter the waterways and upset the ecological balance. As the wastes decay, they consume oxygen in the water, depriving aquatic life forms of oxygen, or causing algal blooms that further deplete the oxygen supply, and eventually turning some water anoxic (without oxygen).

Another danger to the ecology is the poisoning of the food chain through pesticides and fertilizers, or with high concentrations of heavy metals carried into the water supply through runoff from farmlands, factories, and mine tailings.

Skill 7.4 Recognizing the causes and consequences of air pollution and the movements of air pollutants through Earth systems

Pollution also affects our air. Some pollutants are human-produced, including industrial waste, chemical refrigerants, and hydrocarbons released from burning fossil fuels. The uncontrolled burning of fossil fuel hydrocarbons and high-sulfur content coals pose severe health risks, especially to the very young and the very old. Smog alerts are routine in many of the major metropolitan areas, and in Mexico City, air pollution is reaching a critical level.

TEACHER CERTIFICATION STUDY GUIDE

DOMAIN III: LIFE SCIENCE

COMPETENCY 008 UNDERSTAND THE STRUCTURES AND FUNCTIONS OF LIVING ORGANISMS

Skill 8.1 Demonstrating knowledge of the macroscopic structure of a given common organism

TAXONOMY

Carolus Linnaeus is known as the father of **taxonomy**. Taxonomy is the science of classification. Linnaeus based his system on **morphology**, the study of structure. Later on, evolutionary relationships (**phylogeny**) were also used to sort and group species. The modern classification system uses **binomial nomenclature**. This consists of a two-word name for every species. The genus is the first part of the name, and the species is the second part. Notice in the levels explained below that **Homo sapiens** is the scientific name for humans. Starting with the kingdom, the groups get smaller and more alike as one moves down the levels in the classification of humans:

- **Kingdom:** Animalia
- **Phylum:** Chordata
- **Subphylum:** Vertebrata
- **Class:** Mammalia, Order: Primate
- **Family:** Hominidae
- **Genus:** Homo
- **Species:** sapiens

Species are defined by the ability to successfully reproduce with members of their own kind.

Viruses, Bacteria, Protists, and Fungi
The following are the kingdoms of viruses, bacteria, protists, and fungi:

- **Kingdom Monera:** bacteria and blue-green algae, prokaryotic, having no true nucleus, unicellular
- **Kingdom Protista:** eukaryotic, unicellular, some are photosynthetic, some are consumers
- **Kingdom Fungi:** eukaryotic, multicellular, absorptive consumers, contain a chitin cell wall

Viruses
All viruses have a head, or protein capsid, that contains genetic material. This material is encoded in the nucleic acid and can be DNA, RNA, or even a limited number of enzymes. Some viruses also have a protein tail. The tail aids in binding to the surface of

the host cell and penetrating the surface of the host, in order to introduce the virus's genetic material.

Bacteria
Bacteria are classified according to their morphology (shape). **Bacilli** are rod shaped, **cocci** are round, and **spirillia** are spiral shaped. The **gram stain** is a staining procedure used to identify bacteria. **Gram-positive** bacteria pick up the stain and turn purple. **Gram-negative** bacteria do not pick up the stain and are pink in color. Microbiologists use methods of locomotion, reproduction, and feeding to classify protista.

- **Methods of locomotion:** Flagellates have a flagellum; ciliates have cilia; and ameboids move through use of pseudopodia.
- **Methods of reproduction:** binary fission means that the organism divides in half and is asexual. All new organisms are exact clones of the parent. Sexual modes of reproduction provide more diversity. Bacteria can reproduce sexually through conjugation, where genetic material is exchanged.
- **Methods of obtaining nutrition:** photosynthetic organisms or producers convert sunlight to chemical energy; consumers, or heterotrophs, eat other living things. Saprophytes are consumers that live off dead or decaying material.

Plants
Some common divisions of plants and their descriptions are listed below:

- **Nonvascular plants:** Small in size, nonvascular plants do not require **vascular tissue (xylem and phloem)** because individual cells are close to their environment. The nonvascular plants have no true leaves, stems, or roots.
    - Division **Bryophyta** (mosses and liverworts) have a dominant **gametophyte** generation; they possess **rhizoids**, which are root-like structures. Moisture in their environment is required for reproduction and absorption of nutrients.
- **Vascular plants:** The development of vascular tissue enables these plants to grow in size. Xylem and phloem allow for the transport of water and minerals up to the top of the plant as well as transport of food manufactured in the leaves to the bottom of the plant. All vascular plants have a dominant **sporophyte** generation.
    - Division **Lycophyta** (club mosses) reproduce with **spores** and require water for reproduction.
    - Division **Sphenophyta** (horsetails) also reproduce with spores. These plants have small, needle-like leaves and rhizoids; they require moisture for reproduction.
    - Division **Pterophyta** (ferns) reproduce with spores and **flagellated sperm**. These plants have a true stem and need moisture for reproduction.

- **Gymnosperms:** Meaning **"naked seed"** these were the first plants to evolve with seeds, which made them less dependent on water to assist in reproduction. Their seeds and pollen from the male can travel by wind. Gymnosperms have cones that protect their seeds.
    - Division Cycadophyta (cycads) look like palms with cones.
    - Division Ghetophyta (desert dwellers)
    - Division Coniferophyta (pines) have needles and cones.
    - Division Ginkgophyta: The Ginkgo is the only member of this division.
    - Division Anthophyta (Angiosperms) are the largest group in the plant kingdom. They are the flowering plants and produce true seeds for reproduction.

ANIMALS

Listed below are some of the major phyla of animals:

- **Annelida:** segmented worms with specialized tissue. The circulatory system is more advanced in these worms and is a closed system with blood vessels. The **nephridia** are their excretory organs. They are **hermaphrodidic**, and each worm fertilizes the other upon mating. They support themselves with a **hydrostatic** skeleton and have **circular and longitudinal muscles** for movement.
- **Mollusca:** clams, octopus, soft-bodied animals, which have a muscular foot for movement. They breathe through **gills** and most are able to make a shell for protection from predators. They have an **open circulatory system**, with sinuses for bathing the body regions.
- **Arthropoda:** insects, crustaceans, and spiders; this is the largest group of the animal kingdom. Phylum Arthropoda accounts for about 85% of all the animal species. Animals in the phylum Arthropoda possess an **exoskeleton** made of **chitin**. They must molt in order to grow. Some insects, for example, go through four stages of development. They begin as an egg, hatch into a larva, form a pupa, and then emerge as an adult. Arthropods breathe through gills, trachea, or book lungs. Movement varies, with members being able to swim, fly, and/or crawl. There is a division of labor among the appendages (legs, antennae, etc). This is an extremely successful phylum, with members occupying diverse habitats.
- **Echinodermata:** sea urchins and starfish. These animals have spiny skin, and live in a marine habitat. They have **tube feet** for locomotion and feeding.
- **Chordata:** all animals with a **notochord**, or a **backbone**. The classes in this phylum include
    - Agnatha (jawless fish)
    - Chondrichthyes (cartilage fish)
    - Osteichthyes (bony fish)
    - Amphibia (frogs and toads, which have gills that are replaced by lungs during development)
    - Reptilia (snakes, lizards, which lay eggs with a protective covering)

- Aves (birds, which are warm-blooded animals with wings designed for flight)
- Mammalia (warm-blooded animals with body hair that bear their young live and possess mammary glands for milk production).

HOMEOSTASIS

All living organisms respond and adapt to their environments. **Homeostasis** is the result of regulatory mechanisms that help maintain an organism's internal environment within tolerable limits. For example, in humans and mammals, constriction and dilation of blood vessels near the skin help maintain body temperature.

RESPONSE TO STIMULI

Response to stimuli is one of the key characteristics of any living thing. Any detectable change in the internal or external environment (a stimulus) may trigger a response in an organism. Just like physical characteristics, organisms' responses to stimuli are adaptations that allow them to better survive. While these responses may be more noticeable in animals that can move quickly, all organisms are actually capable of responding to changes.

Single-Celled Organisms
These organisms are able to respond to basic stimuli such as the presence of light, heat, or food. Changes in the environment are typically sensed via cell surface receptors. These organisms may respond to such stimuli by making changes in internal biochemical pathways or initiating reproduction or **phagocytosis**. Those capable of simple motility, using flagella, for instance, may respond by moving toward food or away from heat.

Plants
Plants, typically, do not possess sensory organs, so individual cells recognize stimuli through a variety of pathways. When many cells respond to stimuli together, the response becomes apparent. Logically then, the responses of plants occur on a rather longer timescale that those of animals. Plants are capable of responding to a few basic stimuli including light, water, and gravity. Some common examples include the way plants turn and grow toward the sun, the sprouting of seeds when exposed to warmth and moisture, and the growth of roots in the direction of gravity.

Animals
Lower members of the animal kingdom have responses similar to those seen in single-celled organisms. Higher animals, however, have developed complex systems to detect and respond to stimuli. The nervous system, sensory organs (eyes, ears, skin, etc.), and muscle tissue all allow animals to sense and quickly respond to changes in their environment.

As in other organisms, many responses to stimuli in animals are involuntary. For example, pupils dilate in response to the reduction of light. Such reactions are typically called reflexes. However, many animals are also capable of voluntary responses. In many animal species, voluntary reactions are instinctual. For instance, a zebra's response to a lion is a voluntary one, but, instinctually, it will flee quickly as soon as it senses the lion's presence. Complex responses, which may or may not be instinctual, are typically termed behavior. An example is the annual migration of birds when seasons change. Even more complex social behavior is seen in animals that live in large groups.

STABILITY AND DISTURBANCES

Nature replenishes itself continually. Natural disturbances, such as landslides and brushfires, are not only destructive, but following the destruction, they allow for a new generation of organisms to inhabit the land. For every indigenous organism, there exists a natural predator. These predator/prey relationships allow populations to maintain reproductive balance and to avoid overusing food sources, thus keeping food chains intact. Left undisturbed, nature would always find a way to balance itself. Unfortunately, the largest disturbances nature faces are from humans. We have introduced nonindigenous species to many areas, upsetting the predator/prey relationships. Our buildings have caused landslides and disrupted waterfront ecosystems. We have damaged the ozone layer and overused the land entrusted to us.

Skill 8.2 **Demonstrating knowledge of the structure of a plant or animal organ system and the functions of those organ systems**

PLANTS

Roots
Roots absorb water and minerals and exchange gases in the soil. Like stems, roots contain xylem and phloem. The xylem transports water and minerals, called **xylem sap**, upwards. The sugar produced by photosynthesis travels down the phloem in the **phloem sap** to the roots and other nonphotosynthetic parts of the plant. In addition to water and mineral absorption, roots anchor plants in place, preventing erosion by environmental conditions.

Stems
Stems, the major support structure of plants, consist primarily of three types of tissue: dermal tissue, ground tissue, and vascular tissue. **Dermal tissue** covers the outside surface of the stem to prevent excessive water loss and control gas exchange. **Ground tissue** consists mainly of **parenchyma cells** and surrounds the vascular tissue, providing support and protection. Finally, **vascular tissue,** xylem and phloem, provide long distance transport of nutrients and water.

Leaves

Leaves enable plants to capture light and carbon dioxide for photosynthesis. Photosynthesis occurs primarily in the leaves. Plants exchange gases through their leaves via **stomata**, small openings, on the underside of the leaves. Stomata allow oxygen to move in or out of the plant and carbon dioxide to move in. Leaf size and shape varies greatly between species of plants. Botanists often identify plants by their characteristic leaf patterns.

Sexual and asexual reproduction in plants

Reproduction in plants is accomplished through alternation of generations in which a **haploid stage** in the plant's life history alternates with a **diploid stage**. The **diploid sporophyte** divides by **meiosis** to reduce the chromosome number to the haploid gametophyte generation. The haploid gametophytes undergo **mitosis** to produce **gametes** (sperm and eggs), and fertilized haploid gametes then return to the diploid sporophyte stage.

Both the nonvascular plants and the vascular plants that do not produce seeds need water to reproduce. Gymnosperms use seeds for reproduction and do not require water.

Reproduction in Angiosperms

Angiosperms are the most numerous plants and therefore are the main focus of reproduction in this section. The sporophyte is the dominant phase in angiosperm reproduction. Angiosperm reproductive structures are the **flowers**.

The male gametophytes are **pollen grains**, and the female gametophytes are **embryo sacs** that are inside of the **ovules**. The male pollen grains are formed in the **anthers** at the tips of the stamens. The female ovules are enclosed by the **ovaries**. The **stamen** is the reproductive organ of the male and the **carpel** is the reproductive organ of the female.

In a process called **pollination**, the pollen grains are released from the anthers, are carried by animals and the wind, and land on the carpels. The sperm is released to fertilize the eggs. Angiosperms reproduce through a method of **double fertilization**: An ovum is fertilized by two sperm. One sperm produces the new plant, and the other forms the food supply for the developing plant (endosperm). The ovule develops into a seed and the ovary develops into a fruit. The fruit is then carried by wind or animals and the seeds are dispersed to form new plants.

The development of the egg to form a plant occurs in three stages:

- **Growth**
- **Morphogenesis:** the development of form
- **Cellular differentiation:** the acquisition of each cell's specific structure and function

ANIMALS

Skeletal System

The skeletal system functions to support the body. Vertebrates have an **endoskeleton**, with muscles attached to bones. Skeletal proportions are controlled by area to volume relationships: Body size and shape are limited due to the forces of gravity; surface area is increased to improve efficiency in all organ systems.

The **axial skeleton** consists of the bones of the skull and vertebrae. The **appendicular skeleton** consists of the bones of the legs, arms, tail, and shoulder girdle.

Bone is a connective tissue, which includes compact bone, which gives strength; spongy bone, which contains red marrow to make blood cells; yellow marrow in the center of long bones, which stores fat cells; and the periosteum, which is the protective covering on the outside of the bone.

A **joint** is defined as a place where two bones meet. Joints enable movement. **Ligaments** attach bone to bone. **Tendons** attach bones to muscles.

Muscular System

The muscular system enables the organism to move. There are three types of muscle tissue: **Skeletal muscle,** which attaches to bone, is voluntary, meaning the organism has conscious control over it. **Smooth muscle,** found in organs, is involuntary, meaning the organism has no conscious control over it, and enables functions such as digestion and respiration. **Cardiac muscle** is a specialized type of smooth muscle found in the heart. Muscles can only contract; therefore they work in antagonistic pairs to allow back and forward movement. Muscle fibers are made of groups of myofibrils, which, in turn, are made of groups of sarcomeres. Actin and myosin are proteins, which make up the sarcomere.

Physiology of muscle contraction

When a nerve impulse strikes a muscle fiber, it causes calcium ions to flood the sarcomere. Calcium ions allow ATP to expend energy. The myosin fibers creep along the actin fibers causing the muscle to contract. Once the nerve impulse has passed, calcium is pumped out and the contraction ends.

Nervous System

The **neuron** is the basic unit of the nervous system. It consists of an **axon** that carries impulses away from the cell body, the **dendrite** that carries impulses toward the cell body, and the cell body that contains the nucleus. **Synapses** are spaces between neurons. Chemicals called neurotransmitters are found close to the synapse. The myelin sheath, composed of Schwann cells, covers the neurons and provides insulation.

Organization of the nervous system

The **somatic nervous system** is controlled consciously. It consists of the central nervous system (brain and spinal cord) and the peripheral nervous system (nerves that extend from the spinal cord to the muscles). The **hypothalamus** in the brain unconsciously controls the autonomic nervous system, which regulates, for instance, smooth muscles, the heart, and digestion. It is split into two systems: The sympathetic nervous system works in opposition to the parasympathetic nervous system. For example, if the sympathetic nervous system stimulates an action, the parasympathetic nervous system ends that action.

Physiology of a nerve impulse

Nerve action depends on **depolarization** and an imbalance of electrical charges across the neuron. A polarized nerve has a positive charge outside the neuron. A depolarized nerve has a negative charge outside the neuron. Neurotransmitters turn off the sodium pump, which results in depolarization of the membrane. This wave of depolarization (as it moves from neuron to neuron) carries an electrical impulse. This is actually a wave of opening and closing gates that allows for the flow of ions across the synapse. Nerves have an action potential. There is a threshold for the level of chemicals that must be met or exceeded in order for muscles to respond. This is called the "all-or-none" response.

The **reflex arc** is the simplest nerve response and bypasses the brain. When a stimulus (like touching a hot stove) occurs, sensors in the hand send the message directly to the spinal cord, which stimulates motor neurons that contract the muscles to move the hand.

Voluntary nerve responses involve the brain. **Receptor cells** send the message to **sensory neurons,** which lead to **association neurons,** which transport the message to the brain. **Motor neurons** are stimulated and the message is transmitted to **effector cells,** which cause the end effect.

Neurotransmitters

Neurotransmitters are chemicals released by **exocytosis** that either stimulate or inhibit action.

- **Acetylcholine:** The most common neurotransmitter controls muscle contraction and heartbeat. The enzyme acetylcholinesterase breaks it down to end the transmission.
- **Epinephrine:** Also called adrenaline, epinephrine is responsible for the "fight or flight" reaction. It causes an increase in heart rate and blood flow to prepare the body for action.
- **Endorphins and enkephalins:** These natural painkillers and are released during serious injury and childbirth.

Digestive System

The function of the digestive system is to break food down and absorb it into the blood stream where it can be delivered to all the body's cells for use in cellular respiration. The teeth and saliva begin digestion by breaking food down into smaller pieces and lubricating it so it can be swallowed. The lips, cheeks, and tongue form a **bolus** or ball of food, which is carried down the pharynx by the process of **peristalsis** (wavelike contractions). The bolus enters the stomach through the **cardiac sphincter,** which closes to keep food from going back up. In the stomach, pepsinogen and hydrochloric acid form pepsin, the enzyme that breaks down proteins. The food is broken down further by this chemical action and is churned into **chyme**. The **pyloric sphincter muscle** opens to allow the food to enter the small intestine. Most nutrient absorption occurs in the small intestine whose length and protrusions called **villi** and microvilli allow for a great absorptive surface into the bloodstream. Acidic chyme is neutralized to allow the enzymes found there to function. Any food left after the trip through the small intestine enters the large intestine. The large intestine reabsorbs water and produces vitamin K. The feces, or remaining waste, are passed out through the anus.

Accessory organs

Although not part of the digestive tract, these organs function in the production of necessary enzymes and bile. The pancreas makes many enzymes to break down food in the small intestine. The liver makes bile, which breaks down and emulsifies fatty acids

Respiratory System

The respiratory system delivers oxygen to the bloodstream and picks up carbon dioxide for release out of the body. Air enters the mouth and nose, where it is warmed, moistened, and filtered of dust and particles. Cilia in the **trachea** trap unwanted material in mucus, which can be expelled. The trachea splits into two **bronchial tubes** and the bronchial tubes divide into smaller and smaller **bronchioles** in the lungs. The internal surface of the lung is composed of **alveoli**, which are thin-walled air sacs, which provide a large surface area for gas exchange. The alveoli are lined with capillaries. Oxygen diffuses into the bloodstream, and carbon dioxide diffuses out to be exhaled by the lungs. The oxygenated blood is carried to the heart and delivered to all parts of the body.

The thoracic cavity holds the lungs. Below the lungs, the **diaphragm**, a muscle, makes inhalation possible. As the volume of the thoracic cavity increases, the diaphragm muscle flattens out and inhalation occurs. When the diaphragm relaxes, exhalation occurs.

Circulatory System

The circulatory system carries oxygenated blood and nutrients to all cells of the body and returns carbon dioxide waste to be expelled from the lungs. Unoxygenated blood enters the **right atrium** of the heart through the inferior and superior vena cava. The blood flows through the tricuspid valve to the **right ventricle** to the pulmonary arteries and then to the lungs where it is oxygenated. It returns to the heart through the pulmonary vein into the **left atrium**, travels through the bicuspid valve to the **left ventricle** from where it is pumped to all parts of the body through the aorta.

The **sinoatrial node** (SA node), located on the right atrium, is the heart's pacemaker, responsible for contraction of the right and left atrium. The **atrioventricular node** (AV node), located on the left ventricle, is responsible for contraction of the ventricles.

Types of blood vessels

- **Arteries** lead away from the heart. All arteries carry oxygenated blood except the pulmonary artery going to the lungs. Arteries are under high pressure.
- **Arterioles** are smaller vessels that branch off from arteries.
- **Capillaries** are the tiniest vessels that branch off from arterioles and reach every cell. Because the small size of the vessels, blood moves slowest here; only one red blood cell may pass at a time to allow for diffusion of gases into and out of cells and absorption of nutrients.
- **Venules** are the larger vessels formed when capillaries combine. The vessels are now carrying waste products from the cells.
- **Veins** are larger vessels formed when venules combine and lead back to the heart. Veins and venules have thinner walls than arteries because they are not under as much pressure. Veins contain valves to prevent the backward flow of blood due to the force of gravity.

Components of blood

- **Plasma:** Sixty percent of the blood is plasma, which contains salts called electrolytes, nutrients, and waste. Plasma is the liquid part of blood.
- **Erythrocytes:** Also called red blood cells, erythrocytes contain **hemoglobin,** which carries oxygen molecules.
- **Leukocytes:** Also called white blood cells, leukocytes are larger than red cells. They are phagocytic and can engulf invaders. White blood cells are not confined to the blood vessels and can enter the interstitial fluid between cells.
- **Platelets:** Platelets are made in the bone marrow and assist in blood clotting.

The process of blood clotting

The neurotransmitter that initiates blood-vessel constriction following an injury is called serotonin. A material called prothrombin is converted to thrombin with the help of thromboplastin. The thrombin is then used to convert fibrinogen to fibrin, which traps red blood cells to stop blood flow and form a scab.

Lymphatic System (Immune System)

Immunity is the body's ability to recognize and destroy an *antigen* before it causes harm. **Active immunity** develops after recovery from an infectious disease (such as chicken pox) or after a vaccination (for mumps, measles, rubella). **Passive immunity** may be passed from one individual to another but is not permanent. A good example is the immunities passed from a mother to her nursing child.

Nonspecific defense mechanisms do not target specific pathogens, but are a whole body response, seen as symptoms of an infection. These mechanisms include the skin, mucous membranes, and cells of the blood and lymph (i.e., white blood cells, macrophages). **Fever** is a result of an increase in white blood cells. **Pyrogens** are released by white blood cells, which set the body's thermostat to a higher temperature, both to inhibit the growth of microorganisms and to boost metabolism to increase phagocytosis and body repair.

Specific defense mechanisms recognize foreign material, including individual pathogens, and respond by destroying the invader. An **antigen** is any foreign particle that invades the body. In response, the body manufactures **antibodies** that recognize and latch onto antigens, intent on destroying them. These mechanisms are specific and diverse. They also can recognize the self. Memory of the invaders provides immunity upon further exposure.

Excretory System

The excretory system rids the body of nitrogenous wastes in the form of **urea**. The functional unit of excretion is the **nephron**, which make up the kidneys. Antidiuretic hormone (ADH), which is made in the hypothalamus and stored in the pituitary, is released when differences in osmotic balance occur and causes more water to be reabsorbed. As the blood becomes more dilute, ADH release ends.

The Bowman's capsule contains the glomerulus, a tightly packed group of capillaries. The **glomerulus** is under high pressure, causing waste and fluids to leak out. Filtration is not selective in this area. Selective secretion by active and passive transport occur in the proximal convoluted tubule. Unwanted molecules are secreted into the filtrate. Selective secretion also occurs in the **loop of Henle**. Salt is actively pumped out of the tube and much water is lost due to the hyperosmosity of the inner part (medulla) of the kidney. As the fluid enters the distal convoluted tubule, more water is reabsorbed. Urine forms in the collecting duct, which leads to the ureter and then to the bladder where it is stored. Urine is passed from the bladder through the urethra. The amount of water reabsorbed back into the body is dependent upon how much water or fluids an individual has consumed. Urine can be very dilute or very concentrated if dehydration is present.

Endocrine System

The endocrine system manufactures proteins called **hormones** that are released into the bloodstream and carried to a target tissue where they stimulate an action. Hormones may build up over time to cause their effect, as in puberty or the menstrual cycle.

Hormone activation

Hormones are specific and fit receptors on the target tissue cell surface. The receptor activates an enzyme that converts ATP to cyclic AMP. Cyclic AMP (cAMP) is a second messenger from the cell membrane to the nucleus. The genes found in the nucleus turn on or off to cause a specific response. Hormones work on a **feedback system**: The increase or decrease in one hormone may cause the increase or decrease in another.

Classes of hormones

There are two classes of hormones: **Steroid hormones** come from cholesterol. Steroid hormones, such as estrogen and progesterone in females and testosterone in males, cause sexual characteristics and mating behavior. **Peptide hormones** are made in the pituitary, adrenal glands on the kidneys, and the pancreas.

Reproductive System

Sexual reproduction greatly increases diversity because of the many combinations possible through meiosis and fertilization. **Gametogenesis** is the production of the sperm and egg cells. Spermatogenesis begins at puberty in the male. One **spermatozoa** produces four sperm, which mature in the seminiferous tubules located in the testes. **Oogenesis**, the production of egg cells, is usually complete by the birth of a female. Egg cells are not released until menstruation begins at puberty. Meiosis forms one ovum with all the cytoplasm and three polar bodies that are reabsorbed by the body. The ova are stored in the ovaries and released each month from puberty to menopause.

Path of the sperm

Sperm are stored in the **seminiferous tubules** in the testes where they mature. Mature sperm are found in the epididymis located on top of the testes. After ejaculation, the sperm travels up the vas deferens where they mix with semen made in the prostate and seminal vesicles and travel out the urethra.

Path of the egg

Ovulation releases the egg from the ovary into the **fallopian tubes**, which are ciliated to move the egg along. Fertilization normally occurs in the fallopian tube. If pregnancy does not occur, the egg passes through the uterus and is expelled through the vagina during menstruation. Levels of progesterone and estrogen stimulate menstruation and are affected by the implantation of a fertilized egg so menstruation does not occur.

Pregnancy

If fertilization occurs, the **zygote** implants in about two to three days in the uterus. Implantation promotes secretion of **human chorionic gonadotrophin (HCG)**. This is what is detected in pregnancy tests. The HCG keeps the level of progesterone elevated to maintain the uterine lining to feed the developing embryo until the umbilical cord forms. Labor is initiated by **oxytocin**, which causes contractions and dilation of the cervix. Prolactin and oxytocin cause the production of milk.

Skill 8.3 **Demonstrating knowledge of processes used by common organisms (e.g., flowering and nonflowering plants, bacteria, mammals, amphibians) to sustain life**

All living organisms must perform metabolism to maintain homeostasis. Vital metabolic pathways respond either to positive-feedback or negative-feedback loops to maintain parameters within normal ranges. **Feedback loops** typically involve chemical reactions within cells. One of the most-common chemical pathways, **glycolysis**, is found in nearly every living organism. This exergonic pathway splits the sugar molecule glucose into two breakdown products and by doing so releases some of the energy stored in the molecule of sugar. Typically, this energy is used to regenerate ATP (adenosine triphosphate) from ADP (adenosine diphosphate) and inorganic phosphate (glycolysis is more-fully described under Skill 9.2).

The fact that glycolysis occurs in flowering and nonflowering plants, bacteria, mammals, amphibians, and humans is key evidence suggesting that all of life shares a single common ancestor. In fact, many chemical pathways are shared among a wide variety of organisms indicating that complex chemical reactions are highly conserved through evolution. Beyond metabolism, living organisms must be able to grow, respond to external stimuli, and reproduce. All living things also are subject to evolution by means of natural selection—sexually reproducing species are subject to evolution by means of sexual selection.

Skill 8.4 **Recognizing how the structure and function of the components of a living system (e.g., coral reef, estuary, forest, grassland) support the overall function of that system**

POPULATION DYNAMICS

Logistic population growth incorporates the **carrying capacity** into the growth rate. As a population reaches the carrying capacity, the growth rate begins to slow down and level off.

Many populations follow this model of population growth. Humans, however, are an **exponentially growing population**. Eventually, the carrying capacity of the earth will be reached, and the growth rate will level off. How and when this will occur remains unknown.

Population Density

Population density is the number of individuals per unit of area or volume. The spacing pattern of individuals in an area is **dispersion**. Dispersion patterns can be clumped, with individuals grouped in patches; uniform, where individuals are approximately equidistant from each other; or randomly dispersed.

Population densities are usually estimated based on a few representative plots. Aggregation of a population in a relatively small geographic area can have detrimental effects on the environment. Food, water, and other resources will be rapidly consumed, resulting in an unstable environment. A low population density is less harmful to the environment; the use of natural resources will be more widespread, allowing the environment to recover and continue growth.

Niche

The term **niche** describes the relational position of a species or a population in an ecosystem. Niche dynamics include how a population responds to the abundance of its resources and enemies (e.g., by growing when resources are abundant and when predators, parasites, and pathogens are scarce).

A niche also refers to an organism's life history, habitat, and place in the food chain. According to the **competitive exclusion principle,** no two species can occupy the same niche in the same environment for a long time.

The full range of environmental conditions (biological and physical) under which an organism can exist describes its fundamental niche. Because of the pressure from superior competitors, organisms are sometimes driven to occupy a niche much narrower than their previous niche. This is known as the "realized niche."

Examples of niches:

1. Oak trees:
    - Found in forests
    - Absorb sunlight by photosynthesis
    - Provide shelter for many animals
    - Act as support for creeping plants
    - Serve as a source of food for animals
    - Cover their ground with dead leaves in the autumn

If the oak trees were cut down or destroyed by fire or storms, they would no longer be functional within the niche, and this would affect on all the other organisms living in the same habitat.

2. Hedgehogs:
    - Eat a variety of insects and other invertebrates, which live underneath the dead leaves and twigs in the garden
    - The spines are a superb environment for fleas and ticks

- Fleas and ticks put the nitrogen back into the soil when they urinate
- Eat slugs and protect plants from them

If there were no hedgehogs around, the population of slugs would explode and the nutrients in the dead leaves and twigs would not be recycled.

Interspecific Relationships
Predation and **parasitism** both result in a benefit for one species and a detriment for the other. Predation occurs when a predator eats its prey. The common conception of predation is of a carnivore consuming other animals. This is one form of predation. Herbivory is a form of predation although not always resulting in the death of the plant. Some animals eat enough of a plant to cause the plant to die. Parasitism involves a predator that lives on or in its host, causing detrimental effects to the host. Insects and viruses living off and reproducing in their hosts are examples of parasitism. Many plants and animals have defenses against predators. Some plants have poisonous chemicals that will harm the predator if ingested; and some animals are camouflaged, so that they are harder to detect.

Symbiosis occurs when two species live in close relationship to each other. Parasitism is one example of symbiosis described above. Another example of symbiosis is commensalisms. **Commensalism** occurs when one species benefits from the other without harmful effects. **Mutualism** occurs when both species benefit from the other. Species involved in mutualistic relationships must co-evolve to survive. As one species evolves, the other must evolve as well if it is to continue to exist. The grouper and a species of shrimp live in a mutualistic relationship. The shrimp feed off parasites living on the grouper; thus the shrimp are fed and the grouper stays healthy. Many microorganisms have mutualistic relationships with other organisms.

ECOLOGY

Ecology is the study of organisms, their habitat, and their interactions with the environment. A population is a group of the same species in a specific area. A **community** is a group of populations residing in the same area. Communities that are ecologically similar in regards to temperature, rainfall, and the species that live there are called **biomes**. Specific biomes include:

- **Marine:** The marine biome covers 75 percent of the earth and is organized by the depth of the water. The **intertidal zone** stretches from the tide line to the edge of the water. The **littoral zone** covers from the water's edge to the open sea and includes coral reef habitats, the most densely populated area of the marine biome. The **open sea zone** is divided into the epipelagic zone and the pelagic zone. The epipelagic zone receives more sunlight and has a larger number of species. The ocean floor is called the **benthic zone** and is populated with bottom feeders.

- **Tropical rain forest:** Temperature is relatively constant (25° C), and rainfall exceeds 200 cm per year. Located around the area of the equator, the rain forest has abundant, diverse species of plants and animals.
- **Savanna:** Temperatures range from 0° to 25°C, depending on the location. Rainfall ranges from 90 to 150 cm per year. Plants include shrubs and grasses. The savanna is a transitional biome between the rain forest and the desert.
- **Desert:** Temperatures range from 10° to 38°C, and rainfall is under 25 cm per year. Plant species include **xerophytes** and **succulents**. Lizards, snakes, and small mammals are common animals found in this biome.
- **Temperate deciduous forest:** Temperature ranges from -24° to 38°C, and rainfall is between 65 and 150 cm per year. Deciduous trees are common, as well as deer, bear, and squirrels.
- **Taiga:** Temperatures range from -24° to 22° C, and rainfall is between 35 and 40 cm per year. Taiga is located far north and far south of the equator, close to the poles. Plant life includes conifers and plants that can withstand harsh winters. Animals include weasels, mink, and moose.
- **Tundra:** Temperatures range from -28° to 15°C, and rainfall is limited, ranging from 10 to 15 cm per year. The tundra is located even farther north and south than the taiga. Common plants include lichens and mosses. Animals include polar bears and musk ox.
- **Polar or permafrost:** Temperature ranges from -40° to 0°C. It rarely gets above freezing, and rainfall is below 10 cm per year. Most water is bound up as ice. Life is limited.

Succession and Disturbance

The following are some problems and challenges faced by ecosystems:

- **Succession:** Succession is an orderly process in which one community replaces another community that has been damaged, or starts a community where no life has previously existed. **Primary succession** occurs after a community has been totally wiped out by a natural disaster or where life never existed before, as in a flooded area. **Secondary succession** takes place in communities that once flourished but were disturbed by some influence, either human or natural, but were not totally wiped out. A **climax community** is a community that is established and flourishing.
- **Carrying capacity:** Carrying capacity is the total amount of life a habitat can support. Once the habitat runs out of food, water, shelter, or space, the carrying capacity decreases, and then stabilizes.
- **Ecological problems:** Non-renewable resources are fragile and must be conserved for use in the future. Man's impact and knowledge of conservation will directly affect our future.
- **Biological magnification:** Chemicals and pesticides accumulate along the food chain. Tertiary consumers have more accumulated toxins than animals at the bottom of the food chain.

- **Simplification of the food web:** Three major crops feed the world (rice, corn, and wheat). The planting of these foods wipe out habitats and push animals into other habitats causing overpopulation or extinction.
- **Fuel sources:** Strip mining and the overuse of oil reserves have depleted these resources. At the current rate of consumption, conservation and/or alternate fuel sources will help guarantee our future fuel sources.
- **Pollution:** Although technology gives us many advances, pollution is a side effect of production. Waste disposal and the burning of fossil fuels have polluted our land, water, and air. Global warming and acid rain are two results of the burning of hydrocarbons and sulfur.
- **Global warming:** Rainforest depletion and the use of fossil fuels and aerosols have caused an increase in carbon dioxide production. This leads to a decrease in the amount of oxygen, which is directly proportional to the amount of ozone. As the ozone layer is depleted, more heat enters our atmosphere and is trapped. This causes an overall warming effect, which may eventually melt polar ice caps, causing a rise in water levels and changes in climate, which will affect climates worldwide.
- **Endangered species:** Construction of homes to house people in our overpopulated world has caused the destruction of habitat for other animals, leading to their extinction.
- **Overpopulation:** The human race is still growing at an exponential rate. Carrying capacity has not been met due to our ability to use technology to produce more food and housing. Space and water cannot be manufactured, and eventually our non-renewable resources will reach a crisis state. Our overuse of nonrenewable resources affects every living thing on this planet.
- **Biotic factors:** Biotic factors are living things in an ecosystem, such as plants, animals, bacteria, fungi, etc. If one population in a community increases, it affects the ability of another population to succeed by limiting the available amount of food, water, shelter, and space.
- **Abiotic factors:** Abiotic factors are non-living aspects of an ecosystem, such as soil quality, rainfall, and temperature. Changes in climate and soil can cause effects at the beginning of the food chain, thus limiting or accelerating the growth of populations.

SPECIES DIVERSITY

Species diversity is simply a count of the number of different species in a given area. A species is a group of organisms that are similar, able to breed, and able to produce offspring.

Biologists are not sure how many different species live on the earth. The estimates range from 2 to 100 million species. So far, only 2.1 million species living in the middle latitudes have been classified; most of the species that are not classified are invertebrates. This group includes insects, spiders, worms, crustaceans, etc. It is difficult to classify them because of their small size and the inaccessible habitats they live in.

In the tropical rain forest, identifying these species is a difficult task since their habitats are hard to explore. Scientists estimate that this single biome may harbor 50 to 90 percent of the earth's biodiversity.

Extinction

Many species have gone extinct over Earth's geological history. The main reason for these extinctions is a change in the environment and competition from superior species. Because of the Industrial Revolution, a large number of biologically classified species have become extinct. The continued extinction of species on this planet by human activities is one of the greatest environmental problems facing human beings.

Genetic Diversity and Ecosystem Diversity

Species diversity is one of the three categories of biodiversity. The other two are genetic diversity and ecosystem diversity. **Genetic diversity** refers to the total number of genetic characteristics expressed and recessed in all of the individuals that compose a particular species. **Ecosystem diversity** is the variation of habitats, community types, and abiotic environments present in a given area.

Species Richness

In this context, we need to look at species richness, which is one of the components of the ecosystem's species biodiversity. Species richness is a measurable quality and has been found to be a good substitute for other measures of biodiversity that would be difficult to measure.

A few facts about species richness:

- The species richness increases from high latitudes to low latitudes.
- The maximum species richness occurs between 20 and 30 degrees latitude.
- Species richness increases rapidly from the North Pole to the equator, and decreases rapidly from the equator to the South Pole.
- Larger areas contain more species since there are greater opportunities for more species to live there.
- The relationship between endemism (species that are only native to one habitat) and species richness is positively correlated. However, in some oceanic islands, there is a high degree of endemism, but a low level of species richness.
- Species richness is a measure of biodiversity.

FOOD WEBS AND ENERGY FLOW

Trophic levels are based on the feeding relationships that determine energy flow and chemical cycling.

Autotrophs are the primary producers of the ecosystem. Producers mainly consist of plants. Primary consumers are the next trophic level. The **primary consumers** are the herbivores that eat plants or algae. **Secondary consumers** are the carnivores that eat the primary consumers. **Tertiary consumers** eat the secondary consumer. These

trophic levels may go higher, depending on the ecosystem. **Decomposers** are consumers that feed off animal waste and dead organisms. This pathway of food transfer is known as the **food chain**.
For more on food webs, see Skill 11.4.

Skill 8.5   **Analyzing how and why the structures (e.g., skeletal system, respiratory system) for a given function are different in different species**

Evolutionary processes shape species' **phenotype** and morphology. Two species may approach a common problem in different ways because the two species are derived from different ancestors. For example, insect wings and bird wings both allow for flight but they are quite distinct structures. Likewise bat wings allow flight but are not just like either insect or bird wings. This does not infer that insect wings are somehow "better" than bat wings, but simply that the wings of these two groups of organisms are derived from different structures and morphology. This demonstrates a process of evolution called **convergent evolution**. Examples of convergent evolution are quite common in the natural world as a variety of species become adapted to similar environmental paradigms. Other differences might be based in evolution within a different environment. For example, mammalian respiratory systems typically involve relatively constant breathing throughout the organism's lifespan. Whales and some other aquatic mammals, on the other hand, have modified respiratory systems that allow them to 'hold their breath' for prolonged periods of time. This adaptation is simply an evolutionary response to an environmental need. Thus, both convergent evolution and adaptation potentially explain why structures for a given function might vary among species.

Skill 8.6   **Recognizing the origins, transmission, prevention, management, or cures for human diseases (e.g., heart disease, malaria, common cold)**

Many human diseases have a genetic origin wherein the disease is caused by a **mutation** in a given gene. A common example of this is e.g. cystic fibrosis. These genetic diseases typically are transmitted from parent to offspring and, in general, currently are not curable.

Other human diseases have a behavioral origin wherein the disease is either caused by or enabled by a particular behavioral trait. A common example of this is lip cancer, which is highly correlated with tobacco use, or heart disease, which may be caused by obesity. These diseases often can be treated surgically but clearly avoidance is preferable.

Many human diseases are caused by **pathogens**; common pathogens are bacteria, viruses, fungi, protists, and parasites. For example, malaria is caused by a protist organism that is vectored by mosquitoes. Bacteria, viruses, fungi, and protists generally cause disease by living on or in human tissue. Parasites generally cause disease by living in human tissues or in the digestive tract. Most diseases caused by pathogens are transmissible from an infected human to an uninfected human by some **vector**. Common vectors are sexual intercourse, droplet contamination through sneezing and coughing, physical contact, and bodily fluid exchange through insect or rodent vectors. Most diseases use only one vector. Parasites typically propagate through bodily fluid exchange through insect vectors or through fecal contamination of food or water (e.g., ingestion of infected foods). Protist and parasite pathogens sometimes have complex lifecycles and require a nonhuman reservoir between human infections. An emerging class of disease is caused by **prions**: self-replicating proteinaceous infectious particles.

Disease prevention
In virtually all cases, disease prevention is much easier and more cost effective than treatment. Access to clean drinking water, proper sanitation, and personal hygiene can prevent most epidemic diseases. Proper immunization can prevent many epidemic diseases. A balanced and adequate diet helps individuals resist new infections. Behaviors that compromise the immune system or lead to potential exposure should be avoided. In the United States, common behaviors that lead to preventable disease include tobacco use, obesity, sedentary lifestyles, intravenous drug use, and promiscuous sex.

Disease management
Many diseases can be cured through medical practices. Most infectious diseases caused by bacteria can be successfully treated by antibiotics. Some viral infectious diseases can be treated by anti-viral drugs. Many fungal diseases can be cured by topical fungicides. Diseases based in behavioral actions can often be cured or at least ameliorated by behavioral modification. Many diseases, such as the so-called common cold, can be tolerated by infected individuals, who will eventually recover through the operation of their own immune system. Other diseases, such as malaria, so far have resisted attempts at cures. In these cases, prevention or management of symptoms is the best (or only) alternative.

Skill 8.7   Demonstrating knowledge of how a given immunity is established and how a given active or passive immunity functions in a human

Immunity is the ability of the body to repel foreign substances. These may be natural– for example, cancer cells, which are abnormal and hence perceived as foreign by immune cells, or artificial, in the cases of other micro-organisms that attack the body. Active immunity is long lasting. To combat the infections caused by pathogens the human body reacts and fights back through **immune responses** that are staged by the organs that make up the immune system. For example, when an **antigen** enters the body, specific **antibodies** are produced to destroy the antigen. These antibodies will remain in the body forever, providing long-term immunity against that particular antigen. Such long-term immunity also occurs when an individual is vaccinated for certain diseases like polio.

The human immune system is a complex network of defenses that function on a variety of levels. **Passive immunity** is short-term immunity that is gained from an external source—for example, babies obtain passive immunity from their mother's breast milk. **Active immunity** is long-term immunity that relies on a person's own immune response.

Three lines of defense
The human immune system stages three lines of defense against foreign objects that may be infectious: **nonspecific responses**, which include the first and second lines of defense and **specific responses**, which includes the third line of defense. The first and second lines of defense do not differentiate one pathogen from another. The skin and mucous membranes form the first line of defense forming a physical and chemical barrier to prevent the entry of pathogens. Human skin is rigid and prevents the entry of bacteria and other microbes into the body. Glands in the skin secrete chemicals that repel microbes. Similarly, earwax traps germs and the mucous membrane in the nose traps other microbes. Vomiting is another first line of defense, which helps to excrete toxins or other infectious substances.

The second line of defense again is non-specific but at the cellular level. Specific types of white blood cells called **macrophages** indiscriminately attack cells that are presumed to be "foreign." Macrophages are **phagocytes**, which totally engulf and destroy foreign cells. The second line of defense also includes the **inflammatory response** to infection.

Specific immune responses
If a pathogen makes it past the first two lines of defense, the third line of defense is a specific response. This response mainly is performed by another type of white blood cell called **lymphocytes**. There are five different types of white blood cells in humans, one of which is the lymphocyte. Lymphocytes are produced from special cells in the bone marrow called stem cells. The presence of an antigen in the body leads to the production of two different types of lymphocytes—namely the T-lymphocytes (or T-cells) and the B-lymphocytes (or B-cells). These lymphocytes patrol throughout the circulatory and lymphatic systems and are concentrated in the spleen and lymph nodes. The precursors of the T-cells are present in the bone marrow and they mature in the thymus, while the B-cells are produced and also mature in the bone marrow itself.

Immunity by lymphocytes can be divided into two types based on the lymphocyte involved. Cell-mediated immunity is protection provided by T-cells and does not involve antibodies. T-cells find a pathogen, then the memory T-cells identify the pathogen and activate the cytotoxic or the helper T-cells. **Humoral immunity** refers to the protection provided by B-cells and involves antibodies. Once an antigen is encountered, B-cells are activated to produce more antibodies in response. Some B-cells also become memory cells and store the information on the antigen and its specific antibody. This memory gives rise to long-term, active immunity. This is why humans generally do not contract the same infectious disease more than once.

TEACHER CERTIFICATION STUDY GUIDE

COMPETENCY 009 **UNDERSTAND MOLECULAR AND CELLULAR LIFE PROCESSES**

Skill 9.1 Demonstrating knowledge of the cellular structures and related functions of different types of plant and animal cells, including the structural and functional differences between eukaryotic and prokaryotic cells

The cell is the basic unit of all living things. There are two types of cells. Prokaryotic cells include only the bacteria and blue-green algae. Bacteria were most likely the first cells and date back in the fossil record to 3.5 billion years ago.

Prokaryotic cells are distinct because:

- They have no defined nucleus or nuclear membrane. The DNA and ribosomes float freely within the cell.
- They have a thick cell wall to protect the cell, to give it shape, and to keep the cell from bursting.
- The cell walls contain amino sugars (glycoproteins).
- Some have a capsule made of polysaccharides, which make the bacteria sticky (as plaque on your teeth).
- Some have pili, which are protein strands that allow for attachment of the bacteria and may be used for sexual reproduction called conjugation.
- Some have flagella for movement.

Eukaryotic cells are found in protists, fungi, plants, and animals. Some features of eukaryotic cells include:

- They are usually larger than prokaryotic cells.
- They contain many organelles, which are membrane-bound areas for specific cell functions.
- They contain a cytoskeleton that provides a protein framework for the cell.
- They contain cytoplasm to support the organelles and contain the ions and molecules necessary for cell function.

PARTS OF CELLS

1. **Nucleus:** The brain of the cell. The nucleus contains:

   - **Chromosomes**: DNA, RNA, and proteins tightly coiled to conserve space while providing a large surface area.
   - **Chromatin**: Loose structure of chromosomes, called chromatin when the cell is not dividing.
   - **Nucleoli**: The site where ribosomes are made, seen as dark spots in the nucleus.

- **Nuclear membrane:** Contains pores that let RNA out of the nucleus. The nuclear membrane is continuous with the endoplasmic reticulum, which allows the membrane to expand or shrink if needed.

2. **Ribosomes:** The site of protein synthesis. Ribosomes may be free floating in the **cytoplasm** (the non-nucleic interior of the cell) or attached to the endoplasmic reticulum. There may be up to a half a million ribosomes in a cell, depending on how much protein the cell makes.

3. **Endoplasmic reticulum:** The "roadway" of the cell that allows for transport of materials throughout and out of the cell. The endoplasmic reticulum (ER) is folded and provides a large surface area. The lumen of the endoplasmic reticulum helps keep materials out of the cytoplasm and headed in the right direction. The endoplasmic reticulum is capable of building new membrane material.

There are two types:

- Smooth endoplasmic reticulum contains no ribosomes on its surface.
- Rough endoplasmic reticulum contains ribosomes on its surface. This form of ER is abundant in cells that make many proteins, as in the pancreas, which produces many digestive enzymes.

4. **Golgi complex or Golgi apparatus:** A stacked structure that increases surface area and sorts, modifies, and packages molecules that are made in other parts of the cell. These molecules are either sent out of the cell or to other organelles within the cell.

5. **Lysosomes:** Found mainly in animal cells. They contain digestive enzymes that break down food, waste substances, viruses, damaged cell components, and eventually the cell itself. It is believed that lysosomes are responsible for the aging process.

6. **Mitochondria:** Large organelles that make adenosine triphosphate (ATP) to supply energy to the cell. Muscle cells have many mitochondria because they use a great deal of energy. The folds inside the mitochondria, called cristae, provide a large surface area for the reactions of cellular respiration to occur. Mitochondria have their own DNA and are capable of reproducing themselves if a demand is made for additional energy. Mitochondria are found only in animal cells.

7. **Plastids:** Found only in photosynthetic organisms. They are similar to mitochondria because of their double-membrane structure. They also have their own DNA and can reproduce as needed for the increased capture of sunlight. There are several types of plastids:

- Chloroplasts: Green, function in photosynthesis; capable of trapping sunlight.
- Chromoplasts: Make and store yellow and orange pigments; provide color to leaves, flowers, and fruits.

- Amyloplasts: Store starch and are used as a food reserve; abundant in tubers like potatoes.

8. **Cell wall:** Found only in plant cells. Composed of cellulose and fibers, it is thick enough for support and protection, yet porous enough to allow water and dissolved substances to enter. Cell walls are cemented to each other.

9. **Vacuoles:** Hold stored food and pigments. Plant vacuoles' large size allows them to fill with water in order to provide turgor pressure. Lack of turgor pressure causes a plant to wilt.

10. **Cytoskeleton:** Composed of protein filaments attached to the plasma membrane and organelles. They provide a framework for the cell and aid in cell movement. The protein filaments constantly change shape and move about. Three types of fibers make up the cytoskeleton:

- Microtubules: The largest of the three. They make up cilia and flagella for locomotion. Flagella grow from a basal body. Some examples are sperm cells and tracheal cilia. Centrioles, also composed of microtubules, form the spindle fibers that pull the cell apart during cell division. Centrioles are not found in the cells of higher plants.
- Intermediate filaments: Smaller than microtubules but larger than microfilaments. They help the cell keep its shape.
- Microfilaments: Smallest of the three. Made of actin and small amounts of myosin (as in muscle cells), they function in cell movement like cytoplasmic streaming, endocytosis, and ameboid movement. Microfilaments also pinch the two new cells apart after cell division.

Skill 9.2 **Demonstrating knowledge of how plants transform energy from the sun into food through the process of photosynthesis and how energy stored in food molecules is released through cellular respiration**

METABOLISM

Metabolism is the sum of all the chemical changes in a cell that convert nutrients to energy and macromolecules, the complex chemical molecules important to cell structure and function. The four main classes of macromolecules are:

- Polysaccharides (carbohydrates)
- Nucleic acids
- Proteins
- Lipids

Metabolism consists of two contrasting processes, anabolism and catabolism. **Anabolism** is biosynthesis, the formation of complex macromolecules from simple precursors. Anabolic reactions require the input of energy to proceed. **Catabolism** is the breaking down of macromolecules obtained from the environment or cellular reserves to produce energy in the form of ATP and basic precursor molecules. The energy produced by catabolic reactions drives the anabolic pathways of the cell.

Anabolism
The anabolic pathways of a cell diverge, synthesizing a large variety of macromolecules. All anabolic reactions produce complex molecules by linking small subunits, called monomers, together to form a large unit, or polymer. The main mechanisms of anabolism are condensation reactions that covalently link monomer units and release water.

Polysaccharides (carbohydrates) consist of monosaccharide units (e.g., glucose) linked together by glycosidic linkages, which are covalent bonds formed through condensation reactions. Glycogen is the principle storage form of glucose in animal and human cells. Cells produce glycogen by linking glucose monomers to form polymer chains.

Nucleic acids are large polymers of nucleotides. Cells link nucleotides through condensation reactions, consisting of a five-carbon sugar, a phosphate group, and a nitrogenous base. During DNA and RNA synthesis, the template molecule dictates the sequence of nucleotides by complementary base pairing.

Proteins are large polymers of amino acid subunits called polypeptides. Cells synthesize proteins by linking amino acids, forming peptide linkages through condensation reactions. RNA sequences direct the synthesis of proteins.

Lipids are a diverse group of molecules that are hydrophobic, or insoluble in water. Cells synthesize lipids from fatty acid chains formed by the addition of two-carbon units derived from a molecule called acetyl coenzyme A (acetyl-CoA). The reactions involved in lipid synthesis include condensation, oxidation/reduction, and alkylation.

Catabolism
The catabolic pathways of a cell break down macromolecules and produce energy to drive the anabolic pathways. In addition, catabolic pathways release precursor molecules (e.g. amino acids, nucleotides) used in biosynthesis. The basic reaction of catabolism is hydrolysis, the addition of a water molecule across a covalent bond.

Process of Catabolism
Cells break the glycosidic linkages of stored or consumed polysaccharides, releasing glucose or other sugars that can be converted to glucose. The cells further degrade glucose to basic chemical end products, producing energy in the form of ATP.

Cells break down consumed proteins into amino acid units and other simple derivatives. Cells then use the amino acids to form new peptide chains or convert the derivative units into new amino acids. Cells can also acquire energy from the degradation of proteins, but the energy yield is not as high as that of polysaccharides and fatty acids.

Hydrolysis of lipids releases fatty acids that are a rich energy source. Fatty acids contain more than twice as much potential energy as do carbohydrates or proteins. The breakdown of fatty acids produces basic chemical compounds and energy in the form of ATP.

Finally, hydrolysis of nucleic acids by enzymes produces oligonucleotides (short strings of DNA or RNA) that are further degraded to produce free nucleosides (sugar-nitrogenous base units). Cells further digest nucleosides, separating the nitrogenous base from the sugar. Digestion of nucleosides ultimately results in the production of nitrogenous bases, simple sugars, and basic precursor compounds used in the synthesis of new DNA or RNA.

Biologically important organic molecules are involved in the processes of catabolism and anabolism. As described above, they include: polysaccharides, monosaccharides, nucleic acids, proteins, and lipids.

Plants require adequate amounts of nitrogen and phosphorus to build many cellular structures. The availability of the important inorganic minerals phosphorus and nitrogen often is the main limiting factor of biomass production.

RESPIRATION

Cellular respiration is the metabolic pathway in which food (glucose, etc.) is broken down to produce energy in the form of ATP. Both plants and animals use respiration to create energy for metabolism. In respiration, energy is released by the transfer of electrons in a process known as an oxidation-reduction (redox) reaction. The oxidation phase of this reaction is the loss of an electron and the reduction phase is the gain of an electron. Redox reactions are important for the stages of respiration.

Step 1: Glycolysis
Glycolysis is the first step in respiration, which occurs in the cytoplasm of the cell and does not require oxygen. Each of the ten stages of glycolysis is catalyzed by a specific enzyme. The following is a summary of those stages.

In the first stage the reactant is glucose. For energy to be released from glucose, it must be converted to a reactive compound. This conversion occurs through the phosphorylation of a molecule of glucose by the use of two molecules of ATP. This is an investment of energy by the cell. A total of four ATP molecules are made in the four stages. Since two molecules of ATP were needed to start the reaction in stage 1, there is a net gain of two ATP molecules at the end of glycolysis. This accounts for only two percent of the total energy in a molecule of glucose.

Step 2: The Krebs cycle
The Krebs cycle (also known as the citric acid cycle), occurs in four major steps. First, the 2-carbon acetyl CoA combines with a 4-carbon molecule to form a 6-carbon molecule of citric acid. Next, two carbons are lost as carbon dioxide (CO_2) and a 4-carbon molecule is formed, which is available to join with CoA to form citric acid again. Since we started with two molecules of CoA, two turns of the Krebs cycle are necessary to process the original molecule of glucose. In the third step, eight hydrogen atoms are released and picked up by FAD and NAD (vitamins and electron carriers).

Lastly, for each molecule of CoA (remember there were two to start with) you get:

>3 molecules of NADH x 2 cycles
>1 molecule of FADH x 2 cycles
>1 molecule of ATP x 2 cycles

Therefore, this completes the breakdown of glucose. At this point, a total of four molecules of ATP have been made, two from glycolysis and one from each of the two turns of the Krebs cycle. Six molecules of carbon dioxide have been released, two prior to entering the Krebs cycle and two for each of the two turns of the Krebs cycle. Twelve carrier molecules have been made, ten NADH and two FADH . These carrier molecules will carry electrons to the electron transport chain. ATP is made by substrate-level phosphorylation in the Krebs cycle. Notice that the Krebs cycle in itself does not produce much ATP, but functions mostly in the transfer of electrons to be used in the electron transport chain where the most ATP is made.

Step 3: The electron transport chain
In the electron transport chain, NADH transfers electrons from glycolysis and the Kreb's cycle to the first molecule in the chain of molecules embedded in the inner membrane of the mitochondrion. The electron transport chain does not make ATP directly. Instead, it breaks up a large free energy drop into a more manageable amount. The chain uses electrons to pump H+ across the mitochondrion membrane. The H+ gradient is used to form ATP synthesis in a process called chemiosmosis (oxidative phosphorylation). The electron transport chain and oxidative phosphorylation produces 34 ATP.

PHOTOSYNTHESIS

Photosynthesis is an anabolic process that stores energy in the form of a three- carbon sugar. We will use glucose as an example for this section. Only organisms that contain chloroplasts (plants, some bacteria, some protists) perform photosynthesis. There are a few terms to be familiar with when discussing photosynthesis.

An **autotroph** (self-feeder) is an organism that makes its own food from the energy of the sun or other elements. Autotrophs include:

- **Photoautotroph:** makes food from light and carbon dioxide, releasing oxygen that can be used for respiration

- **Chemoautotroph:** oxidizes sulfur and ammonia, as some bacteria

The chloroplast is the site of photosynthesis. It is similar to the mitochondria due to the increased surface area of the thylakoid membrane. The thylakoid membrane contains pigments (chlorophyll) that are capable of capturing light energy. A chloroplast also contains a fluid called stroma between the stacks of thylakoids.

Photosynthesis reverses the electron flow. Water is split by the chloroplast into hydrogen and oxygen. The oxygen is given off as a waste product as carbon dioxide is reduced to sugar (glucose). This requires the input of energy, which comes from the sun.

Stage 1: Light reactions
Photosynthesis occurs in two stages: the light reactions and the Calvin cycle (dark reactions). The conversion of solar energy to chemical energy occurs in the light reactions. Electrons are transferred by chlorophyll, absorbing light and causing the water to split, releasing oxygen as a waste product. The chemical energy that is created in the light reaction is in the form of NADPH. ATP is also produced by a process called photophosphorylation. These forms of energy are produced in the thylakoids and are used in the Calvin cycle to produce sugar.

Stage 2: The Calvin cycle
The second stage of photosynthesis is the Calvin cycle. Carbon dioxide in the air is incorporated into organic molecules already in the chloroplast. The NADPH produced in the light reaction is used as reducing power for the reduction of the carbon to carbohydrate. ATP from the light reaction is also needed to convert carbon dioxide to carbohydrate (sugar).

Skill 9.3 Demonstrating knowledge of the cellular processes of DNA replication and protein synthesis

DNA AND DNA REPLICATION

DNA
The modern definition of a gene is a unit of genetic information. DNA makes up genes, which in turn make up the chromosomes. DNA is wound tightly around proteins in order to conserve space. The DNA/protein combination makes up the chromosome. DNA controls the synthesis of proteins, thereby controlling the total cell activity. DNA is capable of making copies of itself.

Review of DNA structure:

- Made of nucleotides: a five-carbon sugar, phosphate group, and nitrogen base (either adenine, guanine, cytosine, or thymine).
- Consists of a sugar/phosphate backbone, which is covalently bonded. The bases are joined down the center of the molecule and are attached by hydrogen bonds that are easily broken during replication.
- The amount of adenine (A) equals the amount of thymine (T) and the amount of cytosine (C) equals the amount of guanine (G).
- The shape is that of a twisted ladder called a double helix. The sugar/phosphates make up the sides of the ladder and the base pairs make up the rungs of the ladder.

DNA REPLICATION

Enzymes control each step of the replication of DNA. The molecule untwists, and the hydrogen bonds between the bases break and serve as a pattern for replication. Free nucleotides found inside the nucleus join on to form a new strand. Two new pieces of DNA are formed which are identical; this is a very accurate process. There is only one mistake for every billion nucleotides added. This is because there are enzymes (polymerases) present that proofread the molecule. In eukaryotes, replication occurs in many places along the DNA at once. The molecule may open up at many places like a broken zipper. In prokaryotic circular plasmids, replication begins at a point on the plasmid and goes in both directions until it meets itself.

Base pairing rules are important in determining the sequence of a new strand of DNA. For example, our original strand of DNA has the following sequence:

A T C G G C A A T A G C

This may be called our sense strand as it contains a sequence that makes sense or codes for something. The complementary strand (or other side of the ladder) would follow base pairing rules (A and T bond with each other and C and G bond with each other) and would read:

T A G C C G T T A T C G

When the molecule opens up and nucleotides join on, the base pairing rules create two new identical strands of DNA.

A T C G G C A A T A G C   and   A T C G G C A A T A G C
T A G C C G T T A T C G   and   T A G C C G T T A T C G

PROTEIN SYNTHESIS

It is necessary for cells to manufacture new proteins for growth and repair of the organism. Protein synthesis is the process that allows the DNA code to be read and carried out of the nucleus into the cytoplasm in the form of RNA. This is where the ribosomes are found, which are the sites of protein synthesis. The protein is then assembled according to the instructions on the DNA. There are several types of RNA. Here is they are found and their function.

- **Messenger RNA** (mRNA): mRNA copies the code from DNA in the nucleus and takes it to the ribosomes in the cytoplasm.
- **Transfer RNA** (tRNA): Free floating in the cytoplasm, tRNA carries and positions amino acids for assembly on the ribosome.
- **Ribosomal RNA** (rRNA): rRNA is found in the ribosomes and provides a place for the proteins to be made. rRNA is believed to have many important functions, so much research is currently being done currently in this area.

Along with enzymes and amino acids, the RNA's function is to assist in the building of proteins. There are two stages of protein synthesis:

- Transcription
- Translation

Transcription
This phase allows for the assembly of mRNA and occurs in the nucleus where the DNA is found. The DNA splits open, the mRNA reads the code and "transcribes" the sequence onto a single strand of mRNA. For example, if the code on the DNA is T A C C T C G T A C G A, the mRNA will make a complementary strand reading: A U G G A G C A U G C U (uracil replaces thymine in RNA). Each group of three bases is called a codon. The codon will eventually code for a specific amino acid to be carried to the ribosome. "Start" codons begin the building of the protein and "stop" codons end transcription. When the stop codon is reached, the mRNA separates from the DNA and leaves the nucleus for the cytoplasm.

Translation
This is the assembly of the amino acids to build the protein and occurs in the cytoplasm. The nucleotide sequence is translated to choose the correct amino acid sequence. As the rRNA translates the code at the ribosome, tRNAs, which contain an anticodon, seek out the correct amino acid and bring it back to the ribosome. For example, using the codon sequence from the example above:

The mRNA reads A U G / G A G / C A U / G C U

The anticodons are U A C / C U C / G U A / C G A

The amino acid sequence would be: Methionine (start) – Glu – His – Ala.

This whole process is accomplished through the assistance of activating enzymes. Each of the 20 amino acids has its own enzyme. The enzyme binds the amino acid to the tRNA. When the amino acids get close to each other on the ribosome, they bond together using peptide bonds. The start and stop codons are called nonsense codons. There is one start codon (AUG) and three stop codons (UAA, UGA, and UAG). Addition mutations will cause the whole code to shift, thereby producing the wrong protein or, at times, no protein at all.

Skill 9.4 Recognizing how the structures of different types of cells relate to their functions in tissues and organ systems

In multi-cellular organisms such as humans, various cells are differentiated to provide process-specific functions. Whereas all human cells must perform metabolism to survive, many cells have specific functions that require specific structures. Muscle tissue cells, for example, do not look like or function like nervous tissue cells. Each specific cell type has a distinct shape and structure—or form—that is related to its function. For example, macrophages are amorphous and move through other tissues with amoeboid movements so they can locate and destroy invading pathogens. Nervous tissue cells often are very long and thin so they can transmit nerve impulses across large distances very quickly. On the sub-cellular level, organelles are produced and operated to support cellular function. It should come as no surprise that muscle cells, for example, are relatively packed with mitochondria while fat cells have relatively few mitochondria. Cells involved in detoxification can be expected to have an extensive endoplasmic reticulum and numerous lysozomes. In general, form matches function not only at the organismal level but also at the cellular level.

See Skill 9.1 for more discussion on the structure and function of sub-cellular components.

Skill 9.5 Recognizing the stages of mitosis and meiosis and their roles in growth and reproduction

Mitosis is the division of somatic cells, and **meiosis** is the division of sex cells (eggs and sperm). The table below summarizes the major differences between the two processes.

MITOSIS	MEIOSIS
Division of somatic cell	Division of sex cells
Two cells result from each division	Four cells or polar bodies result from each division
Chromosome number is identical to parent cells.	Chromosome number is half the number of parent cells
For cell growth and repair	Recombinations provide genetic diversity

Cell division glossary

- **Gamete:** sex cell or germ cell; eggs and sperm.
- **Chromatin:** loose chromosomes; the state of chromosomes when the cell is not dividing.
- **Chromosome:** tightly coiled, visible chromatin; this state is found when the cell is dividing.
- **Homologues:** chromosomes that contain the same information, are of equal length, and contain the same genes.
- **Diploid:** 2n number; diploid chromosomes are a pair of chromosomes (in somatic cells).
- **Haploid:** 1n number; haploid chromosomes are a half of a pair (in sex cells).

THE STAGES OF MITOSIS ("IPMAT")

- **Interphase:** Chromatin is loose, chromosomes are replicated, cell metabolism is occurring. Technically Interphase is not a stage of mitosis.
- **Prophase:** Once the cell enters prophase, it proceeds through the following steps continuously, without stopping. The chromatin condenses to become visible chromosomes. The nucleolus disappears, and the nuclear membrane breaks apart. Mitotic spindles form, which will eventually pull the chromosomes apart. They are composed of microtubules. The cytoskeleton breaks down, and the spindles are pushed to the poles or opposite ends of the cell by the action of centrioles.

- **Metaphase:** Kinetechore fibers attach to the chromosomes, which cause the chromosomes to line up in the center of the cell (think "middle" for metaphase)
- **Anaphase:** Centromeres split in half and homologous chromosomes separate. The chromosomes are pulled to the poles of the cell, with identical sets at either end.
- **Telophase:** Two nuclei are formed, each with a full set of DNA that is identical to that of the parent cell. The nucleoli become visible, and the nuclear membrane reassembles. A cell plate is visible in plant cells, whereas a cleavage furrow is formed in animal cells. The cell is pinched into two cells. Cytokinesis, or division, of the cytoplasm and organelles occurs.

THE STAGES OF MEIOSIS

Meiosis contains the same five stages as mitosis but is repeated in order to reduce the chromosome number by one half. This way, when the sperm and egg join during fertilization, the diploid number is reached. There are two steps to meiosis.

Meiosis I: chromosomes are replicated; cells remain diploid

- Prophase I: Replicated chromosomes condense and pair with homologues to form a tetrad. Crossing over (the exchange of genetic material between homologues to further increase diversity) occurs during Prophase I.
- Metaphase I: Homologous sets attach to spindle fibers after lining up in the middle of the cell.
- Anaphase I: Sister chromatids remain joined and move to the poles of the cell.
- Telophase I: Two new cells are formed; chromosome number is still diploid.

Meiosis II: reduces the chromosome number in half.

- Prophase II: Chromosomes condense.
- Metaphase II: Spindle fibers form again, sister chromatids line up in center of cell, centromeres divide, and sister chromatids separate.
- Anaphase II: Separated chromosomes move to opposite ends of cell.
- Telophase II: Four haploid cells form for each original sperm germ cell. One viable egg cell gets all the genetic information, and three polar bodies form with no DNA. The nuclear membrane reforms and cytokinesis occurs.

Skill 9.6 Analyzing the inheritance of genetic traits and how sex is determined in plants and animals

Gregor Mendel is recognized as the father of genetics. His work in the late 1800s formed the basis of our knowledge of genetics. Although unaware of the presence of DNA or genes, Mendel realized there were factors (now known as genes) that were transferred from parents to their offspring. Mendel worked with pea plants and fertilized the plants himself, keeping track of subsequent generations, which led to the Mendelian laws of genetics. Mendel found that two "factors" governed each trait, one from each parent. Traits, or characteristics, came in several forms, known as alleles. For example, the trait of flower color had white alleles and purple alleles. Mendel formed three laws:

- **Law of dominance:** In a pair of alleles, one trait may cover up the allele of the other trait. For example, brown eyes are dominant to blue eyes.
- **Law of segregation:** Only one of the two possible alleles from each parent is passed on to the offspring from each parent. During meiosis, the haploid number insures that half the sex cells get one allele; half get the other.
- **Law of independent assortment:** Alleles sort independently of each other. Many combinations are possible, depending on which sperm fertilizes which egg. Compare this to the many combinations of hands possible when dealing a deck of cards.

Punnet squares are used to show the possible ways that genes combine and indicate the probability of the occurrence of a certain **genotype** or **phenotype**. One parent's genes are put at the top of the box, and the other parent's at the side of the box. Genes combine on the square just like numbers that are added in addition tables we learned in elementary school.

Inheritance Glossary

- **Dominant:** Dominant describes the stronger of the two traits. If a dominant gene is present, it will be expressed. It is represented by a capital letter.
- **Recessive:** Recessive describes the weaker of the two traits. In order for the recessive gene to be expressed, there must be two recessive genes present. It is represented by a lowercase letter.
- **Homozygous** (purebred): A homozygote has two of the same genes present. An organism may be homozygous dominant with two dominant genes or homozygous recessive with two recessive genes.
- **Heterozygous** (hybrid): A heterozygote has one dominant gene and one recessive gene. The dominant gene will be expressed due to the law of dominance.
- **Genotype:** Genotype refers to the genes the organism has. Genes are represented with letters. AA, Bb, and tt are examples of genotypes.
- **Phenotype:** Phenotype refers to how the trait is expressed in an organism. Blue eyes, brown hair, and red flowers are examples of phenotypes.
- **Incomplete dominance:** When neither gene masks the other, a new phenotype is formed. For example, red flowers and white flowers may have equal strength. A heterozygote (Rr) would have pink flowers. If a problem occurs with a third phenotype, incomplete dominance is occurring.
- **Co-dominance:** Genes may form new phenotypes. The ABO blood grouping is an example of co-dominance. A and B are of equal strength, and O is recessive. Therefore, type A blood may have the genotypes of AA or AO; type B blood may

have the genotypes of BB or BO. Type AB blood has the genotype A and B, and type O blood has two recessive O genes.
- **Linkage:** Genes that are found on the same chromosome usually appear together unless crossing over has occurred in meiosis. Examples include blue eyes and blonde hair.
- **Lethal alleles:** These genes are usually recessive due to the early death of the offspring. If a 2:1 ratio of alleles is found in offspring, a lethal gene combination is usually the reason. Some examples of lethal alleles include sickle cell anemia, Tay-Sachs, and cystic fibrosis. Usually the coding for an important protein is affected.
- **Inborn errors of metabolism:** These occur when the protein affected is an enzyme. Examples include PKU (phenylketonuria) and albinism.
- **Polygenic characters:** Many alleles code for a phenotype. There may be as many as 20 genes that code for skin color. This is why there is such a variety of skin tones. Another example is height; a couple of medium height may have very tall offspring.
- **Sex-linked traits:** the Y chromosome found only in males (XY) carries very little genetic information, whereas the X chromosome found in females (XX) carries very important information. Since men have no second X chromosome to cover up a recessive gene, the recessive trait is expressed more often in men. Women need the recessive gene on both X chromosomes to show the trait. Examples of sex-linked traits include hemophilia and color-blindness.
- **Sex-influenced traits:** traits are influenced by the sex hormones. Male pattern baldness is an example of a sex-influenced trait. Testosterone influences the expression of the gene; most men lose their hair due to this trait.

The law of independent assortment
The law of independent assortment states that alleles sort independently of each other. (Many combinations are possible depending on which sperm ends up with which egg, just as many combinations of hands are possible when dealing a deck of cards). In a dihybrid cross, two characters are tested, with 16 possible gene combinations. Two of the seven characters Mendel studied were seed shape and color. Yellow is the dominant seed color (Y), and green is the recessive color (y). The dominant seed shape is round (R), and the recessive shape is wrinkled (r). A cross between a plant with yellow round seeds (YYRR) and a plant with green wrinkled seeds (yyrr) produces a first (F1) generation with the genotype YyRr. The production of F2 offspring results in a 9:3:3:1 phenotypic ratio.

Dominance
Based on Mendelian genetics, the more complex hereditary pattern of dominance was discovered. In Mendel's law of segregation, the F1 generation of peas had either purple or white flowers. This is an example of complete dominance, where one trait covers up the allele of the other trait. Incomplete dominance occurs when the F1 generation produces an appearance somewhere between the two parents, for example, when red flowers are crossed with white flowers and result in an F1 generation with pink flowers. The red and white traits are still carried by the F1 generation, resulting in an F2

generation with a phenotypic ratio of 1:2:1. In co-dominance, the genes may form new phenotypes. The ABO blood grouping is an example of co-dominance, as described in the Inheritance Glossary above.

Chromosome theory

In the late 1800s, the processes of mitosis and meiosis and the role of chromosomes in cell division were understood. In the early 1900s, Walter Sutton saw how this explanation confirmed Mendel's "factors." The chromosome theory states that genes are located on chromosomes. The chromosomes undergo independent assortment and segregation.

Skill 9.7   Recognizing how genetic changes (i.e., mutations) are expressed as traits (i.e., phenotypes) and the role these changes play in biological evolution

MUTATIONS

Sometimes DNA is not replicated perfectly. Inheritable changes in DNA are called mutations. Mutations may be errors in replication or a spontaneous rearrangement of one or more segments by factors like radioactivity, drugs, or chemicals. The amount of the change is not as critical as where the change is. Mutations may occur on somatic or sex cells. Usually the ones on sex cells are more dangerous since they contain the basis of all information for the developing offspring. Mutations are not always bad; they are the basis of evolution, and if they make a more favorable variation that enhances the organism's survival, then they are beneficial. But, mutations may also lead to abnormalities, birth defects, and even death. There are several types of mutations:

- **Normal:** A B C D E F
- **Duplication:** One gene is repeated: A B C C D E F
- **Inversion:** A segment of the sequence is flipped around: A E D C B F
- **Deletion:** A gene is left out: A B C E F
- **Insertion or translocation:** A segment from another place on the DNA is inserted in the wrong place: A B C R S D E F
- **Breakage:** A piece is lost: A B C (DEF is lost)
- **Non-disjunction:** This occurs during meiosis when chromosomes fail to separate properly. One sex cell may get both genes and another may get none. Depending on the chromosomes involved, this may or may not be serious. Offspring may end up with either an extra chromosome or a missing one. An example of non-disjunction is Down syndrome, where three of chromosome 21 are present.

EVOLUTION

Charles Darwin defined the **theory of natural selection** in the mid-1800s. Through the study of finches on the Galapagos Islands, Darwin theorized that nature selects the traits that are advantageous to the organism. Those genes that do not possess the desirable trait die and do not pass on to successive generations. Those more fit to survive will reproduce, thus increasing that gene in the population. Darwin listed four principles to define natural selection:

- The individuals in a certain species vary from generation to generation.
- Some of the variations are determined by the genetic makeup of the species.
- More individuals are produced than will survive.
- Some genes allow for better survival of an animal.

Darwin, in contrast to other evolutionary scientists, did not believe that traits acquired during an organism's lifetime (e.g., increased musculature) or the desires and needs of the organism affected evolution of populations. For example, Darwin argued that the evolution of long trunks in elephants resulted from environmental conditions that favored those elephants that possessed longer trunks. The individual elephants did not stretch their trunks to reach food or water and pass on the new, longer trunks to their offspring.

Jean Baptiste Lamarck proposed an alternative mechanism for evolution. Lamarck believed individual organisms developed traits in response to changing environmental conditions and passed on these new, favorable traits to their offspring. For example, Lamarck argued that the trunks of individual elephants lengthen as a result of stretching for scarce food and water, and elephants pass on the longer trunks to their offspring. Thus, in contrast to Darwin's relatively random natural selection, Lamarck believed the mechanism of evolution followed a predetermined plan and depended on the desires and needs of individual organisms.

Causes of evolution
Certain factors increase the chances of variability in a population, thus leading to evolution. Items that increase variability include

- Mutations
- Sexual reproduction
- Immigration
- Large population

Items that decrease variation include

- Natural selection
- Emigration
- Small population
- Random mating

Sexual selection
Genes that come together determine the makeup of the gene pool. Animals that use mating behaviors may be successful or unsuccessful. An animal that lacks attractive plumage or has a weak mating call will not attract the female, thereby eventually limiting that gene in the gene pool. Mechanical isolation, where a male's sex organs do not fit the female, has an obvious disadvantage.

Evidence
The wide range of evidence for evolution provides information on the natural processes by which the variety of life on Earth developed.

Paleontology
Paleontology is the study of past life based on fossil records and their relation to different geologic time periods.

When organisms die, they often decompose quickly or are consumed by scavengers, leaving no evidence of their existence. Occasionally, however, some organisms are preserved. The remains or traces of the organisms from a past geological age embedded in rocks by natural processes are called fossils. They are important for understanding the evolutionary history of life on Earth, since they provide evidence of evolution and detailed information on the ancestry of organisms.

Petrification is one process by which a dead animal gets fossilized. For this to happen, a dead organism must be buried quickly, to avoid weathering and decomposition. When the organism is buried, the organic matter decays. The mineral salts from the mud (in which the organism is buried) will infiltrate into the bones and gradually fill up the pores. The bones will harden and will then be preserved as fossils. If dead organisms are covered by wind-blown sand, and if the sand is subsequently turned into mud by heavy rain or floods, the same process of mineral infiltration may occur.

Besides petrification, the organisms may be well preserved in ice, in hardened resin of coniferous trees (amber), in tar, or in anaerobic acidic peat. Fossilization can sometimes be a trace, an impression of a form (e.g., leaves and footprints).

The horizontal layers of sedimentary rocks (these are formed by silt or mud on top of each other) are called strata, and each layer may contain fossils. The oldest layer is the one at the bottom of the pile. Therefore, fossils found in this layer are the oldest, and this is how the paleontologists determine the relative ages of fossils.

Some organisms appear in a few layers, which indicate that they lived only during that period and then became extinct. A succession of animals and plants can also be seen in fossil records, which supports the theory that organisms tend to progressively increase in complexity.

According to fossil records, some modern species of plants and animals are found to be almost identical to the species that lived in ancient geological ages. They are existing species of ancient lineage that have remained unchanged morphologically, and may be physiologically unchanged as well. Hence, they are called "living fossils." Some examples of living fossils are the tuatara, nautilus, horseshoe crab, gingko, and metasequoia.

Anatomy

Comparative anatomical studies reveal that some structural features of organisms are basically similar (e.g. flowers generally have sepals, petals, stigma, style, and ovary), but the size, color, number of petals, sepals, etc., may differ from species to species. The degree of resemblance between two organisms indicates how closely they are related in evolution

- Groups with little in common are supposed to have diverged from a common ancestor much earlier in geological history than groups that have more in common.
- To decide how closely related two organisms are, anatomists look for the structures that may serve different purposes in the adult, but are basically similar (homologous). .
- In cases where similar structures serve different functions in adults, it is important to trace their origin and embryonic development.

A group of organisms sharing a specialized, homologous structure, to perform a variety of functions, in order to adapt to different environmental conditions, exhibit adaptive radiation. The gradual spreading of organisms with adaptive radiation is known as divergent evolution. Examples of divergent evolution are the pentadactyl limb and insect mouthparts.

Under similar environmental conditions, fundamentally different structures in different groups of organisms may undergo modifications to serve similar functions. This is called convergent evolution. Analogous structures, which have no close phylogenetic links, show adaptations to perform the same functions. Examples include wings of bats, birds, and insects, jointed legs of insects and vertebrates, and the eyes of vertebrates and cephalopods.

Vestigial Organs

Organs that are smaller and simpler in structure than corresponding parts in the ancestral species are called vestigial organs; they are usually underdeveloped or have degenerated. These organs were functional in ancestral species but have become non-functional (e.g., vestigial hind limbs of whales, vestigial leaves of some xerophytes, vestigial wings of flightless birds like ostriches, etc.).

Geographic Distribution
The following are some important components of geographical distribution:

- **Continental distribution:** All organisms are adapted to their environment to some extent. It is generally assumed that the same type of species would be found in a similar habitat in a similar geographic area.
  Examples: Africa has short-tailed monkeys, lions, and giraffes. South America has long-tailed monkeys, jaguars, and llamas.
- **Evidence for migration and isolation:** The fossil record shows that the evolution of camels started in North Africa, from which they migrated across the Bering Strait into Asia and North America and through the Isthmus of Panama into South America.
- **Continental drift:** Fossils of ancient amphibians, arthropods, and ferns, which can be dated to the Paleozoic Era, are found in South America, Africa, India, Australia, and Antarctica indicating a time at which these continents were all joined in a single landmass called Gondwana.
- **Oceanic Island distribution:** Most small isolated islands have only native species. Plant life in Hawaii, for example, could have arrived as airborne spores or as seeds in the droppings of birds. The few large mammals present in remote islands were brought by human settlers.

Comparative Embryology
Comparative embryology shows how embryos start off looking the same. As they develop, their similarities slowly decrease until they take the form of their particular species.

For example, adult vertebrates are diverse, yet their embryos are quite similar at very early stages. Fishlike structures still form in early embryos of reptiles, birds, and mammals. In fish embryos, a two-chambered heart, some veins, and parts of arteries develop and persist in adult fishes. The same structures form early in human embryos but do not persist in adults.

Physiology and Biochemistry
Evolution of widely distributed proteins and molecules supports evolutionary theory All plants and animals make use of DNA and/or RNA. ATP is the metabolic currency. Genetic code is the same for almost every organism. A piece of RNA in a bacterium cell codes for the same protein as in a human cell.

Comparison of the DNA sequence allows organisms to be grouped by sequence and similarity. The resulting phylogenetic trees are typically consistent with traditional taxonomy, and are often used to strengthen or correct taxonomic classifications. DNA sequence comparison is considered strong enough to be used to correct erroneous assumptions in the phylogenetic tree, in cases where other evidence is missing. The sequence of the 168rRNA gene, a vital gene encoding a part of the ribosome was used to find the broad phylogenetic relationships between all life.

The protein and genetic evidence also supports the universal ancestry of life. Vital proteins such as ribosome, DNA polymerase, and RNA polymerase are found in every organism, from the most primitive bacteria to the most complex mammals.

Since metabolic processes do not leave fossils, research into the evolution of the basic cellular processes is done largely by comparing existing organisms.

TEACHER CERTIFICATION STUDY GUIDE

COMPETENCY 010 UNDERSTAND THE DIVERSITY AND BIOLOGICAL EVOLUTION OF LIFE

Skill 10.1 Analyzing the physical and behavioral adaptations that can occur in a given common species in response to environmental stresses

Adaptations are any physical or behavioral changes within a species that allow that species to better exploit its environment—indeed adaptation is the evolutionary process that makes populations better suited to their habitat. As an evolutionary process adaptation takes many generations and a particular adaptation is not "arrived at" but represents a stage in a continuous process of change.

Examples of physical adaptations include a cow's teeth that are broad and suited for grinding, a cheetah's speed that allows it to capture prey, or a human's hand that allow for fine manipulation of the environment. Generally speaking, physical adaptations arise slowly and persist for long geologic periods with little change.

Behavioral adaptations can be found in all of the kingdoms of life though typically they are the most-easily observed and understood among mammals. Behavioral adaptations typically are limited to a small repertoire of behaviors; a given organism can be behaviorally flexible only within fairly well-defined limits. Some animals such as humans, however, have a vast array of possible behaviors. Other animals, such as ants, demonstrate flexible behavior on a much more limited scale. Nevertheless, plastic traits such as behavior are believed to arise fairly quickly through evolution.

All adaptations—physical and behavioral—arise in response to environmental stresses and changes. If the environment is stable for a prolonged period of time there will be little selection pressure for innovative adaptations; instead, existing adaptations will tend to be refined. Environmental upheaval on the other hand is believed to be responsible for selective pressures that lead to novel adaptations.

Skill 10.2 Recognizing the factors (e.g., geographic location, climate, natural and human-caused disturbances, invasive species) that affect species diversity in different ecosystems

Species diversity is a complex paradigm that is only somewhat understood. While diversity exists in all environments, some environments demonstrate much greater diversity than others. Generally speaking, coral reefs, and rain forests demonstrate the greatest species diversity.

Geographical features that fragment environments into distinct niches tend to foster greater species diversity. Examples include island archipelagos, such as the Galapagos (for terrestrial species) and lake systems, such as the African Rift Lakes (for aquatic species). In these niches, novel species can arise that enjoy a competitive edge within the niche. In environments that do not present niches, generalist species tend to dominate large geographical areas, for example, the Great Plains of North America. Factors such as geographic location and climate can account for diversity, though typically seasonal climate changes do not appear to foster great diversity. Environmental disturbances rarely persist long enough to give rise to entire new species, but they do allow so-called **pioneer species** to thrive during the period of disturbance and shortly thereafter.

An **invasive species** is one that arrives in a new habitat to which it is non-native but well-adapted. Unfortunately, examples are only too common. Most invasive species are extremely damaging to the new habitat and markedly decrease local species diversity by outcompeting native species. Well know and destructive examples of invasive species include kudzu in the American Southeast and rabbits in Australia. The starling, a fixture in North American cities, is an invasive species. Environments with many small niches appear to be exceptionally prone to destructive action by invasive species.

Skill 10.3 Demonstrating knowledge of the niches and habitats of common species in different ecosystems in the world's major biomes

The world's major biomes are terrestrial, freshwater aquatic, and marine aquatic. These major groups can be further broken down into smaller biomes—for example, the terrestrial biome can be sub-divided into deserts, grasslands, riparian areas, savannas, taiga (boreal forests), temperate forests, tropical dry forests, tropical moist forests, tundra, etc.

These types of subdivided biomes can in turn be subdivided again into distinct habitats. For example, temperate and broadleaf mixed forests present a canopy layer, a shade-tolerant sub-canopy, a shrub layer, and a ground cover layer. Organisms in temperate and broadleaf mixed forests typically live in (or at least specialize in) one of these four habitats. Thus, animals found in one habitat are said to be characteristic for that habitat (e.g., you wouldn't expect to find a soaring bird living in the understory).

Clearly, a habitat as diverse as the canopy layer further can be subdivided into distinct niches. Niche definition is an actively studied and emerging area of research. Niches also depend largely upon scale. Whereas a human would not consider a single leaf to present multiple niches, an aphid might find the top surface intolerably hot while finding the bottom surface a suitable niche. Biologists expect to find organisms to be very well adapted to their niche, and adapted to their habitat, sub-biome, and biome to less-specific degrees.

Refer to Skill 8.4 for further discussion on biomes.

Skill 10.4 Analyzing the process of speciation (e.g., geographic isolation, founder effect, adaptive radiation) in living populations and the fossil record

The process of one species evolving into two species is called **speciation**. Speciation is nothing more than natural selection driving evolution of two populations in two different ways because of two different local environments. It is critical for the populations to be genetically isolated because, if the two populations of the same species continue to interbreed, then genes will flow back and forth between them and no significant genetic separation will occur. Without distinct genetic separation between two populations speciation does not occur.

The most easily understood barrier providing genetic separation is geographic isolation—a population that is geographically isolated isn't sharing genes with another population. However, other genetic barriers do exist. The so-called **founder effect** is one such type of event. In the founder effect scenario, a small group of individuals becomes isolated from a larger population and effectively founds a new population. Such events occur, for instance, on islands when one or a few individuals arrive on the island and begin a new population. Because all members of the population are descendents from the small founding group, they likely share distinctive allele ratios and are subject to rapid evolution. Adaptive radiation describes the process where a single species rapidly gives rise to multiple species that exploit specific niches. Examples of adaptive radiation include the cichlids of the African Rift Lakes and Darwin's finches on the Galapagos Islands.

In the laboratory, insect speciation has been driven by artificial mechanisms. Other insect speciation events have been observed in urban areas so we know that speciation does occur, and that it can occur in as few as eight generations with some insects. There is also an overwhelming amount of evidence supporting speciation derived from anatomic and molecular studies of closely related species.

Skill 10.5 Identifying organisms using a classification key

Classification keys are logical tools used by systematists to properly classify a given example organism at a particular taxonomic level. At a very basic level, classification keys involve stating diagnostic characteristics that can be compared to a sample organism to determine whether or not it belongs to the defined taxonomic group. An example of a classification key at the class level for mammals would include things like: presence of vertebral column, air breathing, hair and/or fur, three middle ear bones, and a neocortex region of the brain. An organism that possesses some, but not all, of these diagnostic traits would not be classified as a mammal (but perhaps would be classified as a chordate).

Obviously, differing classification keys must be used at each level of taxonomic grouping and different diagnostic characteristics must be chosen for different groups of organisms. The more specific taxonomic groups tend to have more diagnostic traits and tend to be much more specific in these traits (e.g., it's much easier to distinguish a human from a pine tree than it is to distinguish a human from a chimpanzee). Modern practice places a heavy emphasis on molecular diagnostic traits that often does not result in the same classifications as earlier morphologically based classification keys. It should be understood that the goal of classification keys is to support research and there perhaps is no ultimately "right" answer to how scientists choose to classify organisms.

TEACHER CERTIFICATION STUDY GUIDE

COMPETENCY 011 UNDERSTAND THE INTERDEPENDENCE AMONG LIVING THINGS AND THE FLOW OF ENERGY AND MATTER THROUGH ECOSYSTEMS

Skill 11.1 Demonstrating knowledge of factors that influence the diversity and number of species in a given ecosystem

See Skill 10.2.

Skill 11.2 Analyzing species interactions and interdependence in ecosystems (e.g., coral reefs, grasslands, rain forests, estuaries)

In the natural world no organism exists in isolation. Species interaction studies typically attempt to codify the methods that a particular pair or group of species use to interact with each other. Since these studies are based at the species level, they are somewhat abstracted and by design present aggregate responses to given generalized stimuli. In order to survive, every species must exploit its environmental resources and out-compete other species for access to these resources. These species-species interactions usually are classified as:

- **Neutral:** The species interact, but both species are unaffected—presumably very rare.
- **Amensal:** One species is harmed, the other is unaffected.
- **Competitive:** Both species are harmed—probably the most-common type of interaction.
- **Parasitic or antagonistic:** One species is harmed, and one species benefits.
- **Commensal:** One species benefits, the other is unaffected.
- **Mutualistic:** Both species benefit—generally the most intriguing form of species-species interaction

These types of species interactions are found in all ecosystems, though ecosystems that have high species densities (e.g., coral reefs and rain forests) apparently foster more symbiotic relationships. This probably occurs because interspecies competition is quite fierce and thus selective pressures are enormous. Most parasitic and mutualistic relationships are highly complex and demonstrate the phenomenon of co-evolution over prolonged periods of time. Transient ecosystems such as estuaries often exhibit complex and novel species interactions, or interactions that vary on a schedule. For example, tidal movement may change estuarial fauna throughout the day leading to constantly varying—but predictable—species interactions.

For more on symbiotic relationships among organisms, see Skill 8.4.

Skill 11.3 Demonstrating knowledge of the biotic and abiotic components of a given niche, habitat, ecosystem, or biome

Biotic components of the environment are the living components—all of the prokaryotic, fungal, plant, animal, and protist members of the system. Abiotic components of the system include all non-living components, such as the geographic terrain, water, ice, oxygen, carbon dioxide, nitrogen, phosphorous, sunlight, heat, wind, soil, rock, and so forth.

Most environments obviously will have an exceptionally complex array of biotic and abiotic components. Biomes typically are defined not only by their abiotic composition but also by the biotic species mix prevalent in the biome. As the defined ecosystem focus shifts from biome to ecosystem to habitat to niche, biotic factors and complexity tend to decrease while abiotic factors and complexity tend to remain about the same (however, becoming far more granular). In other words, a given niche does not feature every type of organism found in a biome, yet a given niche largely will conform to the abiotic components of the biome in which it is located. Species must be able to survive within a given abiotic paradigm and must be able to compete within a given biotic paradigm. Species failing at either extreme or both will become extinct. Biologically speaking, the most significant factors of any niche, habitat, ecosystem, or biome are energy transfer and the cycling of water, oxygen, carbon, nitrogen, and phosphorous.

Skill 11.4 Analyzing the cycling of matter and the flow of energy in a given ecosystem, and the structure of food webs in different ecosystems, including the roles of decomposers, producers, and consumers

Food webs are complex models that attempt to diagram how organisms obtain energy within their typical habitat. In the simplest terms, a food web might be presented as a food "chain": a rabbit eats grass, a fox eats a rabbit, and a cougar eats a fox. Each of these steps, or trophic levels, encapsulates an energy transfer and the sample food chain in effect converts grass into cougars. In the real world, foxes eat more than just rabbits, and rabbits eat more than just grass. Thus, food webs attempt to be more precise by encapsulating greater complexity and more energy transformations.

Producers are the fundamental basis of all energy flow into organic systems. Producers convert abiotic energy into biotic energy. In nearly all cases this involves plants, photosynthetic algae, and photosynthetic bacteria converting sunlight into chemical energy in the form of ATP, sugars, and other energy-rich molecules. Some rare organisms use other forms of abiotic energy. Photosynthetic producers typically only use about 1% of the sunlight energy that they are exposed to.

Consumers are the higher levels of the food web, and they eat either producers or other consumers. Regardless of how complex or lengthy a food web is, it ultimately relies on producers as the original source of energy. In general, consumers manage to convert only about 10% of the energy consumed from a lower level into their own organic tissues. Because of this inefficiency, food webs rarely involve more than four to six levels. This also explains why a farmer can feed about 100 people on grain but only about 10 people if the same grain crop is first fed to cattle.

When producers and consumers excrete waste or die, their excreta or remains are rich sources of energy. **Decomposers** are organisms that use these sources of energy. Typical decomposers are fungi and bacteria, which help to cycle matter (largely carbon, nitrogen, and phosphorous) back into the ecosystem where it again is used by producers.

Skill 11.5 Recognizing how environmental changes in an organism's habitat can elicit a specific behavioral response in the organism

A fundamental hallmark of all living things is the ability to respond to stimuli. Not all organisms respond to all possible stimuli, and not all responses are obvious to human observers. Yet all organisms respond to appropriate stimuli in appropriate ways. External stimuli are often transient, such as when an herbivore grazes on a plant. Other stimuli are predictable on a timetable, such as the sunrise and sunset, or are predictable roughly by season, such as changes in temperature. Other types of repetitive environmental changes are weather events such as rainfall, tides, seasonal breeding events, and migratory activities.

Typically, species will be able to react to important events in suitable ways. For example, plants may respond to heightened herbivore activity by producing tougher leaves or leaves full of secondary compounds that are noxious to herbivores. Bees may respond to blooming flowers by increased pollen-gathering activities. Elk may respond to increased wolf predation by spending more time in dense woods and less time in the open. Such behavioral responses often have secondary consequences in the environment. For example, elk clustered in dense woods do not graze in meadows and thus relieve pressure on grasses (but elevate pressure on trees). Many behavioral responses are fairly rote (the classic "stimulus-response" scenario), for instance, planaria always can be expected to move away from light sources. Other behaviors are fairly plastic. Squirrels may respond to increased predation with a variety of behaviors. In general, however, the behaviors exhibited are appropriate and effective responses to the driving stimulus.

One type of environmental change that is particularly devastating involves habitat destruction, often by human activity. In this case the species impacted have no suitable response because such a scenario has not previously occurred in their evolutionary history and thus no suitable response is available. In these types of cases, the species typically will be driven into local extinction. Another similar scenario involves invasive species that out-compete local species for the same resources.

TEACHER CERTIFICATION STUDY GUIDE

DOMAIN IV: **PHYSICAL SCIENCE**

COMPETENCY 012   **UNDERSTAND LINEAR MOTION AND FORCES**

Skill 12.1   Analyzing one-dimensional and two-dimensional linear motion (e.g., average speed, direction) using graphs, diagrams, vectors, and simple mathematical relationships

ONE DIMENSIONAL MOTION

Speed

Objects can be stationary, move with a constant speed (v), or move with a changing speed. The average speed is the distance (s) an object travels divided by the time (t) it takes to travel that distance. The distance from Duluth to Minneapolis is 120 miles. If a person travels by car in normal traffic from Duluth to Minneapolis, stopping for rest and gasoline, in 4 hours, the average speed is

$$\bar{v} = \frac{s_{final} - s_{initial}}{t_{final} - t_{initial}} = \frac{\Delta s}{\Delta t} = \frac{120 \text{ miles}}{4 \text{ hours}} = 30 \text{ miles/hour}$$

The instantaneous speed is the speed at any instant in time. It is defined in calculus as the derivative of the position function of the object with respect to time. The speedometer of a car reads the instantaneous speed. In the international system of units (SI), the units of speed are meters/second = m/s.

Acceleration

When an object's speed increases, it is called acceleration, and when an object's speed decreases it is called deceleration. The average acceleration is defined as

$$\bar{a} = \frac{v_{final} - v_{initial}}{t_{final} - t_{initial}} = \frac{\Delta v}{\Delta t}$$

The units of acceleration are m/s^2.

Kinematics

The two above equations can be combined to get equations that describe the motion of an object with a constant acceleration:

$$s_{final} = s_{initial} + v_{initial} t + \frac{1}{2} a t^2$$

$$v_{final}^2 - v_{initial}^2 = 2as$$

In kinematics we generally assume that the acceleration is either zero or a constant value. Hence the average speed is given by

$$v_{average} = \frac{v_{final} + v_{initial}}{2}$$

Graphs
Plotting the position, speed, or acceleration on a vertical axis of a graph and plotting the time on the horizontal axis yields a graph of the motion of objects. There are two cases. In one case, the acceleration is zero and the speed is constant. This means the distance increases linearly:

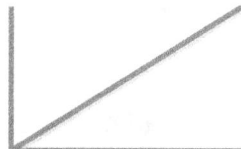

In the other case, the acceleration is not zero and the acceleration, speed, and distance graphs are a horizontal straight line, a sloping straight line, and a parabola.

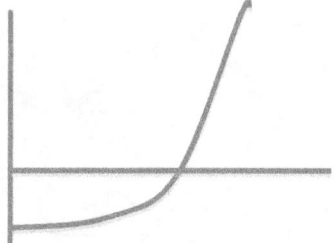

Free fall

When an object near the surface of Earth is free to fall, it always accelerates or decelerates at a rate of 9.8 m/s². If the object has an initial speed upward, its acceleration is negative, and if an object has an initial speed of zero or nonzero, its acceleration is positive.

Vectors

Motion always is motion in a particular direction. A quantity that has direction is called a **vector** and a quantity that does not have direction is called a **scalar**. If we say that a car is going north at 40 meters/second we are giving the velocity of the car. We can represent vectors graphically with arrows. The arrows point in the direction of the vector and the length of the arrow is proportional to the magnitude of the vector. If the vector is graphed on an x-y coordinate system, the direction can be specified by giving the x-component and the y-component of the vector.

Vectors can be added by connecting the tail of one vector to the head of the other. The sum or resultant of the addition is a vector going from the tail of one to the head of the other:

Projectile Motion

When an object is thrown up into the air near Earth's surface at an angle, the motion of the object can be separated into its horizontal and vertical component. For the horizontal motion the acceleration is zero. For the vertical motion, the acceleration is 9.8 m/s². If the coordinate system is located on Earth's surface, the acceleration is negative. When the two solutions are combined, the path of the projectile can be shown to be a parabola:

$$y = ax^2 + bx + c$$

where y is the vertical coordinate and x is the horizontal coordinate.

TEACHER CERTIFICATION STUDY GUIDE

Skill 12.2   Applying Newton's laws to analyze the forces acting on an object represented in free-body vector diagrams, graphs, or descriptions of everyday phenomena

DYNAMICS AND MOTION

Dynamics is the study of the relationship between motion and the forces affecting motion. Force causes motion, and a force can be understood from our experience of pushing or pulling with our own muscles. There is gravity, force from wind, force from magnets, force from rubber bands, etc. See Skill 12.1 for an understanding of motion.

NEWTON'S LAWS OF MOTION

Inertia
Newton's first law of motion is also called the **law of inertia**. It states that an object at rest will remain at rest unless acted upon by a net external force. Also, an object moving at a constant speed in a straight line will continue to move at the same speed and direction unless acted upon by a net external force.

Example: A book resting on a table has two external forces acting on it. The table is exerting an upward force on the book, and gravity is exerting a downward force on the book. The net force is the sum of these two forces. Since they are equal and opposite, the net force acting on the book is zero.

Newton's second law of motion
Newton's second law of motion comes from the observation that whenever an object accelerates, there is a force acting on the object. The object's mass is a measure of how much matter the object consists of. It is an experimental fact that the acceleration of an object is inversely proportional to its mass. If the mass of an object is doubled, the acceleration of the object will be halved for the same force. Thus, $F = ma$. Newton's first law can be derived from the second law. Newton's first law is that when $F =$ zero, the acceleration is zero. In other words, the velocity is constant. The units of force is the newton = kilogram $\times$ m/s^2.

For every action there is a reaction
Newton's third law states that whenever one body exerts a force on a second body, the second body exerts an equal and opposite force on the first. Newton's second law says what happens when a force is exerted on an object. Newton's third law says that

1. Forces on objects come from other objects
2. The forces are equal and opposite.

Middle Level Science

INCLINED PLANE

When an object rests on an inclined plane, the force of gravity acts downward. According to Newton's third law, there is an equal and opposite force upon the center of Earth coming from the object.

There is a component of the force of gravity on the object parallel to the plane and a component perpendicular to the plane. If the plane is not frictionless, there is a frictional force of the plane on the object. There is also a force from the plane to the object called the **normal force**.

WORK, POWER, AND MACHINES

Work and power
When a force (F) acts on an object and the object moves a distance (s), the work (W) done on the object is defined as W = Fs. The unit of work is the joule = newton × meter. Power (P) is the rate at which the work done by a force in moving an object is done. The average power is given by

$$P = \frac{W}{t}$$

The unit of power is a watt = joule/second.

Simple machines
The concept of work explains how machines such as levers, inclined planes, and pulleys work. Lifting a heavy object straight up requires as much work as pushing the object along a ramp or inclined plane (if there is no friction on the ramp). But the inclined plane spreads the work over a greater distance and thereby diminishes the force needed. The inclined plane provides a mechanical advantage. If there is no friction it is called the **ideal mechanical advantage**. When there is friction, it is called the **actual mechanical advantage**.

FRICTION

When a flat object is sliding on a flat surface, there is the force called **kinetic friction** that acts in the direction opposite to the motion. **Static friction** is the force that opposes a force acting on the object and prevents the object from moving.

Example: You are trying to push a heavy sofa across the floor. You have to increase the amount of force until the sofa starts to move. When the sofa is moving, kinetic friction acts on the sofa. Kinetic friction is generally less than static friction.

If the object is on a level surface, the frictional forces depend only on the nature of the two surfaces and the weight of the object. One might think the force would depend on the area of the surface making contact. This is not true because, even for the smoothest surfaces, there is only a small amount of contact between the molecules of the surfaces. It is the binding between the molecules of the two surfaces that causes the frictional forces.

More generally, the frictional force depends on the coefficient of friction and the normal force.

Surfaces	Coefficient of static friction	Coefficient of kinetic friction
Wood on wood	0.4	0.2
Ice on ice	0.1	0.03
Steel on steel	0.6	0.3
Rubber on a solid	1	1 to 4

Skill 12.3 **Analyzing changes in the kinetic and potential energy of a system (e.g., pendulum, mass on a spring) and the transfer of energy into or out of a system of interacting objects (e.g., loss of heat due to friction)**

WORK-ENERGY THEOREM

The kinetic energy of an object is given by

$$K.E = \left(\frac{1}{2}\right) mv^2$$

The work-energy theory can be derived from Newton's second law and the laws of kinematics. It states that the work done on an object by a net external force is equal to the change in the object's kinetic energy. Energy has the same units as work.

Example: Gravity exerts a force on a falling object. The increase in the speed of the object is equal to the work done by gravity. If there is air resistance or friction, the net force is used to calculate the work done.

CONSERVATION OF MECHANICAL ENERGY

A pendulum swinging back and forth and an oscillating weight suspended by a spring are examples of **periodic motion**. In these examples the kinetic energy goes to zero but returns to its highest point if there is not too much friction. Forces that produce round trips like this are considered **conservative forces** and a potential energy can be defined for such forces. The potential energy for gravity near the surface of Earth is

$$P.E. = mgh$$

where g = 9.8 m/s² and h is the height of the object above Earth's surface. The potential energy for a spring is

$$P.E. = \left(\frac{1}{2}\right)kx^2$$

where k is the spring constant. The **law of conservation of mechanical energy** is

$$K.E. + P.E. = \text{a constant}$$

When there is friction, mechanical energy is not conserved. Eventually pendulums come to a stop. However, there is another kind of energy called **internal energy**. When you slide a box on a table against friction, the temperature of the table and the box increase because of the heat generated by friction. In thermodynamics, these kinds of phenomena are studied, and we see that the mechanical energy with friction is converted into internal energy. Whenever it appears that energy is not conserved, it has always been possible to define a new energy so that we can say energy is neither created nor destroyed. It just transforms into different kinds of energy.

Skill 12.4   Analyzing the observed motion of an object in a system of interacting objects in terms of balanced and unbalanced forces and the conservation of energy

MOMENTUM AND IMPULSE

Newton's second law of motion (see Skill 12.2) can be expressed in terms of **momentum** and **impulse**. Momentum is mass times velocity and is a vector quantity, like force. The concept of impulse is used when the force acts for a short length of time. The impulse is force times the length of time the force acts on an object. Newton's second law can be written:

$$\text{Impulse} = Ft = \Delta p = m\Delta v$$

In a system consisting of two objects, Newton's second and third law implies that momentum is always conserved. That is, the total momentum of the two objects always remains the same. This principle is usually applied to collisions between two objects 1 and 2:

$$\vec{p}^{\,1}_{\text{initial}} \, \vec{p}^{\,2}_{\text{initial}} = \vec{p}^{\,1}_{\text{final}} + \vec{p}^{\,1}_{\text{final}}$$

This is a vector equation. It can be considered to be three equations, one equation for each component of the vectors.

The law of conservation of momentum might appear to be violated when a rubber ball collides with a wall and bounces back. The initial momentum of the wall is zero, and it appears that the final momentum is zero. However, there must be some deformation or recoil of the wall so that the final momentum is equal to the initial momentum.

In an elastic collision, not only is momentum conserved, but kinetic energy is also conserved:

$$KE^1_{initial} + KE^2_{initial} = KE^1_{final} + KE^2_{final}$$

Example: Suppose a railroad car of mass m and speed v collides with a stationary car with the same mass. If the cars couple it will be an inelastic collision and the final speed of both cars will be ½ of the initial speed. If it is an elastic collision, the first car will stop and all its kinetic energy and momentum will be transferred to the second car. Elastic collisions are observed when playing billiards.

TEACHER CERTIFICATION STUDY GUIDE

COMPETENCY 013 UNDERSTAND VIBRATIONS, WAVE MOTION, AND THE BEHAVIOR OF LIGHT

Skill 13.1   Analyzing the wavelength, amplitude, period, and frequency of a given oscillating object or wave, including changes in the pitch or intensity of sound waves

MECHANICAL WAVES

A mechanical wave is the transport of energy through a medium at a definite speed, by the regular motion of a disturbance without the bulk motion of the medium. The medium has both **inertia** and **elasticity**. If the motion of the medium is in the same direction as the propagation of energy, the wave is **longitudinal**. If the motion of a medium is perpendicular to the direction of propagation of energy, the wave is **transverse**. Sound waves are longitudinal, and waves in a rope are transverse. Waves in a spring can be either longitudinal or transverse.

The wave equation
If there is a single disturbance in a medium it is called a **pulse**. A **periodic wave** is a series of pulses caused by disturbances that are separated by an amount of time called the **period** of the wave. The **frequency** of the wave is the inverse of the period, or the number of pulses per second. The unit used to measure frequency is the hertz (Hz). The hertz is defined as 1/second. The **wavelength** is the distance between the pulses as they travel along the medium. The speed of the wave is determined by medium. The wave equation is

$$v = \lambda f$$

where v is the speed of the wave, λ is the wavelength, and f is the frequency of the wave.

Amplitude
The amplitude is a measure of the amount of energy that is transported by each pulse. In the case of a transverse wave, the amplitude is the height of the wave above the medium when the medium is not displaced by the wave.

Sound waves
The medium of sound waves is air, and the speed of sound in air is 330 meters per second. The disturbances are caused by vibrating objects, which create areas of high and low air densities or pressures. The waves are longitudinal because the air molecules are vibrating back and forth in the same direction the sound is travelling. Humans can hear sounds with frequencies from 20 Hz to 20,000 Hz. The sensation of frequency is called pitch. The larger the amplitude of the sound wave, that is, the greater the variations in air density, the greater the loudness of the sound.

Middle Level Science

Skill 13.2 Analyzing the wave motion of a standing or traveling wave in a given medium

SUPERPOSITION

When two different mechanical waves are propagated in the same medium and at the same time, the resulting motion of the medium is just the sum of the motions caused by the individual waves. This is called the principle of **superposition**.

Interference
Constructive interference occurs when two crests or two troughs meet. The medium will take on the shape of a crest or a trough with twice the amplitude of the two interfering crests or troughs. If a trough and a crest meet at the same time, the two pulses will cancel each other out, and the medium will assume the equilibrium position. This is called destructive interference.

Beats
When two sound waves differing slightly in frequency are superimposed, beats are created by the superposition of the two waves. The frequency of the beats is equal to the difference between the frequencies of the interfering sound waves.

When a piano tuner tunes a piano, he only uses one tuning fork, even though there are many strings on the piano. He adjusts the first string to be the same pitch as that of the tuning fork. Then he listens to the beats that occur when both the tuned and untuned strings are struck. He adjusts the untuned string until he can hear the correct number of beats per second. This process of striking the untuned and tuned strings together and timing the beats is repeated until all the piano strings are correctly tuned.

STANDING WAVES

Standing waves are produced by musical instruments that use strings and tubes of air to produce the sounds. Standing waves are not really waves because there is no transport of energy through a medium.

When a wave travelling down a taut string strikes a barrier, it will be reflected. The reflected and incident ray will interfere and produce points called **nodes** where there is destructive interference and **antinodes** where there is constructive interference. The number of nodes corresponds to the frequency. In music, harmonics are frequencies that are multiples of the lowest frequency.

Skill 13.3   Analyzing how sound waves are affected when the source of the sound is in motion

DOPPLER EFFECT

Change in experienced frequency due to relative motion of the source of the sound is called the Doppler effect. When a siren approaches, the pitch is high. When it passes, the pitch drops. As a moving sound source approaches a listener, the sound waves are closer together, causing an increase in wave frequency in the sound that is heard. As the source passes the listener, the waves spread out and the wave frequency experienced by the listener is lower.

RADAR AND SONAR DEVICES

Radar and sonar use the Doppler effect to determine the speed of a baseball, automobile, or a submarine. Radar sends out pulses of electromagnetic radiation (See Skill 13.4) and sonar uses pulses of sound. The pulses have a definite frequency. The frequency of the reflected waves is changed when the pulses hit a moving object. The radar or sonar machine detects and measures the frequencies of the reflected waves.

Skill 13.4   Demonstrating knowledge of the chromatic composition of light and how humans perceive an object and its color

ELECTROMAGNETIC RADIATION

Visible light, X-rays, radio waves, infrared radiation, ultraviolet radiation, microwaves, and gamma rays are not mechanical waves because there is no medium. Their nature and properties led to the development of quantum mechanics and relativity. Light consists of photons, or particles of light, that travel in a vacuum at 3.0×10^8 meters/second. Radio waves have a low frequency and large wavelength and gamma rays have a high frequency and short wavelength. The higher the frequency, the more photons behave like particles and not waves.

Electromagnetic spectrum
The electromagnetic spectrum's frequency (f) is measured in hertz, and wavelength (λ) is measured in meters. The frequency times the wavelength of every electromagnetic wave equals the speed of light (3.0×10^9 meters/second).

Common wavelengths of the electromagnetic spectrum

- Radio waves $10^{5} - 10^{-1}$ meters $10^{3} - 10^{9}$ hertz
- Microwaves $10^{-1} - 10^{-3}$ meters $10^{9} - 10^{11}$ hertz
- Infrared radiation $10^{-3} - 10^{-6}$ meters $10^{11.2} - 10^{14.3}$ hertz
- Visible light $10^{-6.2} - 10^{-6.9}$ meters $10^{14.3} - 10^{15}$ hertz
- Ultraviolet radiation $10^{-7} - 10^{-9}$ meters $10^{15} - 10^{17.2}$ hertz
- X-Rays $10^{-9} - 10^{-11}$ meters $10^{17.2} - 10^{19}$ hertz
- Gamma Rays $10^{-11} - 10^{-15}$ meters $10^{19} - 10^{23.25}$ hertz

SENSATION OF COLOR

White is the sensation we experience when light that is a combination of different wavelengths enters our eyes. Black is considered a color because it is the sensation when there is no light striking our eyes. A glass prism separates white light into its component colors: red, orange, yellow, green, blue, indigo, violet (ROYGBIV). The color red has the longest wavelength and violet has the shortest wavelength. Visible light covers a small portion of the electromagnetic spectrum.

Color perception is a complex subject involving many disciplines. When you look at an object and perceive a distinct color, you are not necessarily seeing a single frequency of light. Consider, for instance, looking at a green shirt. There may be several frequencies of light striking your eye, yet your eye-brain system interprets the frequencies as being green.

Color perception can be simplified if we think in terms of primary colors of light. Any three colors (or frequencies) of light when combined with the correct intensity are called primary colors of light. There is a variety of sets of primary colors but the most common are red (R), green (G), and blue (B). Mixing two or three of these three primary colors in varying degrees of intensity can produce a wide range of other colors. The human eye is capable of distinguishing millions of colors and shades.

Atoms are capable of selectively absorbing one or more frequencies of light. A shirt made of a material that absorbs blue light will do so, and it will reflect the other frequencies of the visible spectrum. The apparent color of the shirt is determined by identifying which color or colors of light are subtracted (absorbed) and which are reflected from the original set, a process is called **color subtraction**.

Skill 13.5   Analyzing the reflection, refraction, transmission, and absorption of light when it encounters an object, plane or curved mirror, prism, or convex or concave lens

GEOMETRIC OPTICS

In geometric optics we imagine that there are point sources of light that emit light in rays that travel in straight lines. This is approximately true because the wavelength of light is small compared to what we can see with our eyes unaided with a microscope. It appears, for example, that objects cast sharp shadows. Sound waves, of course, diffract or bend around objects and we can hear sound coming from behind a barrier. We use geometric optics to understand how lenses and mirror create images.

When a light ray hits a smooth surface, like water or a glass plate, part of the beam is reflected and part of the beam enters the water or glass. The part that enters the medium is called the **refracted ray**.

There is no refracted ray if the surface is a mirror. The atoms in a mirror do not absorb any of the incident photons, so there is total reflection. In a transparent substance, such as water or glass, the atoms of the medium absorb and then emit the photons causing the photons to propagate in the medium. The speed of propagation is less than the speed of light in a vacuum. The index of refraction of a transparent substance is a measure of the speed of light in that substance:

$$\text{index of refraction} = n = \frac{3 \times 10^8}{\text{speed of proagation}}$$

Law of reflection and Snell's law
The following diagram shows a ray of light incident upon a glass plate:

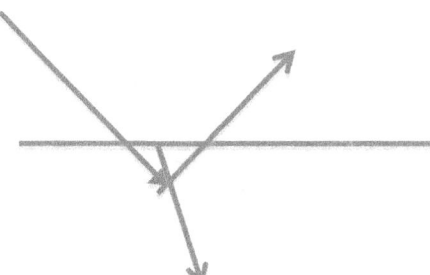

The angle of incidence (i) and the angle of refraction (r) are the angles made by the incident ray and the refraction ray with a line perpendicular to the surface of the medium. The law of reflection is that the angle of the reflected ray is equal to the angle of the refracted ray. The law of refraction or Snell's law is

$$\sin i = n \times \sin r$$

This means the refracted ray bends towards the perpendicular line. This happens because the speed of light is less in the medium. If the ray has an angle of incidence of zero degrees, there is no bending. Also, the slower the speed of propagation, the greater the amount of bending. This equation can be understood with the analogy of a car on pavement hitting mud where the speed of the car is much less. If the car hits the mud at an angle, its direction will be altered because the front wheel in the mud will be going slower than the front wheel on the pavement.

Prisms
A prism is a triangular piece of glass that refracts a ray of light twice. The index of refraction of red light is greater than the index of refraction of violet light. Hence red light bends less when refracted. This is why a prism or droplets of water in the sky can separate out the different frequencies of light that make up white light.

Lenses and curved mirrors
When parallel rays strike a curved mirror or a lens, the refracted or reflected waves converge at a single point called the **focal point**. This occurs because the angle of refraction or reflection increases the farther away the parallel ray is from the center of the lens or mirror.

Skill 13.6   Applying the laws of reflection and refraction to explain magnification and the production of virtual and real images in a pinhole system or in a simple system of lenses and mirrors

PINHOLE CAMERA

A pinhole camera is a light-proof box with a small hole in it. The small hole produces an upside down image of objects placed outside of the box. The creation of this image can be understood by thinking of an object as consisting of an infinite number of point sources, each of which produces an infinite number of rays. Only two rays are needed to understand how the image is created. One from the top of the object, and one from the bottom of the object:

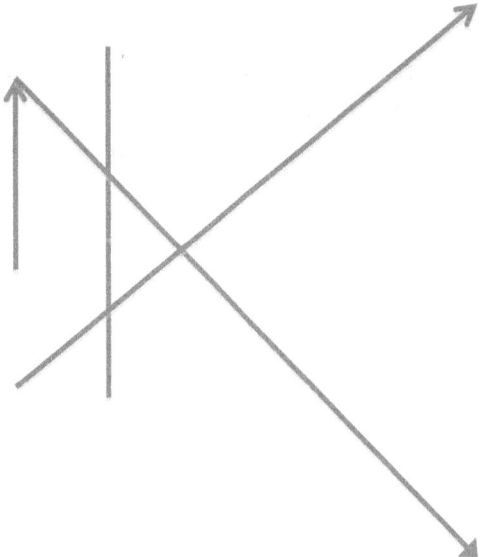

The image created by a pinhole is a **real image** because light rays actually strike the place where the image is located. The image is **inverted** or not **erect** because it is upside down compared to the object. Lenses and mirrors produce real images as well as **virtual images**. In virtual images the light rays appear to be coming from the image location but do not actually do so.

SPHERICAL MIRRORS

The optical axis of a spherical concave mirror is an imaginary line perpendicular to the mirror's surface at the center of the mirror. Light rays parallel to the optical axis are reflected onto a single point on the axis called the focal point (see Skill 13.5). The distance of the focal point from the mirror's surface is called the focal length (f). The focal length is half the radius of the sphere that defines the shape of the mirror.

For objects placed between the mirror and the focal point, a magnified vertical erect image is created. The magnification is the height of the image divided by the height of the object and is the same as the distance of the image from the mirror (dobject) divided by the distance of the object from the mirror (dimage). The location of the image is on the opposite side of the mirror as the object.

For objects where dobject is greater than f, the mirror produces an inverted real image in front of the mirror.

For all locations of the object, the location of the image is determined by the lens equation. The lens equation applies for convex mirrors if the focal length is expressed as a negative number. If the image distance is negative is it located on the opposite side of the mirror.

The location of the image regardless of where the object is located is determined from the lens equation:

$$\frac{1}{d_{image}} + \frac{1}{d_{object}} = \frac{1}{f}$$

This equation also describes the images created by a plane mirror. In this case, the focal length is infinite and dimage = − dobject.

LENSES

The lens equation also applies to convex and concave lenses. For convex lenses, the focal length is positive, and for concave lenses the focal length is negative. dimage is negative if it is on the opposite side of the lens as the object, just as with mirrors.

TEACHER CERTIFICATION STUDY GUIDE

COMPETENCY 014   UNDERSTAND ELECTRICITY AND MAGNETISM

Skill 14.1   Demonstrating knowledge of electrostatics and experiments, and measurements that demonstrate the charge of a given object

Coulomb's Law

Benjamin Franklin defined as **negative** the charge on a rubber rod after being rubbed with fur, and as **positive** the charge on a glass rod after being rubbed by silk. Many experiments show that only these two kinds of charges exist. A negative and a positive charge experience an attractive "action-at-a-distance" force. If the two charges are the same, the force is repulsive. The force between two point charges (q) separated by a distance r is given by Coulomb's law:

$$F = k \frac{q_1 \times q_2}{r^2}$$

The unit of charge is the coulomb. *k* is Coulomb's constant.

Charging by induction and contact

The reason friction can cause objects to be charged is that objects are composed of atoms. Atoms are made of electrons, protons, and neutrons. An atom has no net charge because the number of electrons and protons is the same. An object becomes charged because electrons transfer to one object from another object. The charge on an electron is $-1.6 \times 10-19$ coulomb. A proton has an equal and opposite charge, and a neutron has no charge.

In **charging by induction**, a charged object is placed near a neutral object without touching. If the charge is negative (has excess electrons), it will exert a repulsive force on the electrons in the object forcing the electrons to move to the far side of the object. Thus, the object will have a negative charge on one side and a positive charge on the other.

In **charging by contact**, a charged object touches a neutral object. Electrons will flow either into or from the charged object depending on whether the charged object is negatively charged or positively charged.

This phenomenon can be observed when you charge up a rubber comb by combing your hair. When the comb is brought close to a small bit of paper, the paper will be attracted to the comb and stick to it for a moment. Then, the paper will be repelled by the comb.

This happens because the comb has an excess number of electrons. When brought close to the piece of paper, the electrons near the comb move to the far side of the piece of paper. The near side of the paper is positively charged and is attracted to the comb. Since charges obey the inverse square law, the negative side is not as strongly attracted as the positive side. When the paper is in contact with the comb, electrons transfer from the comb to the paper causing both objects to be negative.

Grounding

Charge can be removed from an object by connecting it to the earth through a conductor. The removal of static electricity by conduction is called grounding.

ELECTRIC AND MAGNETIC FIELDS

A point positive charge produces an electric field throughout all of space. The electric field is a vector quantity directed away from a positive charge. For negative charges, the electric field is directed towards the charge. The electric field is defined as the force acting on a charge divided by the charge:

$$E = \frac{F}{q}$$

Charges also produce magnetic fields when the charge is moving. The magnetic field produced by a moving charge is circular and perpendicular to the direction of motion of the charge.

Skill 14.2 Analyzing experiments and measurements that demonstrate the movement of electrons and changes in the charge of interacting objects

Copper, iron, aluminum, and other metals are solids because their atoms bind together. However, the electrons in the outer shells of metals are not bound to any particular atom and are free to move. In insulators the electrons are more strongly attached to individual atoms.

CONDUCTORS AND INSULATORS

Electrical current requires the free flow of electrons. Various materials allow different degrees of electron movement and are classified as conductors, insulators, or semiconductors (in certain, typically man-made environments, superconductors also exist). When charge is transferred to a mass of material, the response is highly dependent on whether that material is a conductor or insulator.

Conductors are materials that allow for free and easy movement of electrons. Some of the best conductors are metal, especially copper and silver, because these materials are held together with metallic bonds, which involve de-localized electrons shared by atoms in a lattice. If a charge is transferred to a conductor, the electrons will flow freely, and the charge will quickly distribute itself across the material in a manner dictated by the conductor's shape.

Insulators are materials that do not allow conduction. Good insulators include, glass, rubber, and wood. These materials have chemical structures in which the electrons are closely localized to the individual atoms. In contrast to a conductor, a charge transferred to an insulator will remain localized at the point where it was introduced because the movement of electrons will be highly impeded.

BATTERIES

When a copper rod is placed in water, the water molecules pull away the copper ions from the metal leaving behind excess electrons and causing the copper rod to obtain a negative charge. The excess electrons distribute themselves uniformly on the surface of the rod because electrons in metals are free to move. The ionization process stops when the charge on the copper becomes so great that it causes copper ions in the water to reattach to the rod.

An electron on a copper rod or terminal in water has a certain potential energy because of the repulsive force from the other electrons. That potential energy divided by the charge of the electron gives the potential or voltage of the copper metal. Potential is measured in a unit called a volts. A volt = joule/coulomb. The same thing happens with a zinc terminal except that zinc acquires a greater charge than the copper.

If you put the zinc and copper in the same pool of water and use a metal wire to connect the zinc and copper, electrons will flow from the zinc to the copper because the potential of the zinc is greater than the potential of the copper. A device that produces a potential difference is called a battery or **electromotive force**.

Another way of looking at it is that an electric field will be established in a wire that connects the terminals of a zinc-copper battery. The electric field will cause electrons to flow in the wire and will cause zinc ions to leave the zinc and copper ions and zinc ions to reattach to the copper. Hence, an electric current will flow until the copper gets covered with zinc atoms. All the free electrons in the wire flow at a drift velocity of the order of magnitude of 1 centimeter/second. This speed is slow because the electrons are continually colliding with the atoms or ions inside the metal.

OHM'S LAW

The total current (I) flowing in a wire or device connected to a battery is measured in amperes. An ampere = coulomb/second. It is the total flow of charge through a cross-section of wire per unit time. It is determined by how fast the electrons are moving and the number of electrons in the wire. The speed of the electrons is directly proportional to the electric field in the wire. The electric field in the wire is directly proportional to the potential difference (V) between the two terminals of the battery the wire is connected to. The ratio of the current in a wire to the potential difference across the wire is called the resistance of the wire (R). Resistance is measure in the units ohms (ohm = volt/ampere). Ohm's law is

$$V = IR$$

If you have a wire with resistance of 5 ohms and a potential difference of 75 volts, you can calculate the current by

$$I = \frac{75 \text{ volts}}{5 \text{ ohms}} = 15 \text{ amps}$$

The resistance (R) of a metal wire of length (L) and radius (A) is given by

$$R = \rho \frac{L}{A}$$

where ρ is the resistivity of the type of metal the wire is made of. Copper has a very low resistivity, which is why it is used to connect devices to batteries. Tungsten has a high resistivity, which is why thin tungsten wires are used in light bulbs.

CIRCUITS

An electric circuit is a path along which electrons flow. A simple circuit can be created with a battery, light bulb, and a switch. When all are connected, the electrons flow from the negative terminal, through the wire to the device, and back to the positive terminal of the battery. If there are no breaks in the circuit, the device will work. The circuit is closed. Any break in the flow will create an open circuit and cause the device to shut off.

As electrons flow through a wire, they collide with the atoms in the wire and cause the wire to heat up. In the case of incandescent light bulbs, the heat causes the filament to glow.

Series and parallel circuits
A **series circuit** is one where the electrons have only one path along which they can move. When one load in a series circuit goes out, the circuit is open. An example of this is a set of Christmas tree lights that is missing a bulb. None of the bulbs will work.

A **parallel circuit** is one where the electrons have more than one path to move along. If a load goes out in a parallel circuit, the other load will still work because the electrons can still find a way to continue moving along the path.

Direct current and alternating current
Alternating current (AC) is a type of electrical current with cyclically varying magnitude and direction. This is differentiated from **direct current** (DC), which has constant direction. AC is the type of current delivered to businesses and residences. Though other waveforms are sometimes used, the vast majority of AC current is sinusoidal (wavelike). Thus we use wave terminology to help us describe AC current.

Generators are devices that are the opposite of motors in that they convert mechanical energy into electrical energy. The mechanical energy can come from a variety of sources: combustion engines, blowing wind, falling water, or even a hand crank or bicycle wheel. Most generators rely on electromagnetic induction to create an electrical current. These generators consist of magnets and a coil. The magnets create a magnetic field, and the coil is located within this field. Mechanical energy, from whatever source, is used to spin the coil within this field. As stated by Faraday's law, this produces a voltage.

Skill 14.3 Demonstrating knowledge of the properties of magnets, and experiments that demonstrate those properties

LODESTONES

In Earth's crust there are rocks called lodestones that exert magnetic forces on one another. These are called magnets and have a north pole and a south pole. As with electrical charges, like poles repel and unlike poles attract. Unlike electrical charges, there are no particles that have only a south pole or a north pole. When you cut a magnet in half, you get two smaller magnets and two more north and south poles. Magnetic poles obey the inverse square law, just like gravity and electrostatic forces.

Diamagnetism, paramagnetism, and ferromagnetism

Substances are either **diamagnetic** or **paramagnetic**. When a diamagnetic substance is brought close to a magnet it experiences a repulsive force. Very few substances are diamagnetic. A paramagnetic substance is attracted to a magnet. Ferromagnetism is a special case of paramagnetism. The ferromagnetic materials are iron and three other metals. Iron can become permanently magnetized by a lodestone, which is composed of magnetite (Fe_3O_4). Also, the attractive force between a ferromagnetic material and a magnet is much greater than for paramagnetic substances. The force of attraction between a piece of paper and a magnet is so small scientific equipment is needed to measure it.

A bar magnet produces a magnetic field that occupies all of space. Like an electric field, a magnetic field is a vector and has a direction. When a charged particle moves in a magnetic field, it experiences a magnetic force. The direction of the magnetic force and the direction of motion determine the direction of the magnetic field. The magnetic field leaves the north pole and enters the south pole.

CAUSE OF MAGNETISM

A charge moving in a straight line produces a circular magnetic field with a direction determined by the sign of the charge and direction of the motion. Thus an electron moving in a circular path produces a magnetic field very similar to the magnetic field produced by a magnet: it has a north pole and a south pole. For this reason, a single atom can produce a magnetic field.

The magnetic properties of substances are complicated by the fact that electrons spin in addition to orbiting the nucleus of an atom. This spinning produces a magnetic field with a north and a south pole. Most substances are not magnetic because all of the atoms are randomly oriented in the substance. Paramagnetism is largely caused by the magnetic fields produced by spinning electrons. Diamagnetism is associated with the motion of electrons around the nucleus.

In ferromagnetic materials, such as iron, there is an interaction between the nuclei of the iron atoms that produces **magnetic domains** or areas where all of the magnetic poles of the individual atoms are lined up. Hence, when ferromagnetic materials are magnetized, their domains tend to line up to give a strong magnetic field.

MAGNETISM OF EARTH

The earth behaves like a giant magnet with the magnetic south pole located near the geographic north pole. There are theories about what moving charges inside Earth causes the magnetic fields, but none of the theories have been proven.

Skill 14.4 Analyzing the magnetic field of a straight current-carrying wire and a current-carrying solenoid

Negative and positive charges produce magnetic fields when they are moving in addition to the electric fields. When a charge moves, it creates a circular magnetic field. The surface of the circle is perpendicular to the motion of the charge. The direction follows the left-hand rule: If the thumb points in the direction of the motion of a negative charge, the fingers curl in the direction of the magnetic field.

In the case of a permanent magnet, the magnetic field lines leave the north pole and enter the south pole. When a current-carrying wire is shaped to form a loop, one side of the loop can be considered the north pole and the other side the south pole. A solenoid is a series of loops, one next to the other, and produces a magnetic field shaped like the magnetic field of a magnet.

You can make a magnet out of a coil of wire by connecting the ends of the coil to a battery. When the current goes through the wire, the wire acts in the same way that a magnet does: it is called an **electromagnet**.

The poles of the electromagnet will depend upon which way the electric current runs. An electromagnet can be made more powerful in three ways:

- Make more coils
- Put an iron core (nail) inside the coils
- Use more battery power

Applications of electromagnets
Telegraphs use electromagnets to send messages around the world. When a telegraph key is pushed, current flows through a circuit, turning on an electromagnet that attracts

an iron bar. The iron bar hits a sounding board that responds with a click. Release the key and the electromagnet turns off.

Scrap metal can be removed from waste materials by using a large electromagnet suspended from a crane. When the electromagnet is turned on, only the metal in the pile of waste will be attracted to it. All other materials will stay on the ground.

Air conditioners, vacuum cleaners, and washing machines use electric motors. An electric motor uses an electromagnet to change electric energy into mechanical energy.

Transformers and motors
Electromagnetic induction is used in a **transformer**, a device that magnetically couples two circuits together to allow the transfer of energy between the two circuits without requiring motion. Typically, a transformer consists of a couple of coils and a magnetic core. A changing voltage applied to one coil (the primary) creates a flux in the magnetic core, which induces voltage in the other coil (the secondary). All transformers operate on this simple principle though they range in size and function from those in tiny microphones to those that connect the components of the United States power grid. One of the most important functions of transformers is that they allow us to "step-up" and "step-down" between vastly different voltages.

Electric motors are found in many common appliances such as fans and washing machines. The operation of a **motor** is based on the principle that a magnetic field exerts a force on a current-carrying conductor because the current-carrying conductor itself generates a magnetic field, the basic principle that governs the behavior of an electromagnet. In a motor, this idea is used to convert electrical energy into mechanical energy, most commonly rotational energy. Thus the components of the simplest motors must include a strong magnet and a current-carrying coil placed in the magnetic field in such a way that the force on it causes it to rotate.

Motors may be run using DC or AC current and may be designed in a number of ways with varying levels of complexity. A very basic DC motor consists of the following components:

- A field magnet
- An armature with a coil around it that rotates between the poles of the field magnet
- A power supply that supplies current to the armature
- An axle that transfers the rotational energy of the armature to the working parts of the motor
- A set of commutators and brushes that reverse the direction of power flow every half rotation so that the armature continues to rotate

Skill 14.5 Recognizing a circuit consisting of batteries, bulbs, and switches that meets a given design criteria for the brightness and control of the bulbs

An incandescent light bulb with a thin tungsten filament has a high resistance. When a current flows through the light bulb, the electrical potential energy of the electrons is transformed into heat energy by the collision of the electrons with the atoms in the resistor. The heat causes the metal to glow and emit light. The amount of heat generated per second *(P)* by a resistor is given by

$$P = RI^2$$

where *R* is the resistance of the light bulb and *I* is the current through the resistor. The heat generated can be reduced by reducing the current. The current can be reduced by increasing the total resistance of the circuit or by decreasing the voltage of the battery or electromotive force.

A potentiometer is a variable resistor. By inserting a potentiometer in series with an electromotive force and a light bulb, the current in the circuit can be changed.

TEACHER CERTIFICATION STUDY GUIDE

COMPETENCY 015   **UNDERSTAND THE PROPERTIES AND STRUCTURE OF MATTER**

Skill 15.1   Applying knowledge of the properties of matter, including mass, density, volume, concentration, melting and boiling points, and solubility limits of a given substance

A physical property can be observed without changing the chemical makeup of the substance. It can be observed with one of the five senses or measured using an instrument such as a thermometer. Physical properties include state (liquid, solid, gas, or plasma), hardness, color, taste, odor, freezing point, melting point, boiling point, density, electrical conductivity, thermal conductivity, luster, and malleability. Physical properties do not change unless the matter is chemically changed.

A chemical property of matter depends on how the substance reacts with other substances. For example, when exposed to or combined with oxygen, does it rust, does it burn, or is it unaffected? Measuring these properties will change the chemical and physical nature of the substance. Examples of chemical properties include combustibility, rusting, pH, and pOH, reactivity with water and various acids and bases, electromotive force, electronegativity, ionization potential, and preference for various types of bonding. To test these, one has to change the substance chemically.

Volume
Volume is the amount of cubic space that an object occupies. Volume and mass together give a more exact description of the object. Two objects may have the same volume but different mass, or the same mass but different volumes, etc. For instance, consider two cubes that are each one cubic centimeter, one made from plastic, one from lead. They have the same volume, but the lead cube has more mass. The measure that we use to describe the cubes takes into consideration both the mass and the volume.

Density
Density is the mass of a substance contained per unit of volume. If the density of an object is less than the density of a liquid, the object will float in the liquid. If the object is denser than the liquid, then the object will sink.

The density (ρ) of a substance is the mass (m) of an object made of the substance divided by the volume (V) of the object.

$$\rho = \frac{m}{V}$$

PHASE CHANGES

A phase change occurs when a substance changes its physical properties abruptly when the temperature of the substance reaches certain levels. In first-order phase changes, the different states are solid, liquid, and gas.

Water, for example, at temperatures below 0°Celsius, is a solid. When heat is added to the ice, the temperature of the ice increases until the temperature reaches 0°C. At this point, the solid begins to turn into a liquid, and both phases or states exist: solid and liquid. As heat is added, there is no increase in the temperature, but more ice melts. The amount of energy required to melt a solid or transform a liquid to a solid is called the **heat of fusion**. The amount of energy required to transform a liquid to a gas is the **heat of vaporization**.

In the case of water, the two temperatures are called the freezing point and the boiling point.

Skill 15.2 Recognizing the differences between pure elements, compounds, solutions, suspensions, and colloids

MIXTURE

A mixture is a material that can be separated by physical means into two or more substances. Most materials around us are mixtures, and a mixture has a variable composition. Mixtures are classified into two types:

- **Heterogeneous mixture:** a mixture that consists of physically distinct parts, each with different properties, for instance, sugar and salt mixed together
- **Homogeneous mixture (solution):** a mixture that is uniform in its properties throughout a given sample

SOLUTIONS

A solution is a homogeneous mixture. Solutions are composed of a **solvent** and a **solute**. The solute is the dissolved particles in a solution. The solvent is the substance in which the solute is dissolved. For example, consider a glass of sugar water. The solvent in this solution is water. The solute is the sugar. The sugar is dissolved in the water to form a solution. Water is a very common solvent in many chemical reactions.

The solution process depends upon intermolecular forces. Solutions form when the intermolecular forces between solute and solvent molecules are about as strong as those that exist in the solute alone or in the solvent alone. For example, NaCl (salt) dissolves in water because the water molecules interact with the Na+ and Cl– ions with sufficient strength to overcome the attraction between them in the crystalline form.

The intermolecular attraction between solute and solvent molecules is known as **solvation**. When the solvent is water, it is known as **hydration**.

Polar and Nonpolar Solutes and Solvents

A liquid like heptane (C_7H_{16}) is nonpolar because the electrons in it are evenly distributed in the molecule. Water (H_2O) is polar because the electrons tend to stay on the oxygen side of the molecule. Because bonds of similar strength must be broken and formed for solvation to occur, nonpolar substances tend to be soluble in nonpolar solvents, while ionic and polar substances are soluble in polar solvents like water. Polar molecules are often called hydrophilic, and nonpolar molecules are called hydrophobic. This observation is often stated as "like dissolves like." Network solids (e.g., diamond) are soluble in neither polar nor nonpolar solvents because the covalent bonds within the solid are too strong for these solvents to break.

Temperature and solubility

The act of dissolving a solid into a liquid is a process that happens on the surface of the particles of the solute. The smaller the particles (the larger the surface area), the faster the solute dissolves. Confectioner's sugar, for example, has smaller particles than regular table sugar. Rock candy is just regular table sugar that has been crystallized in large lumps. When you put each crystal size of the chemically identical materials in your mouth, which one dissolves faster? The confectioner's sugar tastes sweetest because more of it has dissolved in the shortest amount of time. You can only taste dissolved sugar.

Expose the surface area of the solid to more liquid, and the solute will dissolve faster. Mixing also helps dissolve the solid. You can try this with sugar. Take two glasses of water at the same temperature, and add a spoonful of sugar to each. Mix one, but not the other. In which glass does the sugar dissolve more easily?

Most solid materials will dissolve faster with increased temperature. Since the increased temperature increases the motion of the molecules, you can think of this effect as being similar to mixing. For example, sugar dissolves more quickly in warm tea than iced tea. Table salt dissolves more quickly in hot water than in cold.

Molarity

The concentration of a solute in a solution is frequently expressed as the number of moles of solute per volume of solution. It is called molar concentration or molarity: 1 molar (M) = 1 mole per liter.

How do you create a solution at a specific concentration? First, weigh the solid to obtain the mass. To determine the amount of solute needed, multiply the desired concentration by the volume of solution and by the formula weight of the solute. Place the mass of solute in a volume-measuring device such as a volumetric flask or graduated cylinder. Add water to the volume desired and mix until dissolved.

Gases Dissolved In Liquids

Gases dissolved in liquids are easily measured when you know the pressure, volume, and temperature of the gas. Seltzer water and ammonia water are two good examples of solutions of a gas in a liquid. Seltzer, or carbonated water, consists of pressing the carbon dioxide gas into the water. The bubbles in beer or sparkling wines are also due to carbon dioxide, but the CO_2 is a natural product of the fermentation process. Ammonia water, also called ammonium hydroxide solution, is made from ammonia (NH_3) being pressed into water. It is used as a weak base and as a cleaning material.

Suspensions and colloids
Suspensions and colloids are heterogeneous mixtures of solids in liquids. The solids stay in the solid phase. When a solid is in a solution, the molecules or ions of the solid are mixed in homogenously with the liquid. In a suspension, the solids particles are large enough that they will eventually settle. In a colloid, the particles are so small they will not settle out.

Skill 15.3   Demonstrating knowledge of the processes of distillation, precipitation, extraction, and chromatography

DISTILLATION

Distillation is a method of separating the components of a mixture based on their boiling points. Crude oil, for example, is a mixture of lubricating oils, heating oils, kerosene, and gasoline. Boiling crude oil in a distillation tower will separate the components because the condensation point of the large hydrocarbon molecules is much higher than the condensation of small hydrocarbon molecules.

PRECIPITATION

Precipitation occurs when a solution containing a solid undergoes a chemical reaction that causes the solid to settle out of the solution.

EXTRACTION

Liquid-liquid extraction is a method of separating substances in a mixture by mixing the mixture with, for example, water and oil. Water and oil do not mix. If the substances in the mixture have different solubilities in water and oil, this will cause the substances to separate out.

CHROMATOGRAPHY

Chromatography refers to a variety of laboratory procedures that separate out the components of a mixture. In paper chromatography, a drop of the mixture is placed on a piece of paper suitable for chromatography. The edge of the paper is placed in ethanol or water and the liquid rises in the paper due to capillary action. When the liquid reaches the drop of mixture it dissolves the components of the mixture and continues to move up the paper. The different components of the mixture are deposited on the paper at different points.

Skill 15.4 Demonstrating knowledge of the basic atomic and subatomic constituents of matter

BASIC ATOMIC STRUCTURE

An atom is the smallest particle of an element. A hydrogen atom consists of an electron rotating around a proton. The mass of a proton is around 2000 times greater than the mass of an electron, but the charges are equal and opposite. The diameter of the orbit of the electron, that is, the size of the hydrogen atom, is about 100, 000 times greater than the size of the proton.

The next atom on the periodic table is helium, which has two protons and two neutrons in the nucleus and two electrons rotating around the nucleus. The neutron has a slightly greater mass than the proton but has no charge. In this way, all the elements are built up. The largest well-known element is uranium with 92 electrons and 238 protons and neutrons.

The number of protons in the nucleus of an atom is called the atomic number. All atoms of the same element have the same atomic number. In an atom, the number of protons (with a positive charge) is equal to the number of electrons (with a negative charge). This makes an atom neutral.

Isotopes

An atom's number of protons is always the same. That is, an atom of carbon will always have six protons. But the number of neutrons can vary. For example, carbon can have 5, 6, 7, or even 8 neutrons. This means there are different values for the atomic mass of carbon. There are several different isotopes of carbon as a result. **Isotopes** of an element have the same number of protons in the nucleus, but have different masses. Neutrons explain the difference in mass. They have mass but no charge.

Scientists measure the mass of an atom by comparing it to the mass of carbon atom. Carbon has 6 protons and 6 neutrons and is called carbon-12. It is assigned a mass of 12 atomic mass units (amu), which is the standard unit for measuring the mass of an atom. Therefore, one amu is equal to 1/12 of the mass of a carbon atom.

The mass number of an atom is the sum of its protons and neutrons. In any element, there is a mixture of naturally occurring isotopes, some having slightly more or slightly fewer neutrons. The atomic mass of an element is an average of the mass numbers of its isotopes, based on the abundance of each isotope on Earth.

ENERGY LEVELS

Electrons circle the nucleus of an atom in orbits. Electrons orbiting the nucleus occupy energy levels that are arranged in order, and the electrons tend to occupy the lowest energy level available. A stable electron arrangement is an atom that has all of its electrons in the lowest possible energy levels.

Each energy level holds a maximum number of electrons. The outermost electrons in the atoms are called **valence electrons**. These electrons are involved in the bonding process, and they determine the properties of the element.

Level	Name	Maximum number of electrons
First	K shell	2
Second	L shell	8
Third	M shell	18
Fourth	N shell	32

This can help explain why chemical reactions occur. Atoms react with each other when their outer levels are unfilled. When atoms either exchange or share electrons with each other, these energy levels become filled, and the atom becomes more stable.

Skill 15.5   **Analyzing the properties of a gas, liquid, or solid in terms of kinetic theory, intermolecular forces, and the arrangement and motion of atoms, ions, or molecules**

THE KINETIC THEORY OF GASES

A gas is made up of atoms or molecules that collide with each other and the walls of the container without losing kinetic energy. Gas pressure results from molecular collisions with container walls. The number of molecules striking an area on the walls and the average kinetic energy per molecule are the only factors that contribute to pressure. The average kinetic energy of a gas molecule is directly proportional to the temperature of the gas.

Temperature and pressure
As the temperature (T) of a gas increases, its pressure (p) increases. When you drive a car, the friction between the road and the tire heats the air inside the tire. Because the temperature increases, so does the pressure of the air inside of the tire. Gay-Lussac's law states that the pressure of a fixed amount of gas in a fixed volume is proportional to its temperature, or $p = kT$ where k is a constant.

Temperature and volume
At a constant pressure, an increase in temperature causes an increase in the volume (V) of a gas. Charles's law states that the volume of a fixed amount of gas at constant pressure is directly proportional to temperature, or $V = kT$ where k is a constant.

Pressure and volume
At a constant temperature, a decrease in the volume of a gas causes an increase in its pressure. An example of this is a tire pump. The gas pressure inside the pump gets higher as you press down on the pump handle to compress the gas. This forces it to exist in a smaller volume. This relationship between pressure and volume is called

Boyle's law. Boyle's law states that the volume of a fixed amount of gas at constant temperature is inversely proportional to the gas pressure, or $V = k/P$, where k is a constant.

The ideal gas law

The pressure of a gas also depends on the amount of gas in the container, which can be measured in moles (n). A mole of gas contains Avogadro's number of molecules or atoms: 6.022×10^{23}. The ideal gas law is

$$pV = nRT$$

where R is the universal gas constant. The actual value depends on the units selected for pressure and volume.

The behavior of an ideal gas can be determined by conditions, such as temperature, pressure, volume or quantity of gas—all of which can vary within a system. An ideal gas is an imaginary gas that obeys all of the assumptions of the kinetic molecular theory. While an ideal gas does not exist, most gases will behave like an ideal gas except when at very low temperatures or very high pressures.

STATES OF MATTER

Molecules have kinetic energy (they move around), and they also have intermolecular attractive forces (they stick to each other). The relationship between these two determines whether a collection of molecules will be a gas, liquid, or solid.

A gas has an indefinite shape and an indefinite volume. The kinetic model for a gas is a collection of widely separated molecules, each moving in a random and free fashion, with negligible attractive or repulsive forces between them. Gases will expand to occupy a larger container so there is more space between the molecules. Gases can also be compressed to fit into a small container so the molecules are less separated. **Diffusion** occurs when one material spreads into or through another. Gases diffuse rapidly and move from one place to another.

A liquid assumes the shape of the portion of any container that it occupies and has a specific volume. The kinetic model for a liquid is a collection of molecules attracted to each other with sufficient strength to keep them close to each other but with insufficient strength to prevent them from moving around randomly. Liquids have a higher density and are much less compressible than gases because the molecules in a liquid are closer together. Diffusion occurs more slowly in liquids than in gases because the molecules in a liquid stick to each other and are not completely free to move.

A solid has a definite volume and a definite shape. The kinetic model for a solid is a collection of molecules attracted to each other with sufficient strength to essentially lock them in place. Each molecule may vibrate, but it has an average position relative to its neighbors. If these positions form an ordered pattern, the solid is called **crystalline**.

Otherwise, it is called **amorphous**. Solids have a high density and are almost incompressible because the molecules are close together. Diffusion occurs extremely slowly because the molecules almost never alter their position.

In a solid, the energy of intermolecular attractive forces is much stronger than the kinetic energy of the molecules, so kinetic energy and kinetic molecular theory are not very important. As temperature increases in a solid, the vibrations of individual molecules grow more intense and the molecules spread slightly farther apart, decreasing the density of the solid.

In a liquid, the energy of intermolecular attractive forces is about as strong as the kinetic energy of the molecules, and both play a role in the properties of liquids.

In a gas, the energy of intermolecular forces is much weaker than the kinetic energy of the molecules. Kinetic molecular theory is usually applied to gases and is best applied by imagining ourselves shrinking down to become a molecule and picturing what happens when we bump into other molecules and into container walls.

Skill 15.6 **Applying knowledge of the periodic table and the principles for filling the electron orbitals of atoms in order to explain periodic trends in electrical conductivity and ionization energy and the metallic character of a given set of elements**

THE PERIODIC TABLE

The periodic table of elements is an arrangement of the elements in rows and columns so that it is easy to locate elements with similar properties. The elements of the modern periodic table are arranged in numerical order by atomic number.

The **periods** are the rows numbered down the left side of the table. They are called first period, second period, etc. The columns of the periodic table are called **groups**, or **families**. Elements in a family have similar properties.

There are three types of elements, indicated by three colors on the periodic table:

- Metals
- Nonmetals
- Metalloids

The periodic table arranges metals into families with similar properties. The periodic table has its columns marked IA to VIIIA, which are the traditional group numbers. Arabic numbers 1 to 18 are also used, as suggested by the Union of Physicists and Chemists.

Metals

With the exception of hydrogen, all elements in Group 1 are alkali metals. These metals are shiny, softer, and less dense than other metals and are the most chemically active. Group 2 metals are the alkaline Earth metals. They are harder, denser, have higher melting points, and are chemically active.

The transition elements are in the periods (rows) 4 to 7 under the groups (columns) 3 to 12. They are metals that do not show a range of properties as you move across the chart. They are hard and have high melting points. Compounds of these elements are colorful, such as silver, gold, and mercury.

Elements can be combined to make other metallic objects. An **alloy** is a mixture of two or more elements having properties of metals. The elements do not have to be all metals. For instance, steel is made up of the metal iron and the non-metal carbon.

Nonmetals

Nonmetals are not as easy to recognize as metals because they do not always share physical properties. In general, however, the properties of nonmetals are the opposite of metals. They are dull, brittle, and poor conductors of heat and electricity.
Nonmetals include solids, gases, and one liquid (bromine).

Nonmetals have four to eight electrons in their outermost energy levels and tend to attract electrons. As a result, the outer levels are usually filled with eight electrons. This difference in the number of electrons is what causes the differences between metals and nonmetals. The outstanding chemical property of nonmetals is that they react with metals.

The halogens can be found in Group 17. Halogens combine readily with metals to form salts. Table salt, fluoride toothpaste, and bleach all have an element from the halogen family.

The Noble Gases got their name because they did not react chemically with other elements, much like the nobility did not mix with the masses. These gases (found in Group 18) will only combine with other elements under very specific conditions. They are inert (inactive). In recent years, scientists have found this to be only generally true, since chemists have been able to prepare compounds of krypton and xenon.

Metalloids

Metalloids have properties in between those of metals and nonmetals. They can be found in Groups 13 to 16 but do not occupy the entire group. They are arranged in stair steps across the groups.

Physical Properties:

- All are solids having the appearance of metals.
- All are white or gray, but not shiny.

- They will conduct electricity, but not as well as a metal.

Chemical Properties:

- They have some characteristics of metals and nonmetals.
- Their properties do not follow patterns like those of metals and nonmetals. Each must be studied individually.

Boron is the first element in Group 13; it is a poor conductor of electricity at low temperatures. If its temperature increases, however, it becomes a good conductor of electricity. By comparison, metals, which are good conductors, lose their ability as they are heated. It is because of this property that boron is so useful. Boron is a semiconductor. Semiconductors are used in electrical devices that have to function at temperatures too high for metals.

Silicon is the second element in Group 14; it is also a semiconductor and is found in great abundance in the earth's crust. Sand is made of a silicon compound, silicon dioxide. Silicon is also used in the manufacture of glass and cement.

Skill 15.7 Applying knowledge of the periodic table to predict the covalent, ionic, or metallic nature of a bond in a given substance

Ionic bonding
Ionic bonding occurs when metals combine with nonmetals (see Skill 15.6). Ionic bonding can be understood in terms of the coulombic attraction between the ions that are created when one or two electrons from the metal become attached to the nonmetal.

Covalent bonding
Covalent bonding is an effect that can't be understood in terms of classical physics. It is a phenomenon in quantum mechanics and involves the overlapping of the matter waves associated with electrons. The simplest example of covalent bonding is the hydrogen molecule: H_2.

Metallic bonding
Metallic bonding occurs in a metal. In metal in the solid state, the electrons in the outer shells are not strongly attached to the atoms and are free to move. The bonding between atoms is a result of the interaction of the electrons with the atomic ions in a metal. Whereas there are individual covalent bonds, there are no individual metallic bonds between two atoms.

Skill 15.8 Analyzing the changes in matter and energy that occur in the nuclear processes of radioactive decay, fission, and fusion

NUCLEAR FORCES

The forces that hold a nucleus together are attractive forces between neutrons and protons, neutrons and neutrons, and protons and protons. These forces only act when the nucleons (neutron or proton) are in contact. They are obviously much stronger than the electrostatic force that causes protons to repel one another. The helium nucleus, for example, needs two neutrons to help hold the two protons together. As the number of protons in a nucleus increases, more nucleons are needed to make the nucleus stable. All nuclei with more than 83 protons are unstable because electrostatic repulsion occurs between all 83 protons. The nuclear attractive forces only exist between a limited number of protons and neutrons.

Half-lives of isotopes

The half-life of uranium-238 is 4.5 billion years. It decays into thorium-234 by emitting the nucleus of the helium atom (alpha particle). What this means is that if you have 1000 U-238 atoms, after 4.5 billion years you will have 500 U-238 and 500 thorium-234 atoms.

Nuclear binding energy

The energy that holds protons and neutrons together in a nucleus is called binding energy. The mass of a helium nucleus is much less than the sum of the masses of the two protons and two neutrons. On the sun, protons and neutrons combine to form helium nuclei. The excess mass is transformed into the light and other radiation that the sun emits according to the famous equation $E = \Delta mc^2$. Fusion refers to the nuclear reaction in which small nuclei combine to form larger nuclei. The larger nuclei have a greater binding energy than the smaller nuclei, so energy is emitted.

Fission

The best-known fission nuclear reaction is the splitting of uranium-235 into barium and krypton. If there is a critical mass of U-235, there will be a chain reaction. The chain reaction is uncontrolled in an atomic bomb and is controlled in a nuclear reactor used to generate electricity. For larger nuclei, the binding energy of the smaller nuclei is greater than the binding energy of the larger nuclei, so energy is emitted in the form of electromagnetic radiation and other particles.

Skill 15.9 Applying knowledge of the unique structure of carbon to explain how that structure results in the large variety of organic molecules

ORGANIC MOLECULES

The hundreds of thousands of organic molecules have various chemical and physical properties and three-dimensional structures, but certain similarities exist. Organic compounds are covalently bonded, carbon-based molecules. The ability of carbon atoms to bond with one another allows the formation of long chains, double and triple bonds, and rings.

Trends also exist in physical properties. Organic compounds tend to melt, boil, sublimate, or decompose below 300° C. Typically they are highly flammable. Further, most organic molecules are only slightly soluble in water and dissolve better in organic solvents such as acetones or ethyl alcohol. Solubility and physical properties of organic compounds, however, largely depend on their functional groups. These functional groups, such as hydroxyl or amine groups, also determine the chemical properties of these molecules.

Functional Groups
Many organic molecules contain **functional groups**, which are groups of atoms of a particular arrangement that gives the entire molecule certain characteristics. Functional groups are named according to their composition. The carboxyl group is the arrangement of -COOH atoms to make a molecule exhibiting acidic properties.

Some functional groups are polar and can ionize. For example, the hydrogen atom in the –COOH group can be removed (providing H+ ions in solution). When this occurs, the oxygen retains both the electrons it shared with the hydrogen and will give the molecule a negative charge.

If polar or ionizing functional groups are attached to hydrophobic molecules, the molecule may become hydrophilic due to the functional group. Some ionizing functional groups are: -COOH, -OH, -CO, and -NH_2.

Some common functional groups include:

Hydroxyl Group
The hydroxyl group, -OH, is the functional group that identifies alcohols. The hydroxyl group makes the molecule polar, which increases the solubility of the compound.

Carbonyl Group
The carbonyl group is a -C=O attached to either a carbon chain or a hydrogen atom. It is found in aldehydes and ketones. If the carbon is bonded to a hydrogen atom, the molecule is an aldehyde. If the carbon is attached to two carbon chains, the molecule is a ketone.

The double-bonded oxygen atom is highly electronegative so it creates a polar molecule and will exhibit properties of polar molecules.

Carboxyl Group
The –COOH group has the ability to donate a proton or H+ ion giving the molecule acidic properties.

Amino Group
An amino group contains an ammonia-like functional group composed of a nitrogen atom and two hydrogen atoms, covalently bonded. Since the nitrogen atom has unshared electrons, it can add H+ ions (proton). This gives the molecule its basic properties.

An organic compound that contains an amino group is called an amine. The amines are weak bases because the unshared electron pair of the nitrogen atom can form a coordinate bond with a proton (H+ ion). Another molecule that contains an amino group is an amino acid. It consists of the $-NH_2$ group of an amine and the $-COOH$ group of an acid.

Sulfhydryl Group
A thiol is a compound that contains a functional group that is composed of a sulfur atom and a hydrogen atom (-SH). This functional group is referred to as either a thiol group or a sulfhydryl group. Traditionally, thiols have been referred to as mercaptans.

The small difference in electronegativity between the sulfur and the hydrogen atom produce a nonpolar, covalent bond. This, in turn, prevents hydrogen bonding, which gives thiols lower boiling points and less solubility in water than alcohols of a similar molecular mass.

Phosphate Group
The phosphate ion is contained in a hydrocarbon chain, making a phosphate group present in the molecule. This molecule is ideal for energy transfer reactions (ATP) because of its symmetry and rotating double bond.

In biological systems, phosphates are most commonly found in the form of adenosine phosphates (AMP, ADP and ATP), in DNA and RNA and can be released by the hydrolysis of ATP or ADP.

Hydrocarbons
IUPAC is the International Union of Pure and Applied Chemistry. Organic compounds contain carbon and have their own branch of chemistry because of the huge number of carbon compounds in nature, including most molecules in living things. The simplest organic compounds are called hydrocarbons because they contain only carbon and hydrogen. Hydrocarbon molecules may be divided into classes of **cyclic** and **open-chain** compounds, depending on whether they contain a ring of carbon atoms. Open-chain molecules may be divided into branched or straight-chain categories.

Hydrocarbons are also divided into classes called **aliphatic** and **aromatic**. Aromatic hydrocarbons are related to benzene and always cyclic. Aliphatic hydrocarbons may be open-chain or cyclic. Aliphatic cyclic hydrocarbons are called alicyclic. Aliphatic hydrocarbons are separated into three groups: alkanes, alkenes, and alkynes.

TEACHER CERTIFICATION STUDY GUIDE

COMPETENCY 016   **UNDERSTAND CHEMICAL REACTIONS, THERMODYNAMICS, AND CHEMICAL KINETICS**

Skill 16.1   Demonstrating knowledge of chemical symbols, formulas, and the characteristics of different types of chemical bonds

CHEMICAL BONDS

A **chemical bond** is a force of attraction that holds atoms together. When atoms are bonded chemically, they give up their individual properties. For instance, hydrogen and oxygen combine to form water and no longer look like hydrogen and oxygen. They look like water.

Covalent Bonds

A **covalent bond** is formed when two atoms share electrons. Recall that atoms whose outer shells are not filled with electrons are unstable. When they are unstable, they readily combine with other unstable atoms. By combining and sharing electrons, they act as a single unit. Covalent bonding happens among nonmetals. Covalent bonds are always polar between two non-identical atoms.

Covalent compounds are compounds whose atoms are joined by covalent bonds. Some examples of covalent compounds are:

- Table sugar
- Methane
- Ammonia

Ionic Bonds

An **ionic bond** is formed by the transfer of electrons. It happens when metals and nonmetals bond. Before chlorine and sodium combine, the sodium has one valence electron and chlorine has seven. Neither valence shell is filled, but the chlorine's valence shell is almost full. During the reaction, the sodium gives one valence electron to the chlorine atom. Both atoms then have filled shells and are stable.

Something else happens during the bonding. Before the bonding, both atoms are neutral. When one electron is transferred, it upsets the balance of protons and electrons in each atom. The chlorine atom takes one extra electron, while the sodium atom releases one electron. The atoms now become ions–atoms with an unequal number of protons and electrons. To determine whether the ion is positive or negative, compare the number of protons (+ charge) to the electrons (– charge). If there are more electrons, the ion will be negative. If there are more protons, the ion will be positive. Therefore, the ionic bond is formed from the attraction of the positively charged ion to the negatively charged ion.

Compounds that result from the transfer of electrons from metal atoms to electrons from nonmetal atoms are called **ionic compounds**. Sodium chloride (table salt), sodium hydroxide (drain cleaner), and potassium chloride (salt substitute) are examples of ionic compounds.

CHEMICAL FORMULAS

A formula is a shorthand that uses symbols and subscripts to show what is in a compound. The letter symbols tell us the elements that are involved and the number subscripts tell us how many atoms of each element are involved. No subscript is used if there is only one atom involved. For example, the compound methane gas is CH_4, has one carbon atom and 4 hydrogen atoms.

Let us look at aerobic respiration. Our tissues need energy for growth, repair, movement, excretion, and so on. This energy is obtained from glucose supplied to the tissues by our blood. In aerobic respiration, glucose is broken down in the presence of oxygen into carbon dioxide and water, and energy is released, which is used for our metabolic processes. The above reaction can be written in the form of a word reaction.
glucose + oxygen = carbon dioxide + water + energy

By using chemical symbols and subscripts we can rewrite the above word equation into a proper chemical equation:

$$C_6H_{12}O_6 + 6O_2 = 6CO_2 + 6H_2O + \text{Energy}$$

The compounds on the left side of the equation are called **reactants**, and the compounds on the right side of the reaction are called **products**. The reactants in the above equation have to combine in a fixed proportion for a chemical reaction to take place.

One or more substances are formed during a chemical reaction. Also, energy is released during some chemical reactions. Sometimes the energy release is slow and sometimes it is rapid. In a fireworks display, energy is released very rapidly, but the chemical reaction that produces tarnish on a silver spoon happens very slowly.

Chemical equilibrium is reached when the quantities of reactants and products are at a "steady state" and no longer shifting, but the reaction may still proceed forward and backward. The rate of forward reaction must equal the rate of backward reaction.
In one kind of chemical reaction, two elements combine to form a new substance. We can represent the reaction and the results in a chemical equation.

Carbon and oxygen form carbon dioxide. The equation can be written:

C	+	O_2	=	CO_2
1 atom of carbon	+	1 atom of oxygen	=	1 molecule of carbon dioxide

No matter is ever gained or lost during a chemical reaction; therefore the chemical equation must be balanced. This means that there must be the same number of molecules on both sides of the equation. Remember that the subscript numbers indicate the number of atoms in the elements. The number of molecules is shown by the number in front of an element or compound. If no number appears, assume that it is 1 molecule.

Skill 16.2 Recognizing the properties of acids and bases

ACIDS, BASES, AND SALTS

Acid: a substance that releases a hydrogen ion in solution. An acidic solution has an excess of (H+) ions.

Base: a substance that combines with a hydrogen ion in solution. A base (alkaline) solution has an excess of hydroxide (OH-) ions.

An acid contains one element of hydrogen (H). Although it is never wise to taste a substance to identify it, acids have a sour taste. Vinegar and lemon juice are both acids, and acids occur in many foods in a weak state. Strong acids can burn skin and destroy materials.

Common acids

Acid	Use
Sulfuric acid (H_2SO_4)	Used in medicines, alcohol, dyes, and car batteries
Acetic acid ($HC_2H_3O_2$)	Used in making plastics, rubber, photographic film, and as a solvent.
Nitric acid (HNO_3)	Used in fertilizers, explosives, cleaning materials.
Carbonic acid (H_2CO_3)	Used in soft drinks.

Bases have a bitter taste, and the stronger ones feel slippery. Like acids, strong bases can be dangerous and should be handled carefully. All bases contain the elements oxygen and hydrogen (OH). Many household cleaning products contain bases.

Common bases

Name	Formula	Use
Sodium hydroxide	NaOH	Used in making soap, paper, vegetable oils, and in refining petroleum.
Ammonium hydroxide	NH_4OH	Used in making deodorants, bleaching compounds, cleaning compounds.
Potassium hydroxide	KOH	Used in making soaps, drugs, dyes, alkaline batteries, and in purifying industrial gases
Calcium hydroxide	$Ca(OH)_2$	Used in making cement and plaster

An **indicator** is a substance that changes color when it comes in contact with an acid or a base. Litmus paper is an indicator. Blue litmus paper turns red in an acid. Red litmus paper turns blue in a base. A substance that is neither acid nor base is neutral. Neutral substances do not change the color of litmus paper.

When an acid and a base combine chemically, they form a salt and water, a process called **neutralization**. Table salt (NaCl) is an example of this process. Salts are used in toothpaste, epsom salts, and cream of tartar. Calcium chloride ($CaCl_2$) is used on frozen streets and walkways to melt ice.

Oxides are compounds that are formed when oxygen combines with another element. Rust is an oxide formed when oxygen combines with iron.

pH and the effects of buffers

Maintaining a proper balance between acids and bases is critical to sustaining life. This balance is measured on the pH scale, which measures the concentration of hydrogen ions in a solution.

Pure water is considered neutral and is pegged at a pH of 7.0. As the numbers drop, the acidity increases. As the numbers rise, the alkaline (base) properties increase.

The increase or decrease from a neutral pH is based on the interactions of the hydrogen and hydroxide ions in the water. Hydrogen ions (H+) and hydroxide ions (OH-) are found in equal concentrations in pure water.

Seawater is not pure water. It actually is slightly alkaline with a pH of 7.4 to 8.4 with a median acidity around 8.0-8.1.

This alkalinity is maintained despite the high concentrations of carbon dioxide because of the forms the CO_2 takes in the seawater. Although the CO_2 does combine with the water to make carbonic acid (H_2CO_3), some of this acid breaks down to produce hydrogen ions (H+), bicarbonate ions (HCO_3^-), and carbonate ions (CO_3^{2-}). This breakdown results in maintaining the alkalinity, because as the pH of the ocean drops (increases in acidity), a reaction occurs which removes more H+ ions, returning the water to the proper balance.

Likewise, if the pH level increases (becomes more alkaline), more H+ ions are added to the water, once again maintaining the proper balance. This self-correcting feature of the seawater is called **buffering**.

Buffers usually are composed of weak acids and their salts, or weak bases and their salts. An appropriate acid or base/salt combination will buffer a solution only when it is at sufficient concentration and has a pKa close to the desired pH of the solution. Thus, a buffered solution can be created as follows:

- Select a compound with a pKa close the desired pH.
- Determine what the buffer concentration must be; typical concentrations are between 1mM and 200 mM.
- Using the pKa, calculate the number of moles of acid/salt or base/salt that must be present at the desired pH.
- Convert moles to grams and weigh out the components.
- If both salt and acid (or base) are available, use the appropriate amount of each.
- If only the acid is available, add the entire needed compound in acid form; then use enough base (NaOH) to convert the proper portion to salt.
- Dissolve all components in slightly less water than is needed to reach the final volume.
- Check the pH and adjust if necessary. Add water to reach the final volume.

Naming acids
There are special naming rules for acids that correspond with the suffix of their corresponding anion (negatively charged ion) if hydrogen were removed from the acid. Anions ending with –ide correspond to acids with the prefix hydro– and the suffix –ic. Anions ending with –ate correspond to acids with no prefix that end with –ic. Oxoanions ending with –ite have associated acids with no prefix and the suffix –ous. The hypo– and per– prefixes are maintained.

Anion	Anion name	Acid	Acid name
Cl^-	chloride	HCl(aq)	hydrochloric acid
CN^-	cyanide	HCN(aq)	hydrocyanic acid
CO_3^{2-}	carbonate	H_2CO_3(aq)	carbonic acid
SO_3^{2-}	sulfite	H_2SO_3(aq)	sulfurous acid
SO_4^{2-}	sulfate	H_2SO_4(aq)	sulfuric acid
ClO^-	hypochlorite	HClO(aq)	hypochlorous acid

ClO_2^-	chlorite	$HClO_2(aq)$	chlorous acid
ClO_3^-	chlorate	$HClO_3(aq)$	chloric acid
ClO_4^-	perchlorate	$HClO_4(aq)$	perchloric acid

Skill 16.3 Demonstrating knowledge of balancing chemical equations, and the changes in the energy and arrangement of atoms for a given chemical reaction

CHEMICAL REACTIONS

A **chemical reaction** is a process where one or more molecules change into different molecules.

Also, energy is released during some chemical reactions. Sometimes the energy release is slow (as in the tarnishing of silver), and sometimes it is rapid (as in a fireworks display).

For the basics of a chemical reaction, see "Chemical Formulas," Skill 6.1.

Kinds of Chemical Reactions
There are four kinds of chemical reactions:

In a **composition reaction**, two or more substances combine to form a compound.

$$A + B \rightarrow AB$$
i.e., silver and sulfur yield silver dioxide

In a **decomposition reaction**, a compound breaks down into two or more simpler substances.

$$AB \rightarrow A + B$$
i.e., water breaks down into hydrogen and oxygen

In a **single replacement reaction**, a free element replaces an element that is part of a compound.

$$A + BX \rightarrow AX + B$$
i.e., iron plus copper sulfate yields iron sulfate plus copper

In a **double replacement reaction**, parts of two compounds replace each other. In this case, the compounds switch partners.

$$AX + BY \rightarrow AY + BX$$
i.e., sodium chloride plus mercury nitrate yields sodium nitrate plus mercury chloride

Chemists use a set of rules to properly balance equations:

1. Determine the correct formulas for all reactants and products, using subscripts to balance ionic charges.
2. Write formulas for reactants on the left of the arrow and predict the products and write their formulas to the right of the arrow.
3. Under the reactants list all the elements in the reactants, starting with metals, then nonmetals, listing oxygen last and hydrogen next to last. Under the products, list all the elements in the same order as those under the reactants (straight across from them).
4. Count the atoms of each element on the left side and list the numbers next to the elements. Repeat for products. Don't forget that subscripts outside a parenthesis multiply everything inside the parenthesis, including subscripts inside the parenthesis.
5. For the first element in the list that has unequal numbers of atoms, use a coefficient (large numeral to the left of the compound or element) to give the correct number of atoms. Never change the subscripts to balance an equation.
6. Go to the next unbalanced element and balance it, moving down the list until all are balanced.
7. Start back at the beginning of the list and actually count the atoms of each element on each side of the arrow to make sure the number listed is the actual number. Rebalance and recheck as needed.

Skill 16.4 Recognizing different types of chemical reactions (e.g., oxidation-reduction, acid-base, free radical, precipitation)

TYPES OF CHEMICAL REACTIONS

An **oxidation-reduction reaction** (or **redox reaction**) involves the transfer of electrons from one molecule to another.

An **acid-base reaction** is a reaction that occurs between an acid and a base.

A **precipitation reaction** is a reaction in which a solid, or **precipitate**, is formed.

Also see Skill 16.3.

Skill 16.5 Demonstrating knowledge of the first and second laws of thermodynamics, and the changes in the enthalpy and entropy that occur during a given chemical reaction

WORK AND ENERGY

Energy is the ability to do work or supply heat. Work is the transfer of energy to move an object a certain distance. It is motion against an opposing force. Lifting a chair into the air is work; the opposing force is gravity. Pushing a chair across the floor is work; the opposing force is friction.

According to the **first law of thermodynamics**, energy is neither created nor destroyed; rather it is converted from one form of energy to another. This also means that energy is neither created nor destroyed in ordinary (nonnuclear) physical and chemical processes. Energy, in all of its forms, must be conserved. The following equation reflects the aforementioned statement: In any system, $\Delta E = q + w$ (Δ = change, E = energy, q = heat and w = work). This means that the change in energy is always equal to the energy used plus the work done.

Kinetic and Potential Energy
The two most commonly encountered forms of energy are potential and kinetic energy. **Kinetic energy** is the energy of a moving object. **Potential energy** is the energy stored in matter due to its position relative to other objects.

In any object—solid, liquid, or gas—the atoms and molecules that make up the object are constantly moving and colliding with each other. They are not stationary.

Due to this motion, the object's particles have varying amounts of kinetic energy. A fast-moving atom can push a slower-moving atom during a collision, so it has energy. All moving objects have energy, and that energy depends on the object's mass and velocity. Kinetic energy is calculated as: $KE = \frac{1}{2} mv^2$.

An object's temperature is proportional to the average kinetic energy of the particles in the substance. When the temperature of a substance is increased its particles move faster, so their average kinetic energies increase as well. Temperature is not energy, it is not conserved.

The energy an object has due to its position or arrangement of its parts is called potential energy. Potential energy due to position is equal to the mass of the object times the gravitational pull on the object times the height of the object, or: $PE = mgh$. Where PE = potential energy, m = mass of object, g = gravity, and h = height.

Heat
Heat is energy that is transferred between objects caused by differences in their temperatures. Heat is transferred from an object of higher temperature to one of lower temperature. This transfer continues until both objects reach the same temperature. Both kinetic energy and potential energy can be transformed into heat energy. When you step on the brakes in your car, the kinetic energy of the car is changed to heat energy by friction between the brake and the wheels. Other transformations can occur from kinetic to potential as well. Since most of the energy in our world is in a form that is not easily used, both humans and nature have developed some clever ways of changing one form of energy into another form that may be more readily used.

Temperature

We cannot rely on our sense of touch to determine an object's temperature because it is not an accurate measurement. **Thermometers** are used to measure temperature. When a thermometer is heated, a small amount of mercury—or colored alcohol, as is more commonly used today—expands in a capillary tube. The metal end of the thermometer and the object whose temperature it is measuring are put in contact long enough for them to reach thermal equilibrium. Then the temperature can be read from the thermometer scale.

Three temperature units are used:

- **Celsius:** The freezing point of water is set at 0 and the boiling point is 100 degrees. The interval between the two is divided into 100 equal parts called degrees Celsius.
- **Fahrenheit:** The freezing point of water is 32 degrees and the boiling point is 212. The interval between is divided into 180 equal parts called degrees Fahrenheit.
- **Kelvin:** This scale has degrees the same size as the Celsius scale, but the zero point is moved down to a hypothetical absolute zero, determined by the triple point of water. Water inside a closed vessel is in thermal equilibrium in all three states (ice, water, and vapor) at 273.15 Kelvin. This temperature is equivalent to .01 degrees Celsius. Because the degrees are the same in the two scales, temperature changes are the same in Celsius and Kelvin.

Units of Heat Measure

The **heat capacity** of an object is the amount of heat energy that it takes to raise the temperature of the object by one degree.

Heat capacity per unit mass is called **specific heat**.
A **calorimeter** uses the transfer of heat from one substance to another to determine the specific heat of the substance. Specific heats for many materials have been calculated and can be found in tables.

There are a number of ways that heat is measured. In each case, the measurement depends on raising the temperature of a specific amount of water by a specific amount. These conversions of heat energy and work are called the **mechanical equivalent of heat.**

The **calorie** is the amount of energy that it takes to raise one gram of water one degree Celsius.

The **kilocalorie** is the amount of energy that it takes to raise one kilogram of water by one degree Celsius. Food "calories" are actually kilocalories.

In the International System of Units (SI), the calorie is equal to 4.184 **joules**.

A **British thermal unit (BTU)** = 252 calories = 1.054 kJ

Heat transfer
Heat energy that is transferred into or out of a system is **heat transfer.** The temperature change is positive for a gain in heat energy and negative when heat is removed from the object or system.

The formula for heat transfer is Q = mcT where Q is the amount of heat energy transferred, m is the amount of substance (in kilograms), c is the specific heat of the substance, and T is the change in temperature of the substance. It is important to assume that the objects in thermal contact are isolated and insulated from their surroundings. Because energy is neither created nor destroyed, if a substance in a closed container loses heat, then another substance in the container must gain heat.

Phase Change and Heat Transfer
When an object undergoes a change of phase, it goes from one physical state (solid, liquid, or gas) to another. For instance, water can go from liquid to solid (freezing) or from liquid to gas (boiling). The heat that is required to change from one state to the other is called **latent heat**.

The **heat of fusion** is the amount of heat that it takes to change a substance from a solid to a liquid or the amount of heat released during the change from liquid to solid. The **heat of vaporization** is the amount of heat that it takes to change a liquid to a gas.

Methods of Heat Transfer
Heat is transferred in three ways: conduction, convection, and radiation.

Conduction is the transfer of heat with no actual transfer of matter. Conduction takes place between two substances in contact with each other, or within one substance. Conduction is the movement of thermal energy (heat) between molecules that are in contact with each other.

The **transfer rate** is the ratio of the amount of heat per amount of time it takes to transfer heat from one area of an object to another. For example, if you place an iron pan on a flame, the handle will eventually become hot. How fast the handle gets hot is a function of the amount of heat and how long it is applied. The shorter the amount of time it takes to heat the handle, the greater the transfer rate.

Convection is the transfer of thermal energy within a fluid. The particles in a fluid (which could be air or a liquid) transfer the thermal energy from hot areas to cooler areas. Hot fluids rise and cooler fluids sink due to differences in their densities. This is the basic premise behind the transfer of heat energy by convection. The warmed, rising air from a heat source such as a fire or electric heater is a common example of convection. Convection ovens make use of circulating air to more efficiently cook food.

Radiation is the transfer of energy by waves such as the electromagnetic waves emitted by stars. The sun warms the earth by emitting radiant energy.

The first law of thermodynamics is sometimes known as the law of conservation of energy. This law states that energy is conserved. This means that if energy is added to a system one of two things must happen. Either the thermal energy of the system must increase. Or work must be done. But that energy added to the system must be accounted for in some way—it is conserved. The change in heat energy supplied to a system (Q) is equal to the sum of the change in the internal energy (U) and the change in the work done by the system against internal forces: $Q = U + W$

The second law of thermodynamics says that thermal energy can move from a colder system to a warmer system only if work is done. It is intuitive that heat will move from a warm object to a cooler object. But is it important to recognize that it can move the other way as well, with a little help. Heat cannot spontaneously pass from a colder to a hotter object. An ice cube sitting on a hot sidewalk will melt into a little puddle; but a puddle of water will not spontaneously cool and form the same ice cube.

Entropy is the measure of how much energy or heat is available for work. Work occurs only when heat is transferred from warmer to cooler objects. Once this is accomplished, no more work can be done. The energy is still conserved but is not available for work as long as the objects are the same temperature. According to this theory, all things in the universe will eventually reach the same temperature. If this happens, energy will no longer be usable.

Skill 16.6   Demonstrating knowledge of factors (e.g., effective particle collisions, temperature, concentration) that can affect the spontaneity and rate of a given chemical reaction

KINETIC MOLECULAR THEORY

Kinetic molecular theory may be applied to reaction rates in addition to physical constants like pressure. Reaction rates increase with reactant concentration because more reactant molecules are present, and more molecules are likely to collide with one another in a certain volume at higher concentrations. The nature of these relationships determines the rate law for the reaction. For ideal gases, the concentration of a reactant is its molar density, and this varies with pressure and temperature.

Kinetic molecular theory also predicts that reaction rate constants increase with temperature (values for k) because of two reasons:

- More reactant molecules will collide with each other per second.
- These collisions will each occur at a higher energy, which is more likely to overcome the activation energy of the reaction.

Electrochemistry

Electrochemistry is the field that studies electrically driven reactions. A specific reaction that is driven by electricity is called an **electrolysis reaction.** An example would be adding electricity to split a water molecule into its components. It is also commonly used for the synthesis of organic molecules.

Practical applications for electrochemistry include pH measuring devices and electroplating. An example of an electrochemical device is a pH meter, which measures pH by comparing the electrical properties of a solution to those of a reference electrode. Electroplating is done by immersing a metal object in a bath containing the salt of a second metal. You can uniformly plate on a coating of that metal by running an electric current through the solution. The object being plated is called a cathode.

Skill 16.7   **Recognizing how changes in the concentration of reactants and products, the introduction of a catalyst, or changes in temperature or pressure can be used to predict the change in the equilibrium state of a given chemical reaction**

Endothermic and exothermic chemical reactions

If during a chemical reaction, more energy is needed to break the reactant bonds than is released when product bonds form, the reaction is **endothermic**, heat is absorbed from the environment, and the environment becomes colder.

On the other hand, if more energy is released through the formation of product bonds than is needed to break reactant bonds, the reaction is **exothermic**, and the excess energy is released to the environment as heat. The temperature of the environment goes up.

The total energy absorbed or released in the reaction can be determined by using bond energies. The total energy change of the reaction is equal to the total energy of all of the bonds of the products minus the total energy of all of the bonds of the reactants.

Effects of temperature, pressure, concentration, and the presence of catalysts on chemical reactions

The rate of most simple reactions increases with temperature because a greater fraction of molecules have the kinetic energy required to overcome the reaction's **activation energy.** The graph below shows the effect of temperature on the distribution of kinetic energies in a sample of molecules. These curves are called Maxwell-Boltzmann distributions. The shaded areas represent the fraction of molecules containing sufficient kinetic energy for a reaction to occur. This area is larger at a higher temperature so more molecules are above the activation energy threshold, and more molecules react per second.

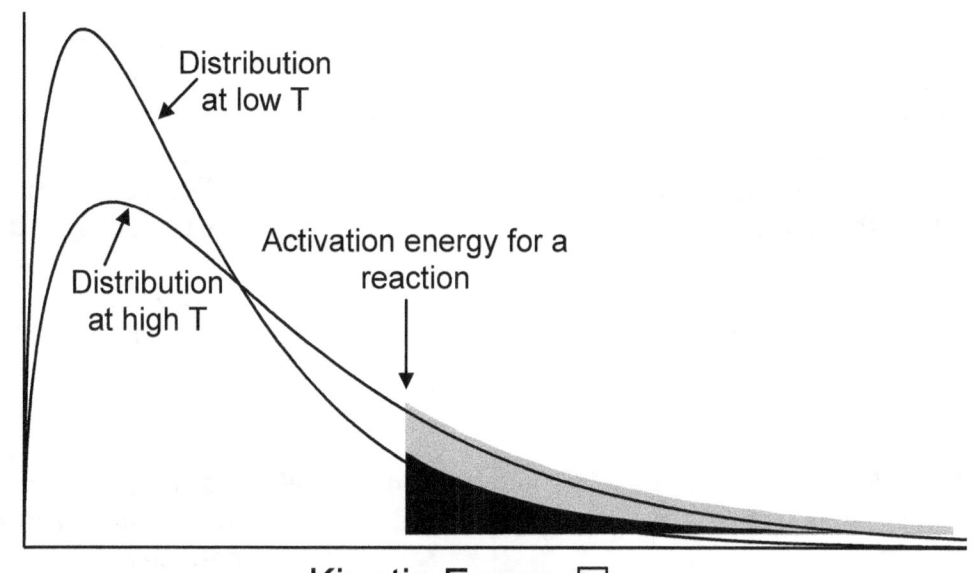

Kinetic molecular theory may be applied to reaction rates as well as to physical constants like pressure. Reaction rates increase with reactant concentration because more reactant molecules are present and more are likely to collide with one another in a certain volume at higher concentrations. The nature of these relationships determines the rate law for the reaction. For ideal gases, the concentration of a reactant is its molar density, and this varies with pressure and temperature as discussed in Skill 15.5.

A **catalyst** is a material that increases the rate of a chemical reaction without changing itself permanently in the process. Catalysts provide an alternate reaction mechanism for the reaction to proceed in the forward and in the reverse direction. Therefore, catalysts have no impact on the chemical equilibrium of a reaction. They will not make a less favorable reaction more favorable.

Catalysts reduce the activation energy of a reaction. Molecules with such low energies that they would have taken a long time to react will react more rapidly if a catalyst is present.

Biological catalysts are called enzymes.

Sample Test

Directions: Select the best answer in each group.

CONCEPTS AND APPLICATIONS IN MIDDLE LEVEL GENERAL SCIENCE

1. Which is the correct order of methodology?

   1. Collecting data
   2. Planning a controlled experiment
   3. Drawing a conclusion
   4. Hypothesizing a result
   5. Revisiting a hypothesis to answer a question

   (Average) (Skill 1.1)

   A. 1,2,3,4,5
   B. 4,2,1,3,5
   C. 4,5,1,3,2
   D. 1,3,4,5,2

2. When measuring the volume of water in a graduated cylinder, where does one read the measurement?
   (Average) (Skill 1.2)

   A. At the highest point of the liquid
   B. At the bottom of the meniscus curve
   C. At the closest mark to the top of the liquid
   D. At the top of the plastic safety ring

3. Which of the following data sets is properly represented by a line graph?
   (Rigorous) (Skill 1.3)

   A. The activity of different enzymes at varying temperatures
   B. The ages of children in a classroom
   C. The percent of time students spend on various after-school activities
   D. The concentrations of bacteria colonies on a petri dish

4. What is the prefix in the metric system for one thousandth?
   (Average) (Skill 1.3)

   A. Kilo
   B. Centi
   C. Milli
   D. Deca

5. **Which of these is the *best* example of negligence?**
   (Easy) (Skill 1.4)

   A. A teacher fails to give oral instructions to those with reading disabilities.
   B. A teacher fails to exercise ordinary care to ensure safety in the classroom.
   C. A teacher does not supervise a large group of students.
   D. A teacher reasonably anticipates that an event may occur, and plans accordingly.

6. **Experiments may be done with any of the following animals except:**
   (Rigorous) (Skill 1.5)

   A. Birds
   B. Invertebrates
   C. Lower order life
   D. Frogs

7. **Formaldehyde should not be used in school laboratories for the following reason:**
   (Average) (Skill 1.5)

   A. It smells unpleasant.
   B. It is a known carcinogen.
   C. It is expensive to obtain.
   D. It is explosive.

8. **Which of the following biologists discovered that microorganisms exist?**
   (Easy) (Skill 1.6)

   A. Robert Koch
   B. Anton van Leeuwenhoek
   C. Louis Pasteur
   D. James Watson

9. **Which discovery is part of modern physics?**
   (Easy) (Skill 1.6)

   A. Periodic table
   B. Theory or relativity
   C. Heliocentrism
   D. Evolution

10. **What are the four steps in the systems model?**
    (Average) (Skill 2.1)

    A. Input, process, output, feedback
    B. Input, process, reaction, feedback
    C. Method, process, reaction, feedback
    D. Method, process, output, feedback

11. **Which of the following is a science-based consumer good?**
    (Easy) (Skill 2.3)

    A. Plastics
    B. Genetically modified foods
    C. Cosmetics
    D. All of the above

12. **Which of the following is an example of genetic engineering?**
    (Easy) (Skill 2.3)

    A. Dairy cows are given bovine growth hormone to increase milk production
    B. Plants are fertilized with manure for optimal growth
    C. A child is vaccinated against chicken pox
    D. All of the above

13. **Which statement about graphs and computer models is true?**
    (Average) (Skill 2.5)

    A. Any type of graph can be used for any type of graphical representation.
    B. Computer models can be used before an investigation to predict results.
    C. Flowcharts are generally used to display large amounts of data.
    D. Textual descriptions are not needed for color-coded computer models.

14. **Which of the following is the *best* use for graphs?**
    (Rigorous) (Skill 2.5)

    A. Presenting large amounts of text
    B. Presenting long lists of numerical data
    C. Presenting large amounts of aggregated numerical data
    D. Presenting steps of a process in graphical form

15. **Approximately what percentage of the water on our planet is not safe to drink because of its high salinity?**
    (Average) (Skill 2.6)

    A. 95
    B. 50
    C. 35
    D. 3

16. **What is biomass?**
    (Rigorous) (Skill 2.6)

    A. Electricity produced by deflecting and diverting strong tidal currents through offshore turbines that drive electric generators
    B. Plant and animal wastes that can be burned to produce heat for steam turbine electrical generators
    C. Electricity produced from solar radiation
    D. Energy produced from hot, igneous rocks within the earth

17. Mr. Sanchez is having his students work with one-syllable words, removing the first consonant and substituting another, as in changing mats to hats. What reading skill are they working on?
    (Rigorous) (Skill 3.1)

    A. Morphemic inflections
    B. Pronouncing short vowels
    C. Invented spelling
    D. Phonemic awareness

18. Which of the following is not a primary way to differentiate instruction?
    (Rigorous) (Skill 3.2)

    A. Product
    B. Content
    C. Quantity
    D. Process

19. A Venn diagram is an example of which type of comprehension strategy?
    (Easy) (Skill 3.3)

    A. Text structure
    B. Graphic organizer
    C. Summarization
    D. Textual marking

20. To summarize a passage, a student should:
    (Average) (Skill 3.3)

    A. Answer the key questions raised in the passage
    B. Paraphrase the main idea
    C. Create a list of key words in the passage
    D. State the main idea and supporting details

21. Which of the following is true about content area vocabulary?
    (Easy) (Skill 3.4)

    A. Content area vocabulary should be taught by connecting new words to familiar ideas, words, and experiences.
    B. Content area vocabulary should be taught beginning in middle school.
    C. Content area vocabulary should be taught primarily in language arts classes.
    D. Content area vocabulary should be introduced once and then used occasionally for review.

EARTH AND SPACE SYSTEMS

22. **Approximately how thick is the earth's crust?**
    (Rigorous) (Skill 4.1)

    A. Between 1 and 2 m thick
    B. Between 5 and 70 m thick
    C. Between 1 and 2 km thick
    D. Between 5 and 70 km thick

23. **Which statement is true?**
    (Rigorous) (Skill 4.1)

    A. The slow convection of rocks in the core is responsible for the shifting of tectonic plates on the crust.
    B. The slow convection of rocks in the mantle is responsible for the shifting of tectonic plates in the core.
    C. The slow convection of rocks in the mantle is responsible for the shifting of tectonic plates on the crust.
    D. The slow convection of rocks on the crust is responsible for the shifting of tectonic plates in the mantle.

24. **Which type of rock is formed from magma?**
    (Average) (Skill 4.2)

    A. Sedimentary
    B. Igneous
    C. Metamorphic
    D. Both sedimentary and igneous

25. **Foliated rocks and unfoliated rocks are two types of:**
    (Rigorous) (Skill 4.2)

    A. Sedimentary rocks
    B. Igneous rocks
    C. Metamorphic rocks
    D. Minerals

26. **Which type of mountain is formed as magma tries to push up through the crust but fails to break the surface?**
    (Average) (Skill 4.4)

    A. Folded
    B. Fault-block
    C. Dome
    D. Upwarped

27. **Which type of volcano creates the largest type of volcanic mountain?**
    (Rigorous) (Skill 4.4)

    A. Composite
    B. Shield
    C. Caldera
    D. Cinder cone

28. During which era did birds undergo an explosion of evolution?
(Rigorous) (Skill 4.5)

   A. Cenozoic
   B. Archean
   C. Mesozoic
   D. Paleozoic

29. Which is the correct order, from largest units to smallest units?
(Rigorous) (Skill 4.6)

   A. Eons, eras, periods, epochs
   B. Eras, eons, periods, epochs
   C. Eons, epochs, eras, periods
   D. Eons, eras, epochs, periods

30. Energy is transferred between the hydrosphere, lithosphere, and atmosphere by all of the following processes except:
(Easy) (Skill 5.1)

   A. Convection
   B. Radiation
   C. Evaporation
   D. Conduction

31. Boundaries form between spreading plates where the crust is forced apart in a process called:
(Average) (Skill 5.2)

   A. Folding
   B. Faulting
   C. Subduction
   D. Rifting

32. In the ocean, water that has a salinity that is different from the surrounding water is most likely to form a:
(Rigorous) (Skill 5.3)

   A. Density current
   B. Surface current
   C. Cold current
   D. Warm current

33. What is the most accurate description of the water cycle?
(Rigorous) (Skill 5.4)

   A. Rain comes from clouds, filling the ocean. The water then evaporates and becomes clouds again.
   B. Water circulates from rivers into groundwater and back, while water vapor circulates in the atmosphere.
   C. Water is conserved except for chemical or nuclear reactions, and any drop of water could circulate through clouds, rain, groundwater, and surface water.
   D. Water flows toward the oceans, where it evaporates and forms clouds, which causes rain, which in turn flow back to the oceans after it falls.

34. **What is a front?**
    (Average) (Skill 5.5)

    A. A latitude of high or low pressure
    B. A zone of transition between air masses of different densities
    C. A continental landform that affects the movement of air masses
    D. A jet stream

35. **Which front's movement causes lighter warm air to advance, while denser cold air retreats?**
    (Rigorous) (Skill 5.5)

    A. Warm front
    B. Cold front
    C. Occluded front
    D. Stationary front

36. **Which of the following is a variable radio source that emits signals in short, regular bursts?**
    (Average) (Skill 6.1)

    A. Quasar
    B. Corona
    C. Pulsar
    D. Black hole

37. **Which of the following proposes that the solar system began with rotating clouds of dust and gas?**
    (Average) (Skill 6.2)

    A. Steady state theory
    B. Big Bang theory
    C. Tidal hypothesis
    D. Condensation hypothesis

38. **Which is the largest planet in the solar system?**
    (Average) (Skill 6.3)

    A. Uranus
    B. Neptune
    C. Jupiter
    D. Saturn

39. **During a partial lunar eclipse:**
    (Average) (Skill 6.4)

    A. The moon does not completely enter the earth's shadow, so part of the moon is visible
    B. The moon appears as a small, dark spot in the center of the sun
    C. The earth is in the moon's shadow, making the sun invisible
    D. The moon is in the earth's shadow, making the moon invisible

40. **The change in seasons is caused by:**
 (Easy) (Skill 6.5)

 A. The distance between the Earth and sun
 B. The distance between the Earth and moon
 C. The distance between the Earth and other planets
 D. The tilt of the Earth

41. **Which of these is most responsible for the shrinking of arable farmland?**
 (Average) (Skill 7.2)

 A. Urbanization
 B. Demand for lumber
 C. Overgrazing
 D. Natural disasters

42. **How does sewage upset the ecological balance in waterways?**
 (Rigorous) (Skill 7.3)

 A. It increases the salinity of water, making it unsafe to drink.
 B. As it decays, it kills algal blooms.
 C. As it decays, it consumes carbon dioxide in the water.
 D. As it decays, it consumes oxygen in the water.

LIFE SCIENCE

43. **Mollusca have an open circulatory system. Their sinuses serve which purpose?**
 (Rigorous) (Skill 8.1)

 A. Breathing
 B. Bathing
 C. Filtering food
 D. Circulating blood

44. **Members of the same animal species:**
 (Easy) (Skill 8.1)

 A. Look identical
 B. Never adapt differently
 C. Are able to reproduce with each other
 D. Are found in the same geographic location

45. **Animals with a notochord or backbone are in the phylum:**
 (Average) (Skill 8.1)

 A. Arthropoda
 B. Chordata
 C. Mollusca
 D. Animalia

46. **Which part of a plant is responsible for transporting water?**
 (Easy) (Skill 8.2)

 A. Phloem
 B. Xylem
 C. Stomata
 D. Cortex

47. Which of the following is not a necessary characteristic of living things?
    (Average) (Skill 8.3)

    A. Movement
    B. Reduction of local entropy
    C. Composition of cells
    D. Reproduction

48. Which of the following animals are most likely to live in a tropical rain forest?
    (Rigorous) (Skill 8.4)

    A. Reindeer
    B. Monkeys
    C. Puffins
    D. Bears

49. A wrasse (fish) cleans the teeth of other fish by eating plaque. This is an example of _____ between the fish.
    (Average) (Skill 8.4)

    A. parasitism
    B. symbiosis (mutualism)
    C. competition
    D. predation

50. Which of the following human diseases is caused by a bacterial infectious agent?
    (Average) (Skill 8.6)

    A. Cystic fibrosis
    B. AIDS
    C. Malaria
    D. Tuberculosis

51. Which of the following is/are involved in the human immune system's first line of defense?
    (Rigorous) (Skill 8.7)

    A. Earwax and vomit
    B. Macrophages
    C. Antigens
    D. Interleukin 2

52. Which cellular organelle contains the food and other materials needed by the cell?
    (Rigorous) (Skill 9.1)

    A. Vacuoles
    B. Golgi Apparatus
    C. Ribosomes
    D. Lysosomes

53. Which of the following biological processes is/are carried out only by producers?
    (Easy) (Skill 9.2)

    A. Metabolism
    B. Evolution
    C. Mitosis and meiosis
    D. Photosynthesis

54. Which of the following is not a nucleotide?
    (Average) (Skill 9.3)

    A. Adenine
    B. Alanine
    C. Cytosine
    D. Guanine

55. The first stage of mitosis is called:
    (Average) (Skill 9.5)

    A. Telophase
    B. Anaphase
    C. Prophase
    D. Metaphase

56. A child has type O+ blood. Her father has type A+ blood, and her mother has type B- blood. What are the genotypes of the father and mother, respectively?
    (Rigorous) (Skill 9.6)

    A. AO+ - and BO - -
    B. AO+ + and BO - -
    C. AO+ + and BO + -
    D. Cannot determine both parents' genotype from the information provided

57. A genetic mutation is:
    (Easy) (Skill 9.7)

    A. A substance that increases the likelihood of cancer
    B. Any change to the DNA sequence that may result in the production of an altered protein
    C. A change in the phenotypes of individuals in a given population over time
    D. A change that identifies as a separate species all populations with a unique lineage

58. A duck's webbed feet are an example of:
    (Easy) (Skill 9.7)

    A. Mimicry
    B. Structural adaptation
    C. Protective resemblance
    D. Protective coloration

59. **Which of the following is the best example of an explanation of the theory of evolution?**
(Rigorous) (Skill 9.7)

   A. Giraffes need to reach higher for leaves to eat, so their necks stretch. The giraffe babies are then born with longer necks. Eventually, there are more long-necked giraffes in the population.
   B. Giraffes with longer necks are better able to reach more leaves, so they eat more and have more babies than other giraffes. Eventually, there are more long-necked giraffes in the population.
   C. Giraffes want to reach higher for leaves to eat, so they release enzymes into their bloodstream, which in turn causes fetal development of longer-necked giraffes. Eventually, there are more long-necked giraffes in the population.
   D. Giraffes with long necks are more attractive to other giraffes, so they get the best mating partners and have more babies. Eventually, there are more long-necked giraffes in the population.

60. **Extensive use of antibacterial soap has been found to increase the virulence of certain bacterial infections in hospitals. Which of the following might be an explanation for this phenomenon?**
(Average) (Skill 9.7)

   A. Antibacterial soaps do not kill viruses.
   B. Antibacterial soaps do not incorporate the same antibiotics used in medicines.
   C. Antibacterial soaps kill a lot of bacteria, and only the hardiest ones survive to reproduce.
   D. Antibacterial soaps can be very drying to the skin.

61. **What is the general term or phrase that describes phenotypic features that allow organisms to exploit their environment?**
(Rigorous) (Skill 10.1)

   A. Reproductive isolation
   B. Carrying capacity
   C. Adaptation
   D. Zona pellucida

62. Species diversity is highest in which of the following groups of biomes?
    (Easy) (Skill 10.2)

    A. Coral reefs and tropical forests
    B. Temperate forests and tundra
    C. Boreal forests and grasslands
    D. Mountains and deserts

63. The founder effect takes place when:
    (Average) (Skill 10.4)

    A. A small group of individuals joins a larger population
    B. A small group of individuals becomes isolated from a larger population
    C. One large population joins another population
    D. A large population moves from one geographic area to another

64. In what type of species-species interaction does one species benefit and the other is unaffected?
    (Rigorous) (Skill 11.2)

    A. Competitive
    B. Commensal
    C. Amensal
    D. Parasitic

65. What is an example of a biotic component of an ecosystem?
    (Average) (Skill 11.3)

    A. Sunlight
    B. Oxygen
    C. Water
    D. Fungus

66. Which of the following convert abiotic energy into biotic energy?
    (Rigorous) (Skill 11.4)

    A. Decomposers
    B. Producers
    C. Consumers
    D. Both producers and consumers

67. A species would be *least* likely to have an appropriate response to which environmental change?
    (Rigorous) (Skill 11.5)

    A. Sunrise
    B. Rainfall
    C. An increase in predation
    D. Habitat destruction

PHYSICAL SCIENCE

68. The force of gravity on Earth causes all bodies in free fall to:
(Rigorous) (Skill 12.1)

A. Fall at the same speed
B. Accelerate at the same rate
C. Reach the same terminal velocity
D. Move in the same direction

69. All of the following are considered Newton's Laws except:
(Easy) (Skill 12.2)

A. An object in motion will continue in motion unless acted upon by an outside force
B. For every action force, there is an equal and opposite reaction force
C. Nature abhors a vacuum
D. Mass can be considered the ratio of force to acceleration

70. The Law of Conservation of Energy states that:
(Average) (Skill 12.3)

A. There must be the same number of products and reactants in any chemical equation
B. Objects always fall toward large masses such as planets
C. Energy is neither created nor destroyed, but may change form
D. Lights must be turned off when not in use, by state regulation

71. A boy is playing in the mud and makes a mud ball. He throws the mud ball against a brick wall and it sticks there. Which of the following statements is true about the mechanical energy and momentum of the mud ball and the wall?
(Rigorous) (Skill 12.4)

A. Neither momentum nor mechanical energy is conserved.
B. Mechanical energy is conserved, but not momentum.
C. Momentum is conserved, but not mechanical energy.
D. Mechanical energy and momentum are conserved.

72. Sound waves are produced by:
(Easy) (Skill 13.1)

A. Pitch
B. Noise
C. Vibrations
D. Sonar

73. Which statement describes the principle of superposition for mechanical waves?
(Average) (Skill 13.2)

A. Mechanical waves interfere destructively or constructively.
B. Two waves can occupy the same space at the same time.
C. The total displacement of a medium caused by two waves is the sum of the two displacements caused by each wave.
D. Waves produce crests and troughs in a medium.

74. As a train approaches, the whistle sounds:
(Rigorous) (Skill 13.3)

A. Higher, because it has a higher apparent frequency
B. Lower, because it has a lower apparent frequency
C. Higher, because it has a lower apparent frequency
D. Lower, because it has a higher apparent frequency

75. The electromagnetic radiation with the longest wave length is:
(Rigorous) (Skill 13.4)

A. Radio waves
B. Red light
C. X-rays
D. Ultraviolet light

76. A ray of light strikes a glass surface at an angle of 30 degrees with the horizontal. What equation determines the angle of refraction?
(Rigorous) (Skill 13.5)

A. $\sin 30° = (1.4) \sin r$
B. $\sin 60° = (1.4) \sin r$
C. $(1.4) \sin 30° = \sin r$
D. $i = r$

77. A converging lens produces a real image:
(Rigorous) (Skill 13.6)

   A. Never
   B. When the object is exactly at a distance of one focal length
   C. When the object is within one focal length of the lens
   D. When the object is farther than one focal length from the lens

78. Which of the following statements describes charging by induction?
(Average) (Skill 14.1)

   A. Rubbing two objects together
   B. Putting a charged object in contact with another object
   C. Grounding a charged object
   D. Placing a charged object near another object

79. Resistance is measured in units called:
(Average) (Skill 14.2)

   A. Watts
   B. Volts
   C. Ohms
   D. Current

80. The magnetic property that most elements possess is:
(Easy) (Skill 14.3)

   A. Ferromagnetism
   B. Paramagnetism
   C. Diamagetism
   D. North and south magnetic poles

81. Which describes the magnetic field produced by a moving charge?
(Average) (Skill 14.4)

   A. The magnetic field is circular in a plane perpendicular to the direction of motion.
   B. The magnetic field is parallel to the electric field.
   C. The magnetic field is antiparallel to the electric field.
   D. The magnetic field is too small to be observed without instruments.

82. Which formula describes the amount of heat generated per second (P) by a resistor?
(Average) (Skill 14.5)

   A. $P = VI^2$
   B. $P = IR^2$
   C. $P = RI^2$
   D. $P = IR$

83. Which of the following are physical properties?

    I   Color
    II Density
    III Taste
    IV Combustibility
    (Rigorous) (Skill 15.1)

    A. I only
    B. I and II only
    C. I, II, and III only
    D. III and IV only

84. Which of the following occur when NaCl dissolves in water?
    (Rigorous) (Skill 15.2)

    A. Heat is required to break bonds in the NaCl crystal lattice.
    B. Heat is released when hydrogen bonds in water are broken.
    C. Heat is required to form bonds of hydration.
    D. The oxygen end of the water molecule is attracted to the Cl⁻ ion.

85. Which method of separating the components of a mixture uses capillary action?
    (Easy) (Skill 15.3)

    A. Extraction
    B. Chromatography
    C. Precipitation
    D. Distillation

86. Which of the following statements describes an isotope of an element?
    (Rigorous) (Skill 15.4)

    A. An isotope has a different number of electrons.
    B. An isotope has a different number of neutrons.
    C. The arrangement of the electrons is different.
    D. An isotope has a different number of protons.

87. When heat is added to most solids, they expand. Why is this the case?
    (Rigorous) (Skill 15.5)

    A. The molecules get bigger.
    B. The faster molecular motion leads to greater distance between the molecules.
    C. The molecules develop greater repelling electric forces.
    D. The molecules form a more rigid structure.

88. Which statement is true about groups and periods on the periodic table? (Average) (Skill 15.6)

   A. Groups are associated with rows on the periodic table.
   B. Periods are associated with columns on the periodic table.
   C. Elements in the same period have similar properties.
   D. The three types of elements are metals, non-metals, and metalloids.

89. Bronze is an alloy of copper and tin. It melts at a very high temperature. What is the kind of bonding that exists between the elements in bronze? (Easy) (Skill 15.7)

   A. Ionic bonding
   B. Metallic bonding
   C. Covalent bonding
   D. Molecular bonding

90. Iodine-131 decays into xenon, which has a half-life of about 8 days. If you have a 100-gram sample of pure I-131, how much iodine will be left after one year? (Average) (Skill 15.8)

   A. 50 grams
   B. 100 grams
   C. No iodine atoms at all
   D. Less than 0.00001 grams

91. Which of the following is found in the least abundance in organic molecules? (Rigorous) (Skill 15.9)

   A. Phosphorus
   B. Potassium
   C. Argon
   D. Oxygen

92. A covalent bond: (Average) (Skill 16.1)

   A. Is formed when two atoms share electrons
   B. Is formed by the transfer of electrons
   C. happens when metals and nonmetals bond
   D. happens when metals bond to metals

93. Which of the following is *not* true about a base? (Rigorous) (Skill 16.2)

   A. It has a bitter taste.
   B. It is a substance that combines with a hydrogen ion in solution.
   C. Many household cleaning products contain bases.
   D. Vinegar is an example of a base.

94. In which type of chemical reaction is a compound broken down into two or more simpler substances?
(Average) (Skill 16.3)

   A. Composition
   B. Decomposition
   C. Single replacement
   D. Double replacement

95. In which type of chemical reaction is a solid formed?
(Average) (Skill 16.4)

   A. Oxidation-reduction
   B. Acid-base
   C. Decomposition
   D. Precipitation

96. If you lift a book into the air, what is the opposing force?
(Average) (Skill 16.5)

   A. The force applied by the book
   B. The force applied by your arm
   C. Gravity
   D. Friction

97. Which of the following statements about heat is true?
(Average) (Skill 16.5)

   A. Heat is transferred from an object of higher temperature to one of lower temperature.
   B. Heat is transferred from an object of lower temperature to one of higher temperature.
   C. Heat is transferred evenly between objects of different temperatures.
   D. Heat is not transferred between objects of different temperatures.

98. According to kinetic molecular theory, reaction rate increases with temperature. Why is this true?
(Average) (Skill 16.6)

   A. More reactant molecules will collide with each other per second.
   B. Collisions between molecules will each occur at a higher energy, which is more likely to overcome the activation energy of the reaction.
   C. Both A and B
   D. Neither A nor B

Middle Level Science

99. A material that increases the rate of a chemical reaction without changing itself permanently in the process is called a: *(Easy) (Skill 16.7)*

    A. Reactant
    B. Catalyst
    C. Precipitate
    D. Product

100. A chemical reaction in which more energy is needed to break the reactant bonds than is released when product bonds form is called: *(Rigorous) (Skill 16.7)*

    A. Endothermic
    B. Exothermic
    C. Composition
    D. Decompostion

Answer Key

1. B	35. A	69. C
2. B	36. C	70. C
3. A	37. D	71. C
4. C	38. C	72. C
5. B	39. A	73. C
6. A	40. D	74. A
7. B	41. A	75. A
8. B	42. D	76. B
9. B	43. B	77. D
10. A	44. C	78. D
11. D	45. B	79. C
12. A	46. B	80. B
13. B	47. A	81. A
14. C	48. B	82. C
15. A	49. B	83. C
16. B	50. D	84. A
17. D	51. A	85. B
18. C	52. A	86. B
19. B	53. D	87. B
20. D	54. B	88. D
21. A	55. C	89. B
22. D	56. D	90. D
23. C	57. B	91. C
24. B	58. B	92. A
25. C	59. B	93. D
26. C	60. C	94. B
27. B	61. C	95. D
28. A	62. A	96. C
29. A	63. B	97. A
30. C	64. B	98. C
31. D	65. D	99. B
32. A	66. B	100. A
33. C	67. D	
34. B	68. B	

Rigor Table

	Easy 20%	Average Rigor 40%	Rigorous 40%
Question	5, 8, 9, 11, 12, 19, 21, 30, 40, 44, 46, 53, 57, 58, 62, 69, 72, 80, 85, 89, 99	1, 2, 4, 7, 10, 13, 15, 20, 24, 26, 31, 34, 36, 37, 38, 39, 41, 45, 47, 49, 50, 54, 55, 60, 63, 65, 70, 71, 73, 78, 79, 81, 82, 88, 90, 92, 94, 95, 96, 97, 98	3, 6, 14, 16, 17, 18, 22, 23, 25, 27, 28, 29, 32, 33, 35, 42, 43, 48, 51, 52, 56, 59, 61, 64, 66, 67, 68, 74, 75, 76, 77, 83, 84, 86, 87, 91, 93, 100

TEACHER CERTIFICATION STUDY GUIDE

Rationales with Sample Questions

Directions: Select the best answer in each group.

CONCEPTS AND APPLICATIONS IN MIDDLE LEVEL GENERAL SCIENCE

1. Which is the correct order of methodology?

   1. Collecting data
   2. Planning a controlled experiment
   3. Drawing a conclusion
   4. Hypothesizing a result
   5. Revisiting a hypothesis to answer a question
   (Average) (Skill 1.1)

   A. 1,2,3,4,5

   B. 4,2,1,3,5

   C. 4,5,1,3,2

   D. 1,3,4,5,2

Answer: B. 4,2,1,3,5
The correct methodology for the scientific method is first to make a meaningful hypothesis (educated guess); then plan and execute a controlled experiment to test that hypothesis. Using the data collected in that experiment, the scientist then draws conclusions and attempts to answer the original question related to the hypothesis.

TEACHER CERTIFICATION STUDY GUIDE

2. **When measuring the volume of water in a graduated cylinder, where does one read the measurement?**
   (Average) (Skill 1.2)

   A. At the highest point of the liquid

   B. At the bottom of the meniscus curve

   C. At the closest mark to the top of the liquid

   D. At the top of the plastic safety ring

Answer: B. At the bottom of the meniscus curve
When water is in a glass, a meniscus (curved surface at the top of the water) forms because water molecules adhere to the sides of the glass, which is a slightly stronger force than their cohesion to each other. This leads to a U-shaped top of the liquid column, the bottom of which gives the most accurate volume measurement.

3. **Which of the following data sets is properly represented by a line graph?**
   (Rigorous) (Skill 1.3)

   A. The activity of different enzymes at varying temperatures

   B. The ages of children in a classroom

   C. The percent of time students spend on various after-school activities

   D. The concentrations of bacteria colonies on a petri dish

Answer: A. The activity of different enzymes at varying temperatures
A line graph shows change over time, so it would best represent the activity of different enzymes at varying temperatures.

TEACHER CERTIFICATION STUDY GUIDE

4. **What is the prefix in the metric system for one thousandth?**
   (Average) (Skill 1.3)

   A. Kilo

   B. Centi

   C. Milli

   D. Deca

Answer: C. Milli
In the metric system, milli is the prefix for 1/1000, as in *millimeter*. Kilo is the prefix for 1000.

5. **Which of these is the *best* example of negligence?**
   (Easy) (Skill 1.4)

   A. A teacher fails to give oral instructions to those with reading disabilities.

   B. A teacher fails to exercise ordinary care to ensure safety in the classroom.

   C. A teacher does not supervise a large group of students.

   D. A teacher reasonably anticipates that an event may occur, and plans accordingly.

Answer: B. A teacher fails to exercise ordinary care to ensure safety in the classroom.
Negligence is the failure to "exercise ordinary care" to ensure an appropriate and safe classroom environment. It is best for a teacher to meet all special requirements for disabled students and to be good at supervising large groups. However, if a teacher can prove that he has done a reasonable job to ensure a safe and effective learning environment, then it is unlikely that he would be found negligent. Therefore, the answer is B.

TEACHER CERTIFICATION STUDY GUIDE

6. **Experiments may be done with any of the following animals except:**
   (Rigorous) (Skill 1.5)

   A. Birds

   B. Invertebrates

   C. Lower order life

   D. Frogs

Answer: A. Birds
No dissections or biological experiments may be performed on living mammals or birds. Lower order life and invertebrates may be used. Therefore the answer is A.

7. **Formaldehyde should not be used in school laboratories for the following reason:**
   (Average) (Skill 1.5)

   A. It smells unpleasant.

   B. It is a known carcinogen.

   C. It is expensive to obtain.

   D. It is explosive.

Answer: B. It is a known carcinogen.
Formaldehyde is a known carcinogen, so it is too dangerous for use in schools. In general, teachers should not use carcinogens in school laboratories.

8. **Which of the following biologists discovered that microorganisms exist?**
   (Easy) (Skill 1.6)

   A. Robert Koch

   B. Anton van Leeuwenhoek

   C. Louis Pasteur

   D. James Watson

Answer: B. Anton van Leeuwenhoek
Robert Koch and Louis Pasteur made discoveries showing that microorganisms caused disease and that diseases could be prevented by sterilizations and vaccinations. James Watson discovered DNA with Francis Crick.

TEACHER CERTIFICATION STUDY GUIDE

9. **Which discovery is part of modern physics?**
   (Easy) (Skill 1.6)

   A. Periodic table

   B. Theory of relativity

   C. Heliocentrism

   D. Evolution

Answer: B. Theory of relativity
Heliocentrism refers to the idea—conceived in the third century BC—that the sun was the center of the solar system. Evolution and the periodic table are part of the scientific revolution that occurred from the 16th century to the end of the 19th century. Modern physics refers to the discovery of quantum mechanics and relativity at the beginning of the 20th century.

10. **What are the four steps in the systems model?**
    (Average) (Skill 2.1)

    A. Input, process, output, feedback

    B. Input, process, reaction, feedback

    C. Method, process, reaction, feedback

    D. Method, process, output, feedback

Answer: A. Input, process, output, feedback
The systems model graphically represents scientific processes. It breaks a system down into four steps: input, process, output, and feedback.

TEACHER CERTIFICATION STUDY GUIDE

11. Which of the following is a science-based consumer good? *(Easy) (Skill 2.3)*

    A. Plastics

    B. Genetically modified foods

    C. Cosmetics

    D. All of the above

Answer: D. All of the above
The production of a large number of popular consumer products requires scientific knowledge and technology. Genetically modified foods, plastics, and cosmetics are examples of science-based consumer goods.

12. Which of the following is an example of genetic engineering? *(Easy) (Skill 2.3)*

    A. Dairy cows are given bovine growth hormone to increase milk production

    B. Plants are fertilized with manure for optimal growth

    C. A child is vaccinated against chicken pox

    D. All of the above

Answer: A. Dairy cows are given bovine growth hormone to increase milk production
Genetic engineering has benefited agriculture. For example, many dairy cows are given bovine growth hormone to increase milk production.

TEACHER CERTIFICATION STUDY GUIDE

13. **Which statement about graphs and computer models is true?**
    (Average) (Skill 2.5)

    A. Any type of graph can be used for any type of graphical representation.

    B. Computer models can be used before an investigation to predict results.

    C. Flowcharts are generally used to display large amounts of data.

    D. Textual descriptions are not needed for color-coded computer models.

Answer: B. Computer models can be used before an investigation to predict results.
Computer models are suitable for use at any point during a process—they can be used before an investigation commences to predict results; they can be used during an investigation to demonstrate progress; and they can be used so summarize final results.

14. **Which of the following is the *best* use for graphs?**
    (Rigorous) (Skill 2.5)

    A. Presenting large amounts of text

    B. Presenting long lists of numerical data

    C. Presenting large amounts of aggregated numerical data

    D. Presenting steps of a process in graphical form

Answer: C. Presenting large amounts of aggregated numerical data
Graphs are used to present large amounts of aggregated numerical data in easily interpreted formats; numerous types of graphs exist, all more or less suited to specific types of data presentation

15. **Approximately what percentage of the water on our planet is not safe to drink because of its high salinity?**
    (Average) (Skill 2.6)

    A. 95

    B. 50

    C. 35

    D. 3

Answer: A. 95
We live on a watery planet. Unfortunately, a large percentage (97 percent) of the water is not fit for human consumption or agricultural use because of its high salinity.

Middle Level Science

TEACHER CERTIFICATION STUDY GUIDE

16. **What is biomass?**
    (Rigorous) (Skill 2.6)

    A. Electricity produced by deflecting and diverting strong tidal currents through offshore turbines that drive electric generators

    B. Plant and animal wastes that can be burned to produce heat for steam turbine electrical generators

    C. Electricity produced from solar radiation

    D. Energy produced from hot, igneous rocks within the earth

Answer: B. Plant and animal wastes that can be burned to produce heat for steam turbine electrical generators
Biomass is the name for plant and animal wastes (decaying or decayed) can be burned to produce heat for steam turbine electrical generators.

17. **Mr. Sanchez is having his students work with one-syllable words, removing the first consonant and substituting another, as in changing mats to hats. What reading skill are they working on?**
    (Rigorous) (Skill 3.1)

    A. Morphemic inflections

    B. Pronouncing short vowels

    C. Invented spelling

    D. Phonemic awareness

Answer: D. Phonemic awareness
Phonemic awareness is the acknowledgement of sounds and words; a child's realization that some words rhyme is one of the skills that fall under this category.

18. Which of the following is not a primary way to differentiate instruction? (Rigorous) (Skill 3.2)

    A. Product

    B. Content

    C. Quantity

    D. Process

Answer: C. Quantity
Teachers can differentiate instruction by modifying content, process, or product. Differentiation does not distinguish differences in quantity of work for different students; it distinguishes differences in types of work.

19. A Venn diagram is an example of which type of comprehension strategy? (Easy) (Skill 3.3)

    A. Text structure

    B. Graphic organizer

    C. Summarization

    D. Textual marking

Answer: B. Graphic organizer
Graphic organizers are graphical representations of content. Venn diagrams, a type of graphic organizer, show the similarities and differences between two concepts.

20. To summarize a passage, a student should: (Average) (Skill 3.3)

    A. Answer the key questions raised in the passage

    B. Paraphrase the main idea

    C. Create a list of key words in the passage

    D. State the main idea and supporting details

Answer: D. State the main idea and supporting details
To create a summary, a student should identify the main idea of a passage and the details that support the main idea.

TEACHER CERTIFICATION STUDY GUIDE

21. **Which of the following is true about content area vocabulary?**
    (Easy) (Skill 3.4)

    A. Content area vocabulary should be taught by connecting new words to familiar ideas, words, and experiences.

    B. Content area vocabulary should be taught beginning in middle school.

    C. Content area vocabulary should be taught primarily in language arts classes.

    D. Content area vocabulary should be introduced once and then used occasionally for review.

Answer: A. Content area vocabulary should be taught by connecting new words to familiar ideas, words, and experiences.
When teachers explicitly teach vocabulary, it is best if they can connect new words to ideas, words, and experiences with which students are already familiar. This will help to reduce the strangeness of the new words.

EARTH AND SPACE SYSTEMS

22. **Approximately how thick is the earth's crust?**
    (Rigorous) (Skill 4.1)

    A. Between 1 and 2 m thick

    B. Between 5 and 70 m thick

    C. Between 1 and 2 km thick

    D. Between 5 and 70 km thick

Answer: D. Between 5 and 70 km thick
The crust of the earth is the outermost layer and is between 5 and 70 km thick. Thin areas generally exist under ocean basins (oceanic crust), and thicker crust underlies the continents (continental crust).

23. **Which statement is true?**
    (Rigorous) (Skill 4.1)

    A. The slow convection of rocks in the core is responsible for the shifting of tectonic plates on the crust.

    B. The slow convection of rocks in the mantle is responsible for the shifting of tectonic plates in the core.

    C. The slow convection of rocks in the mantle is responsible for the shifting of tectonic plates on the crust.

    D. The slow convection of rocks on the crust is responsible for the shifting of tectonic plates in the mantle.

Answer: C. The slow convection of rocks in the mantle is responsible for the shifting of tectonic plates on the crust.
There is a great deal of interaction between the mantle and the crust. The slow convection of rocks in the mantle is responsible for the shifting of tectonic plates on the crust.

24. **Which type of rock is formed from magma?**
    (Average) (Skill 4.2)

    A. Sedimentary

    B. Igneous

    C. Metamorphic

    D. Both sedimentary and igneous

Answer: B. Igneous
Igneous rocks form from melted rock. This melted rock is called magma when it is under Earth's surface.

TEACHER CERTIFICATION STUDY GUIDE

25. **Foliated rocks and unfoliated rocks are two types of:**
    (Rigorous) (Skill 4.2)

    A. Sedimentary rocks

    B. Igneous rocks

    C. Metamorphic rocks

    D. Minerals

Answer: C. Metamorphic rocks
Metamorphic rocks are classified into two groups: foliated rocks and unfoliated rocks. Foliated rocks consist of compressed, parallel bands of minerals, which give the rocks a striped appearance. Unfoliated rocks are not banded.

26. **Which type of mountain is formed as magma tries to push up through the crust but fails to break the surface?**
    (Average) (Skill 4.4)

    A. Folded

    B. Fault-block

    C. Dome

    D. Upwarped

Answer: C. Dome
Dome mountains are formed as magma tries to push up through the crust but fails to break the surface. Dome Mountains resemble a huge blister on the earth's surface.

27. **Which type of volcano creates the largest type of volcanic mountain?**
    (Rigorous) (Skill 4.4)

    A. Composite

    B. Shield

    C. Caldera

    D. Cinder cone

Answer: B. Shield
Shield volcanoes are associated with quiet eruptions. Lava emerges from the vent or opening in the crater and flows freely out over the earth's surface until it cools and hardens into a layer of igneous rock. A repeated lava flow builds this type of volcano into the largest type of volcanic mountain.

28. **During which era did birds undergo an explosion of evolution?**
    (Rigorous) (Skill 4.5)

    A. Cenozoic

    B. Archean

    C. Mesozoic

    D. Paleozoic

Answer: A. Cenozoic
Birds had just started to appear in the late Mesozoic era. During the Cenozoic era, birds underwent an explosion of evolution as they diversified and multiplied.

29. **Which is the correct order, from largest units to smallest units?**
    (Rigorous) (Skill 4.6)

    A. Eons, eras, periods, epochs

    B. Eras, eons, periods, epochs

    C. Eons, epochs, eras, periods

    D. Eons, eras, epochs, periods

Answer: A. Eons, eras, periods, epochs
Earth's history extends over more than four billion years and is reckoned in terms of a scale. Paleontologists who study the history of the earth have divided this huge period of time into four large time units called eons. Subsequent eons, which encompass the biological history of the earth, are divided into four smaller units of time called eras, which are further divided into major periods. Periods are refined into groupings called epochs.

30. Energy is transferred between the hydrosphere, lithosphere, and atmosphere by all of the following processes except:
    (Easy) (Skill 5.1)

    A. Convection

    B. Radiation

    C. Evaporation

    D. Conduction

Answer: C. Evaporation
While the hydrosphere (water layer), lithosphere (solid outer layer), and atmosphere (gasses surrounding Earth) can be described and considered separately, they are actually constantly interacting with one another. Energy flows freely among these different spheres by means of convection, conduction, and radiation.

31. Boundaries form between spreading plates where the crust is forced apart in a process called:
    (Average) (Skill 5.2)

    A. Folding

    B. Faulting

    C. Subduction

    D. Rifting

Answer: D. Rifting
Boundaries form between spreading plates where the crust is forced apart in a process called rifting. Rifting generally occurs at mid-ocean ridges. Rifting can also take place within a continent, splitting the continent into smaller landmasses that drift away from each other.

TEACHER CERTIFICATION STUDY GUIDE

32. **In the ocean, water that has a salinity that is different from the surrounding water is most likely to form a:**
    (Rigorous) (Skill 5.3)

    A. Density current

    B. Surface current

    C. Cold current

    D. Warm current

Answer: A. Density current
Differences in water density can create ocean currents. Water that is denser tends to flow to a less dense area. Currents that flow because of a difference in the density of the ocean's water are called density currents. Water with a higher salinity is denser than water with a lower salinity. Therefore, water that has a salinity that is different from the surrounding water may form a density current.

33. **What is the most accurate description of the water cycle?**
    (Rigorous) (Skill 5.4)

    A. Rain comes from clouds, filling the ocean. The water then evaporates and becomes clouds again.

    B. Water circulates from rivers into groundwater and back, while water vapor circulates in the atmosphere.

    C. Water is conserved except for chemical or nuclear reactions, and any drop of water could circulate through clouds, rain, groundwater, and surface water.

    D. Water flows toward the oceans, where it evaporates and forms clouds, which causes rain, which in turn flow back to the oceans after it falls.

Answer: C. Water is conserved except for during chemical or nuclear reactions; and any drop of water could circulate through clouds, rain, groundwater, and surface water.
All natural chemical cycles, including the water cycle, depend on the principle of conservation of mass. (For water, unlike for elements such as nitrogen, chemical reactions may cause sources or sinks of water molecules.) Any drop of water may circulate through the hydrologic system, ending up in a cloud, as rain, or as surface water or groundwater. Although answers A, B, and D describe parts of the water cycle, the most comprehensive and correct answer is C.

Middle Level Science

34. **What is a front?**
    (Average) (Skill 5.5)

    A. A latitude of high or low pressure

    B. A zone of transition between air masses of different densities

    C. A continental landform that affects the movement of air masses

    D. A jet stream

Answer: B. A zone of transition between air masses of different densities
A front is a narrow zone of transition between air masses of different densities that is usually due to temperature differences. Because they are associated with temperature, fronts are usually referred to as either warm or cold.

35. **Which front's movement causes lighter warm air to advance, while denser cold air retreats?**
    (Rigorous) (Skill 5.5)

    A. Warm front

    B. Cold front

    C. Occluded front

    D. Stationary front

Answer: A. Warm front
A warm front's movement causes lighter warm air to advance, while denser cold air retreats. A warm front usually triggers a cloud development and may result in an onset of light rain or snowfall immediately ahead of the front, which gives way, as the cloud sequence forms, to steady precipitation until the front passes, a time frame that may exceed 24 hours.

36. Which of the following is a variable radio source that emits signals in short, regular bursts?
    (Average) (Skill 6.1)

    A. Quasar

    B. Corona

    C. Pulsar

    D. Black hole

Answer: C. Pulsar
A pulsar is defined as a variable radio source that emits signals in very short, regular bursts. A pulsar is believed to be a rotating neutron star.

37. Which of the following proposes that the solar system began with rotating clouds of dust and gas?
    (Average) (Skill 6.2)

    A. Steady state theory

    B. Big Bang theory

    C. Tidal hypothesis

    D. Condensation hypothesis

Answer: D. Condensation hypothesis
The condensation hypothesis proposes that the solar system began with rotating clouds of dust and gas. Condensation occurred in the center forming the sun and the smaller parts of the cloud formed the nine planets. This example is widely accepted by many astronomers.

38. Which is the largest planet in the solar system?
    (Average) (Skill 6.3)

    A. Uranus

    B. Neptune

    C. Jupiter

    D. Saturn

Answer: C. Jupiter
Jupiter is largest planet in the solar system. It has 16 moons and was named after the Roman king of the gods.

TEACHER CERTIFICATION STUDY GUIDE

39. **During a partial lunar eclipse:**
    (Average) (Skill 6.4)

    A. The moon does not completely enter the earth's shadow, so part of the moon is visible

    B. The moon appears as a small, dark spot in the center of the sun

    C. The earth is in the moon's shadow, making the sun invisible

    D. The moon is in the earth's shadow, making the moon invisible

Answer: A. The moon does not completely enter the earth's shadow, so part of the moon is visible
A partial lunar eclipse occurs when the moon does not completely enter the earth's shadow, so part of the moon is visible.

40. **The change in seasons is caused by:**
    (Easy) (Skill 6.5)

    A. The distance between the Earth and sun

    B. The distance between the Earth and moon

    C. The distance between the Earth and other planets

    D. The tilt of the Earth

Answer: D. The tilt of the Earth
The result of the tilt of the earth's axis allows for the seasonable changes called summer, spring, autumn, and winter. As the earth continues to revolve around the sun, it is the angle of the earth's axis that contributes to the amount of sunlight that is received on Earth, resulting in the changing seasons.

TEACHER CERTIFICATION STUDY GUIDE

41. **Which of these is most responsible for the shrinking of arable farmland?** *(Average) (Skill 7.2)*

    A. Urbanization

    B. Demand for lumber

    C. Overgrazing

    D. Natural disasters

Answer: A. Urbanization
The drive to urbanization affects our soil. Arable farmland is shrinking as the press to develop home and commercial sites increases. Of the approximately 15 billion hectares of dry land on the earth, only 2 billion are suitable for agriculture.

42. **How does sewage upset the ecological balance in waterways?** *(Rigorous) (Skill 7.3)*

    A. It increases the salinity of water, making it unsafe to drink.

    B. As it decays, it kills algal blooms.

    C. As it decays, it consumes carbon dioxide in the water.

    D. As it decays, it consumes oxygen in the water.

Answer: D. As it decays, it consumes oxygen in the water.
Sewage is produced by both humans and animals. Left untreated, it can enter the waterways and upset the ecological balance. As it decays, it consumes oxygen in the water, depriving aquatic life forms of oxygen, or causing algal blooms that further deplete the oxygen supply, and eventually turning some water anoxic (without oxygen).

TEACHER CERTIFICATION STUDY GUIDE

LIFE SCIENCE

43. **Mollusca have an open circulatory system. Their sinuses serve which purpose?**
    (Rigorous) (Skill 8.1)

    A. Breathing

    B. Bathing

    C. Filtering food

    D. Circulating blood

Answer: B. Bathing
Creatures in the Mollusca genus include clams, octopi, and soft-bodied animals that have a muscular foot for movement. Most of these creatures breathe through gills. With the open circulatory system, the sinuses are for bathing the body regions of the creature.

44. **Members of the same animal species:**
    (Easy) (Skill 8.1)

    A. Look identical

    B. Never adapt differently

    C. Are able to reproduce with each other

    D. Are found in the same geographic location

Answer: C. Are able to reproduce with each other
Although members of the same animal species may look alike (A), adapt alike (B), or be found near each other (D), the only requirement is that they be able to reproduce with one another. This ability to reproduce within the group is considered the hallmark of a species. Therefore, the answer is C.

Middle Level Science

45. Animals with a notochord or backbone are in the phylum:
(Average) (Skill 8.1)

    A.   Arthropoda

    B.   Chordata

    C.   Mollusca

    D.   Animalia

Answer: B. Chordata.
The phylum Arthropoda includes spiders and insects, and the phylum Mollusca contains snails and squid. Mammalia is a class in the phylum Chordata. The answer is B.

46. Which part of a plant is responsible for transporting water?
(Easy) (Skill 8.2)

    A.   Phloem

    B.   Xylem

    C.   Stomata

    D.   Cortex

Answer: B. Xylem
The phloem transports a plant's food. Stomata are openings on the underside of a leaf that allow for the passage of carbon dioxide, oxygen, and water. The cortex is where a plant stores food. The correct answer is B the xylem, which transports water up the plant.

47. Which of the following is not a necessary characteristic of living things?
(Average) (Skill 8.3)

    A.   Movement

    B.   Reduction of local entropy

    C.   Composition of cells

    D.   Reproduction

Answer: A. Movement
There are many definitions of "life," but in all cases, a living organism reduces local entropy, changes chemical energy into other forms, and reproduces. Not all living things move, however, so the correct answer is A.

TEACHER CERTIFICATION STUDY GUIDE

48. **Which of the following animals are most likely to live in a tropical rain forest?**
    (Rigorous) (Skill 8.4)

    A.   Reindeer

    B.   Monkeys

    C.   Puffins

    D.   Bears

Answer: B. Monkeys
The tropical rain forest biome is hot and humid, and is very diverse—it is thought to contain almost half of the world's species. Reindeer (A), puffins (C), and bears (D), however, are usually found in much colder climates. There are several species of monkeys that thrive in hot, humid climates, so answer B is correct.

49. **A wrasse (fish) cleans the teeth of other fish by eating plaque. This is an example of _____ between the fish.**
    (Average) (Skill 8.4)

    A.   parasitism

    B.   symbiosis (mutualism)

    C.   competition

    D.   predation

Answer: B. symbiosis (mutualism)
When both species benefit from their interaction in their habitat, this is called "symbiosis," or "mutualism." In this example, the wrasse benefits from having a source of food, and the other fish benefit by having healthier teeth.

TEACHER CERTIFICATION STUDY GUIDE

50. **Which of the following human diseases is caused by a bacterial infectious agent?**
    (Average) (Skill 8.6)

    A. Cystic fibrosis

    B. AIDS

    C. Malaria

    D. Tuberculosis

Answer: D. Tuberculosis
Cystic fibrosis is a genetic disease. AIDS is caused by HIV (human immunodeficiency virus). Malaria is caused by protozoans from the genus *Plasmodium*. Tuberculosis is caused by bacteria and is the correct answer.

51. **Which of the following is/are involved in the human immune system's first line of defense?**
    (Rigorous) (Skill 8.7)

    A. Earwax and vomit

    B. Macrophages

    C. Antigens

    D. Interleukin 2

Answer: A. Earwax and vomit
Macrophages are involved in the human immune system's second line of defense. Antigens and Interleukin 2 are involved in the human immune system's third line of defense. Earwax and vomit are involved with the human immune systems' first line of defense, and this is the correct answer.

52. **Which cellular organelle contains the food and other materials needed by the cell?**
    (Rigorous) (Skill 9.1)

    A. Vacuoles

    B. Golgi Apparatus

    C. Ribosomes

    D. Lysosomes

Answer: A. Vacuoles
In a cell, the subparts are called organelles. Of these, the vacuoles hold stored food (and water and pigments). The Golgi Apparatus sorts molecules from other parts of the cell; the ribosomes are sites of protein synthesis; the lysosomes contain digestive enzymes. The correct answer is A.

53. **Which of the following biological processes is/are carried out only by producers?**
    (Easy) (Skill 9.2)

    A. Metabolism

    B. Evolution

    C. Mitosis and meiosis

    D. Photosynthesis

Answer: D. Photosynthesis
Metabolism, evolution, mitosis, and meiosis are all carried out by producers, consumers, and decomposers. Only producers, however, carry out photosynthesis. The correct answer is D.

TEACHER CERTIFICATION STUDY GUIDE

54. **Which of the following is not a nucleotide?**
    (Average) (Skill 9.3)

    A. Adenine

    B. Alanine

    C. Cytosine

    D. Guanine

Answer: B. Alanine
Alanine is an amino acid. Adenine, cytosine, guanine, thymine, and uracil are nucleotides. The correct answer is B.

55. **The first stage of mitosis is called:**
    (Average) (Skill 9.5)

    A. Telophase

    B. Anaphase

    C. Prophase

    D. Metaphase

Answer: C. Prophase
In mitosis, the division of somatic cells, prophase is the stage where the cell enters mitosis. The four stages of mitosis, in order, are: prophase, metaphase, anaphase, and telophase.

56. **A child has type O+ blood. Her father has type A+ blood, and her mother has type B- blood. What are the genotypes of the father and mother, respectively?**
   (Rigorous) (Skill 9.6)

   A. AO+ - and BO - -

   B. AO+ + and BO - -

   C. AO+ + and BO + -

   D. Cannot determine both parents' genotype from the information provided

Answer: D. Cannot determine both parents genotype from the information provided
Because O blood is recessive, the child must have inherited two Os—one from each of her parents. Since her father has type A blood, his genotype must be AO; likewise her mother's blood must be BO. Because the lack of the Rh factor (-) is recessive, the child must have inherited at least one Rh+ from a parent. The father contributed the Rh+ to the child; it cannot be determined, however, if the father is heterozygous for the Rh factor (answer A), or homozygous for the Rh factor (answer B). Answer C is impossible because the mother cannot be heterozygous for the Rh factor and express the recessive trait. Since both answers A and B are possible then the answer must be D. With additional family information it may be possible to determine the father's genotype.

57. **A genetic mutation is:**
   (Easy) (Skill 9.7)

   A. A substance that increases the likelihood of cancer

   B. Any change to the DNA sequence that may result in the production of an altered protein

   C. A change in the phenotypes of individuals in a given population over time

   D. A change that identifies as a separate species all populations with a unique lineage

Answer: B. Any change to the DNA sequence that may result in the production of an altered protein
Answer A defines a mutagen; answer C partially describes evolution; answer D partially describes the genealogical species concept. Answer B defines a genetic mutation and is correct.

TEACHER CERTIFICATION STUDY GUIDE

58. **A duck's webbed feet are an example of:**
    (Easy) (Skill 9.7)

    A. Mimicry

    B. Structural adaptation

    C. Protective resemblance

    D. Protective coloration

Answer: B. Structural adaptation
Ducks (and other aquatic birds) have webbed feet, which make them more efficient swimmers. This is most likely due to evolutionary patterns where web-footed birds were more successful at feeding and reproducing and eventually became the majority of aquatic birds. Because this structure of the duck adapted to its environment over generations, this is termed "structural adaptation."

59. **Which of the following is the best example of an explanation of the theory of evolution?**
    (Rigorous) (Skill 9.7)

    A. Giraffes need to reach higher for leaves to eat, so their necks stretch. The giraffe babies are then born with longer necks. Eventually, there are more long-necked giraffes in the population.

    B. Giraffes with longer necks are better able to reach more leaves, so they eat more and have more babies than other giraffes. Eventually, there are more long-necked giraffes in the population.

    C. Giraffes want to reach higher for leaves to eat, so they release enzymes into their bloodstream, which in turn causes fetal development of longer-necked giraffes. Eventually, there are more long-necked giraffes in the population.

    D. Giraffes with long necks are more attractive to other giraffes, so they get the best mating partners and have more babies. Eventually, there are more long-necked giraffes in the population.

Answer: B. Giraffes with longer necks are better able to reach more leaves, so they eat more and have more babies than other giraffes. Eventually, there are more long-necked giraffes in the population.
Evolution occurs via natural selection. Organisms with a reproductive advantage will produce more offspring. Giraffes with longer necks who are able to eat more leaves will have that reproductive advantage.

TEACHER CERTIFICATION STUDY GUIDE

60. **Extensive use of antibacterial soap has been found to increase the virulence of certain bacterial infections in hospitals. Which of the following might be an explanation for this phenomenon?**
    (Average) (Skill 9.7)

    A. Antibacterial soaps do not kill viruses.

    B. Antibacterial soaps do not incorporate the same antibiotics used in medicines.

    C. Antibacterial soaps kill a lot of bacteria, and only the hardiest ones survive to reproduce.

    D. Antibacterial soaps can be very drying to the skin.

Answer: C. Antibacterial soaps kill a lot of bacteria, and only the hardiest ones survive to reproduce.
This phenomenon is due to natural selection. The bacteria that can survive contact with antibacterial soap are the strongest ones, and without other bacteria competing for resources, they have more opportunity to flourish.

61. **What is the general term or phrase that describes phenotypic features that allow organisms to exploit their environment?**
    (Rigorous) (Skill 10.1)

    A. Reproductive isolation

    B. Carrying capacity

    C. Adaptation

    D. Zona pellucida

Answer: C. Adaptation
Adaptations are any physical or behavioral changes within a species that allow that species to better exploit its environment—indeed adaptation is the evolutionary process that makes populations better suited to their habitat.

Middle Level Science

TEACHER CERTIFICATION STUDY GUIDE

62. **Species diversity is highest in which of the following groups of biomes?**
    (Easy) (Skill 10.2)

    A.   Coral reefs and tropical forests

    B.   Temperate forests and tundra

    C.   Boreal forests and grasslands

    D.   Mountains and deserts

Answer: A. Coral reefs and tropical forests
Coral reefs and tropical forests exhibit more biodiversity than any other biomes.

63. **The founder effect takes place when:**
    (Average) (Skill 10.4)

    A.   A small group of individuals joins a larger population

    B.   A small group of individuals becomes isolated from a larger population

    C.   One large population joins another population

    D.   A large population moves from one geographic area to another

Answer: B. A small group of individuals becomes isolated from a larger population
In the founder effect scenario, a small group of individuals becomes isolated from a larger population and effectively founds a new population. Such events occur, for instance, on islands when one or a few individuals arrive on the island and begin a new population.

64. **In what type of species-species interaction does one species benefit and the other is unaffected?**
    (Rigorous) (Skill 11.2)

    A.   Competitive

    B.   Commensal

    C.   Amensal

    D.   Parasitic

Answer: B. Commensal
In a commensal relationship, one species benefits, and the other is unaffected.

TEACHER CERTIFICATION STUDY GUIDE

65. What is an example of a biotic component of an ecosystem? *(Average) (Skill 11.3)*

    A. Sunlight

    B. Oxygen

    C. Water

    D. Fungus

Answer: D. Fungus
Biotic components of an environment are the living components—all of the prokaryotic, fungal, plant, animal, and protist members of the system.

66. Which of the following convert abiotic energy into biotic energy? *(Rigorous) (Skill 11.4)*

    A. Decomposers

    B. Producers

    C. Consumers

    D. Both producers and consumers

Answer: B. Producers
Producers are the fundamental basis of all energy flow into organic systems. Producers convert abiotic energy into biotic energy.

67. A species would be *least* likely to have an appropriate response to which environmental change?
    (Rigorous) (Skill 11.5)

    A. Sunrise

    B. Rainfall

    C. An increase in predation

    D. Habitat destruction

Answer: D. Habitat destruction
One type of environmental change that is particularly devastating involves habitat destruction, often by human activity. In this case the species impacted have no suitable response because such a scenario has not previously occurred in their evolutionary history and thus no suitable response is available. In these types of cases, the species typically will be driven into local extinction.

PHYSICAL SCIENCE

68. The force of gravity on Earth causes all bodies in free fall to:
    (Rigorous) (Skill 12.1)

    A. Fall at the same speed

    B. Accelerate at the same rate

    C. Reach the same terminal velocity

    D. Move in the same direction

Answer: B. Accelerate at the same rate
When an object near the surface of Earth is free to fall, it always accelerates or decelerates at a rate of 9.8 m/s^2.

TEACHER CERTIFICATION STUDY GUIDE

69. All of the following are considered Newton's Laws except:
    (Easy) (Skill 12.2)

    A. An object in motion will continue in motion unless acted upon by an outside force

    B. For every action force, there is an equal and opposite reaction force

    C. Nature abhors a vacuum

    D. Mass can be considered the ratio of force to acceleration

Answer: C. Nature abhors a vacuum
Newton's Laws include his law of inertia (A), which states that an object in motion (or at rest) will stay in motion (or at rest) until acted upon by an outside force; (D) his law that (Force)=(Mass)(Acceleration); and (B), his equal and opposite reaction force law. Therefore, the answer to this question is C, because "Nature abhors a vacuum" is not one of these.

70. The Law of Conservation of Energy states that:
    (Average) (Skill 12.3)

    A. There must be the same number of products and reactants in any chemical equation

    B. Objects always fall toward large masses such as planets

    C. Energy is neither created nor destroyed, but may change form

    D. Lights must be turned off when not in use, by state regulation

Answer: C. Energy is neither created nor destroyed, but may change form
Answer C is a summary of the law of conservation of energy (for non-nuclear reactions). In other words, energy can be transformed into various forms such as kinetic, potential, electric, or heat energy, but the total amount of energy remains constant. Answer A is untrue, as demonstrated by many synthesis and decomposition reactions. Answers B and D may be sensible, but they are not relevant in this case.

71. A boy is playing in the mud and makes a mud ball. He throws the mud ball against a brick wall and it sticks there. Which of the following statements is true about the mechanical energy and momentum of the mud ball and the wall?
(Rigorous) (Skill 12.4)

   A. Neither momentum nor mechanical energy is conserved.

   B. Mechanical energy is conserved, but not momentum.

   C. Momentum is conserved, but not mechanical energy.

   D. Mechanical energy and momentum are conserved.

Answer: C. Momentum is conserved, but not mechanical energy.
Momentum is a vector quantity and is always conserved in a collision because of Newton's second and third laws: The change in momentum of one object is equal and opposite to the change in momentum of the other object. In the above collision, there is a loss of mechanical energy to heat energy, so mechanical energy is not conserved.

72. **Sound waves are produced by:**
(Easy) (Skill 13.1)

   A. Pitch

   B. Noise

   C. Vibrations

   D. Sonar

Answer: C. Vibrations
Sound waves are produced by a vibrating body. The vibrating object moves forward and compresses the air in front of it, then reverses direction so that the pressure on the air is reduced, and expansion of the air molecules occurs. The vibrating air molecules move back and forth parallel to the direction of motion of the wave as they pass the energy from adjacent air molecules closer to the source to air molecules farther away from the source. Therefore, the answer is C.

TEACHER CERTIFICATION STUDY GUIDE

73. **Which statement describes the principle of superposition for mechanical waves?**
    (Average) (Skill 13.2)

    A. Mechanical waves interfere destructively or constructively.

    B. Two waves can occupy the same space at the same time.

    C. The total displacement of a medium caused by two waves is the sum of the two displacements caused by each wave.

    D. Waves produce crests and troughs in a medium.

Answer: C. The total displacement of a medium caused by two waves is the sum of the two displacements caused by each wave.
The crest is the maximum displacement of a wave above an undisplaced point on the medium, and the trough is the maximum displacement below an undisplaced point. Interference refers to the ability of two waves to produce a new wave form. Constructive and destructive interference refers to whether the two displacements are moving in the same or different directions. That two waves can occupy the same point at the same time is called superposition.

74. **As a train approaches, the whistle sounds:**
    (Rigorous) (Skill 13.3)

    A. Higher, because it has a higher apparent frequency

    B. Lower, because it has a lower apparent frequency

    C. Higher, because it has a lower apparent frequency

    D. Lower, because it has a higher apparent frequency

Answer: A. Higher, because it has a higher apparent frequency
According to the Doppler effect, when a source of sound is moving toward an observer, the wave fronts are released closer together, i.e., with a greater apparent frequency. Higher frequency sounds are higher in pitch.

TEACHER CERTIFICATION STUDY GUIDE

75. **The electromagnetic radiation with the longest wave length is:**
    (Rigorous) (Skill 13.4)

    A. Radio waves

    B. Red light

    C. X-rays

    D. Ultraviolet light

Answer: A. Radio waves
As one can see on a diagram of the electromagnetic spectrum, radio waves have longer wave lengths (and smaller frequencies) than visible light, which, in turn, has longer wave lengths than ultraviolet or X-ray radiation. If you did not remember this sequence, you might recall that wave length is inversely proportional to frequency, and that radio waves are considered much less harmful (less energetic, i.e. lower frequency) than ultraviolet or X-ray radiation.

76. **A ray of light strikes a glass surface at an angle of 30 degrees with the horizontal. What equation determines the angle of refraction?**
    (Rigorous) (Skill 13.5)

    A. $\sin 30° = (1.4) \sin r$

    B. $\sin 60° = (1.4) \sin r$

    C. $(1.4) \sin 30° = \sin r$

    D. $i = r$

Answer: B. $\sin 60° = (1.4) \sin r$
Snell's law uses the angle made by the incident ray with a line perpendicular to the surface. Choice D is the law of reflection. Choice C would apply to the case of a ray inside glass going into air.

Middle Level Science

77. **A converging lens produces a real image:**
    (Rigorous) (Skill 13.6)

    A. Never

    B. When the object is exactly at a distance of one focal length

    C. When the object is within one focal length of the lens

    D. When the object is farther than one focal length from the lens

Answer: D. When the object is farther than one focal length from the lens.
A converging lens produces real images when the object is far enough from the lens (outside one focal length) so that the rays of light that bounce off the object can hit the lens and be focused into a real image on the other side of the lens.

78. **Which of the following statements describes charging by induction?**
    (Average) (Skill 14.1)

    A. Rubbing two objects together

    B. Putting a charged object in contact with another object

    C. Grounding a charged object

    D. Placing a charged object near another object

Answer: D. Placing a charged object near another object
Answer A is called charging by friction. Answer B is charging by contact. Answer C means only the earth acquires a charge. In Answer D, the nearby charge causes charges to separate in the object. One side of the object has a positive charge and the other side a negative charge.

79. **Resistance is measured in units called:**
    (Average) (Skill 14.2)

    A. Watts

    B. Volts

    C. Ohms

    D. Current

Answer: C. Ohms
A *watt* is a unit of energy. Potential difference is measured in a unit called the *volt*. *Current* is the number of electrons per second that flow past a point in a circuit. An *ohm* is the unit for resistance. The correct answer is C.

80. **The magnetic property that most elements possess is:**
    (Easy) (Skill 14.3)

    A. Ferromagnetism

    B. Paramagnetism

    C. Diamagetism

    D. North and south magnetic poles

Answer: B. Paramagnetism
When a north pole comes close to most objects made of a single element, a south pole is induced in the object. This causes the object to be attracted to the north pole and is called paramagnetism. For iron and three other elements the force is very large, and the elements are said to be ferromagnetic. In diamagnetic substances, a north pole induces a north pole. Few substances are diamagnetic.

81. **Which describes the magnetic field produced by a moving charge?**
    (Average) (Skill 14.4)

    A. The magnetic field is circular in a plane perpendicular to the direction of motion.

    B. The magnetic field is parallel to the electric field.

    C. The magnetic field is antiparallel to the electric field.

    D. The magnetic field is too small to be observed without instruments.

Answer: A. The magnetic field is circular in a plane perpendicular to the direction of motion.
When a charge moves, it creates a circular magnetic field. The surface of the circle is perpendicular to the motion of the charge.

TEACHER CERTIFICATION STUDY GUIDE

82. Which formula describes the amount of heat generated per second (P) by a resistor?
    (Average) (Skill 14.5)

    A. $P = VI^2$

    B. $P = IR^2$

    C. $P = RI^2$

    D. $P = IR$

Answer: C. $P = RI^2$
The amount of heat generated per second (P) by a resistor is given by $P = RI^2$ where R is the resistance of the light bulb and *I* is the current through the resistor.

83. Which of the following are physical properties?
    I Color
    II Density
    III Taste
    IV Combustibility
    (Rigorous) (Skill 15.1)

    A. I only
    B. I and II only
    C. I, II, and III only
    D. III and IV only

Answer: C. I, II, and III only
A physical property can be observed without changing the chemical makeup of the substance. Combustibility is not a physical property because it cannot be found without altering the substance itself.

TEACHER CERTIFICATION STUDY GUIDE

84. **Which of the following occur when NaCl dissolves in water?**
    (Rigorous) (Skill 15.2)

    A. Heat is required to break bonds in the NaCl crystal lattice.

    B. Heat is released when hydrogen bonds in water are broken.

    C. Heat is required to form bonds of hydration.

    D. The oxygen end of the water molecule is attracted to the Cl⁻ ion.

Answer: A. Heat is required to break bonds in the NaCl crystal lattice.
The lattice does break apart, H-bonds in water are broken, and bonds of hydration are formed, but the first and second process require heat while the third process releases heat. The oxygen end of the water molecule has a partial negative charge and is attracted to the Na+ ion.

85. **Which method of separating the components of a mixture uses capillary action?**
    (Easy) (Skill 15.3)

    A. Extraction

    B. Chromatography

    C. Precipitation

    D. Distillation

Answer: B. Chromatography
Chromatography uses paper and the ability of liquid to move up paper by capillary action to separate substances. Extraction uses differing solubility properties, distillation uses different boiling points, and precipitation uses chemical reactions.

TEACHER CERTIFICATION STUDY GUIDE

86. Which of the following statements describes an isotope of an element? (Rigorous) (Skill 15.4)

    A. An isotope has a different number of electrons.

    B. An isotope has a different number of neutrons.

    C. The arrangement of the electrons is different.

    D. An isotope has a different number of protons.

Answer: B. An isotope has a different number of neutrons.
A change in the number of electrons (A) creates an ion. The change in the arrangement of the electrons (C) could change the reactivity of an atom temporarily. A change of the number of protons (D), will change the atom a new element. Answer B is the only one that does not change the relative charge of an atom, while changing the weight of and atom, which in essence is what an isotope is.

87. When heat is added to most solids, they expand. Why is this the case? (Rigorous) (Skill 15.5)

    A. The molecules get bigger.

    B. The faster molecular motion leads to greater distance between the molecules.

    C. The molecules develop greater repelling electric forces.

    D. The molecules form a more rigid structure.

Answer: B. The faster molecular motion leads to greater distance between the molecules
The atomic theory of matter states that matter is made up of tiny, rapidly moving particles. These particles move more quickly when warmer, because temperature is a measure of average kinetic energy of the particles. Warmer molecules therefore move farther away from each other, with enough energy to separate from each other more often and for greater distances.

88. **Which statement is true about groups and periods on the periodic table? (Average) (Skill 15.6)**

    A. Groups are associated with rows on the periodic table.

    B. Periods are associated with columns on the periodic table.

    C. Elements in the same period have similar properties.

    D. The three types of elements are metals, non-metals, and metalloids.

Answer: D. The three types of elements are metals, non-metals, and metalloids.

There are three types of elements, indicated by three colors on the periodic table: Metals, Nonmetals, and Metalloids.

89. **Bronze is an alloy of copper and tin. It melts at a very high temperature. What is the kind of bonding that exists between the elements in bronze? (Easy) (Skill 15.7)**

    A. Ionic bonding

    B. Metallic bonding

    C. Covalent bonding

    D. Molecular bonding

Answer: B. Metallic bonding
Metallic bonding occurs in a metal. Bronze is an alloy of copper and tin, which are both metals, so the answer is B0, metallic bonding.

90. Iodine-131 decays into xenon, which has a half-life of about 8 days. If you have a 100-gram sample of pure I-131, how much iodine will be left after one year?
    (Average) (Skill 15.8)

    A. 50 grams

    B. 100 grams

    C. No iodine atoms at all

    D. Less than 0.00001 grams

Answer: D. Less than 0.00001 grams
After 8 days there will be 50 grams of iodine and 50 grams of xenon, and after 16 days, 25 grams of iodine and 75 grams of xenon. A year is equivalent to about 40 half-lives. Answer C is wrong because there are so many atoms of iodine in a 100-gram sample. Also, even if you have only one radioactive iodine atom, there is a 50 percent chance it will not have decayed in 8 days, and a very small chance it will not decay in one year.

91. Which of the following is found in the least abundance in organic molecules?
    (Rigorous) (Skill 15.9)

    A. Phosphorus

    B. Potassium

    C. Argon

    D. Oxygen

Answer: C. Argon
Organic molecules consist mainly of carbon, hydrogen, and oxygen, and also contain significant amounts of nitrogen, phosphorus, and sulfur. Other elements, such as potassium, are present in much smaller quantities. Argon is a noble gas, so its atoms rarely bond to any other atoms, making it extremely rare for argon to be part of an organic compound. Therefore the answer is C.

TEACHER CERTIFICATION STUDY GUIDE

92. **A covalent bond:**
    (Average) (Skill 16.1)

    A. Is formed when two atoms share electrons

    B. Is formed by the transfer of electrons

    C. happens when metals and nonmetals bond

    D. happens when metals bond to metals

Answer: A. Is formed when two atoms share electrons
A covalent bond is formed when two atoms share electrons. Atoms whose outer shells are not filled with electrons are unstable. When they are unstable, they readily combine with other unstable atoms. By combining and sharing electrons, they act as a single unit. Covalent bonding happens among nonmetals.

93. **Which of the following is *not* true about a base?**
    (Rigorous) (Skill 16.2)

    A. It has a bitter taste.

    B. It is a substance that combines with a hydrogen ion in solution.

    C. Many household cleaning products contain bases.

    D. Vinegar is an example of a base.

Answer: D. Vinegar is an example of a base.
Although it is never wise to taste a substance to identify it, acids have a sour taste. Vinegar and lemon juice are both acids, and acids occur in many foods in a weak state.

Middle Level Science

94. In which type of chemical reaction is a compound broken down into two or more simpler substances?
    (Average) (Skill 16.3)

    A. Composition

    B. Decomposition

    C. Single replacement

    D. Double replacement

Answer: B. Decomposition
In a decomposition reaction, a compound breaks down into two or more simpler substances, e.g., water breaking down into hydrogen and oxygen.

95. In which type of chemical reaction is a solid formed?
    (Average) (Skill 16.4)

    A. Oxidation-reduction

    B. Acid-base

    C. Decomposition

    D. Precipitation

Answer: D. Precipitation
A precipitation reaction is a reaction in which a solid, or precipitate, is formed.

96. **If you lift a book into the air, what is the opposing force?**
    (Average) (Skill 16.5)

    A. The force applied by the book

    B. The force applied by your arm

    C. Gravity

    D. Friction

Answer: C. Gravity
Work is the transfer of energy to move an object a certain distance. It is motion against an opposing force. Lifting an object into the air is work; the opposing force is gravity.

97. **Which of the following statements about heat is true?**
    (Average) (Skill 16.5)

    A. Heat is transferred from an object of higher temperature to one of lower temperature.

    B. Heat is transferred from an object of lower temperature to one of higher temperature.

    C. Heat is transferred evenly between objects of different temperatures.

    D. Heat is not transferred between objects of different temperatures.

Answer: A. Heat is transferred from an object of higher temperature to one of lower temperature.
Heat is energy that is transferred between objects caused by differences in their temperatures. Heat is transferred from an object of higher temperature to one of lower temperature. This transfer continues until both objects reach the same temperature.

TEACHER CERTIFICATION STUDY GUIDE

98. **According to kinetic molecular theory, reaction rate increases with temperature. Why is this true?**
    (Average) (Skill 16.6)

    A. More reactant molecules will collide with each other per second.

    B. Collisions between molecules will each occur at a higher energy, which is more likely to overcome the activation energy of the reaction.

    C. Both A and B

    D. Neither A nor B

Answer: C. Both A and B
Kinetic molecular theory also predicts that reaction rate constants increase with temperature (values for k) because of two reasons: More reactant molecules will collide with each other per second. Also, these collisions will each occur at a higher energy, which is more likely to overcome the activation energy of the reaction.

99. **A material that increases the rate of a chemical reaction without changing itself permanently in the process is called a:**
    (Easy) (Skill 16.7)

    A. Reactant

    B. Catalyst

    C. Precipitate

    D. Product

Answer: B. Catalyst
A catalyst is a material that increases the rate of a chemical reaction without changing itself permanently in the process. Catalysts reduce the activation energy of a reaction.

TEACHER CERTIFICATION STUDY GUIDE

100. A chemical reaction in which more energy is needed to break the reactant bonds than is released when product bonds form is called:
    (Rigorous) (Skill 16.7)

    A. Endothermic

    B. Exothermic

    C. Composition

    D. Decompostion

Answer: A. Endothermic
If during a chemical reaction, more energy is needed to break the reactant bonds than is released when product bonds form, the reaction is endothermic, heat is absorbed from the environment, and the environment becomes colder.

www.ingramcontent.com/pod-product-compliance
Lightning Source LLC
Chambersburg PA
CBHW080537300426
44111CB00017B/2768